Oxford Shakespeare Topics

Shakespeare and Masculinity

D0706412

OXFORD SHAKESPEARE TOPICS
Published and Forthcoming Titles Include:

Oxford Shakespeare Topics

GENERAL EDITORS: PETER HOLLAND AND STANLEY WELLS

Shakespeare and Masculinity

BRUCE R. SMITH

OXFORD
UNIVERSITY PRESS

Great Clarendon Street, Oxford OX2 6DP
Oxford University Press is a department of the University of Oxford.
It furthers the University's objective of excellence in research, scholarship,
and education by publishing worldwide in

Oxford New York

Athens Auckland Bangkok Bogotá Buenos Aires Calcutta
Cape Town Chennai Dar es Salaam Delhi Florence Hong Kong Istanbul
Karachi Kuala Lumpur Madrid Melbourne Mexico City Mumbai
Nairobi Paris São Paulo Shanghai Singapore Taipei Tokyo Toronto Warsaw
and associated companies in Berlin Ibadan

Oxford is a registered trade mark of Oxford University Press
in the UK and certain other countries

Published in the United States
by Oxford University Press Inc., New York

British Library Cataloguing in Publication Data
Data available

Library of Congress Cataloging in Publication Data

Smith, Bruce R., 1946–
   Shakespeare and masculinity / Bruce R. Smith.
      p.   cm. — (Oxford Shakespeare topics)
Includes bibliographical references (p.) and index.
1. Shakespeare, William, 1564–1616–Characters—Men. 2. Masculinity in literature. 3. Men in
literature. I. Title. II. Series.

PR2992.M28 S65 2000   822.3′3—dc21   00–024419

ISBN 0-19-871188-3
ISBN 0-19-871189-1 (pbk.)
10 9 8 7 6 5 4 3 2 1

Typeset by Kolam Information Services Pvt Ltd, Pondicherry, India
Printed in Great Britain
on acid-free paper by Biddles Ltd, Guildford and Kings Lynn

For my students at Georgetown University
1972–2000

Acknowledgements

For inviting me to contribute a volume to the series and for reading my drafts with critical sympathy I am especially grateful to the editors of 'Oxford Shakespeare Topics', Peter Holland and Stanley Wells. Additional counsel and advice came from Will Fisher, Mary Fuller, John Gillies, Margaret Rose Jaster, Arthur Little, and Peter Stallybrass. The customary courtesy and efficiency of Betsy Walsh and the reading-room staff of the Folger Shakespeare Library made research for this book an absolute pleasure. I would also like to thank Sylvia Morris of the Shakespeare Centre Library in Stratford-upon-Avon for her help in locating the production shot that appears here as Figure 6. The expert splicing of Figures 2a and 2b was carried out by Sally Blakemore and Betsy Armstrong of Arty Projects Studio, Santa Fe. For various forms of logistical support I extend thanks to Ken Collins, Dottie Indyke, David Jenness, Gail Paster, and Diane Winters. Funds for completing research and writing were provided by a Summer Grant from the National Endowment for the Humanities and a Summer Academic Research Grant from Georgetown University. This book would have been quite impossible without the encouragement and understanding of my partner, Gordon Davis. To all these institutions and individuals I express sincere appreciation.

Santa Fe, New Mexico   B.R.S.
July 1999

Contents

List of Illustrations

1. Hendrik Goltzius, *The Farnese Hercules* (1592).

About a quarter of the way through *The Tragedy of King Lear* there comes a moment in which Lear, in a phrase widely understood today, 'loses it'. What he loses is not just his self-control but his masculinity. The Fool has been taunting Lear with Goneril and Regan's ingratitude, when Lear exclaims:

> O, how this mother swells up toward my heart!
> *Histerica passio* down, thou climbing sorrow;
> Thy element's below.
>
> (2.2.231–3)[1]

The precise terms in which Lear expresses his passion are gendered: 'this mother' he calls it and visualizes it as a womb inside his body. *Hystera* is the Greek word for womb, which in Galenic medicine was imagined to have no fixed place but to wander about the entire body cavity, producing 'hysterical' behaviour. True to early modern ideas about such things, Lear divides his person into an 'above' and a 'below': '*Histerica passio* down . . .; | Thy element's below'. In this divided sense of his own body Lear as fictional king repeats an early modern commonplace, affirmed by an actual king, James I, who is reported to have been fond of observing that

God made one part of man of earth, the basest element, to teach him humility; his soul proceeded from the bosom of Himself, to teach him goodness; so that if he looks downward nothing is viler, if he cast his eyes to heaven he is of a matter more excellent than Angels; the former part was a type of Adam, the second of Christ, which gives life to that which was dead in itself.[2]

Framed within the Great Chain of Being, man's upper body figures as the seat of reason, purer in spirit, closer to God and the angels; his lower body, as the seat of passion, contaminated with the flesh, closer to the Devil. In Lear's own view, this division into upper and lower is also gendered: the heart that he calls 'mine' is threatened by 'this mother' from below. Lear's loss of reason in the subsequent action can be seen, then, as the triumph of this female passion within, a loss of both masculine authority and masculine identity.

Quite aside from its political gains, feminist criticism since the 1970s has altered fundamentally the way scholars, critics, actors, and audiences think about gender. 'Female' may be a biological given, 'feminine' may be a social identity that all cultures recognize, but the *content* of 'femininity' does not make up a universal category. It varies from culture to culture and from one historical era to another. In Judith Butler's formulation, gender is a matter of *performance*: 'there is no gender identity behind the expressions of gender...identity is performatively constituted by the very "expressions" that are said to be its results.'[3] Because theatre is also a matter of performance, plays provide a perfect means of investigating cultural and historical differences with respect to gender identity. Only recently has masculinity been subjected to the same critical scrutiny as femininity. In every binary, one term implicitly serves as the standard that marks the other term as being different. In the binary 'masculine'/'feminine' the criterion has usually been taken to be 'masculine'. As a result, 'masculine' has managed to deflect attention from itself. It is 'feminine' that is different, or so the implication goes; it is 'feminine' that deserves study. 'Masculinity' is, however, just as much a social construction as 'femininity'. In a survey of cultures through history and across the world, David Gilmore has demonstrated that masculinity is something quite different from biological maleness, and that different cultures define masculinity in markedly different ways. In every culture men are expected to propagate, provide, and defend, but the ways in which they are expected to do those things vary from one culture to another. What remains constant across these differences, however, is the fact that masculinity must be *achieved*. It is not a natural given:

Among most of the peoples that anthropologists are familiar with, true manhood is a precious and elusive status beyond mere maleness, a hortatory image that men and boys aspire to and that their culture demands of them as a measure of belonging....Its vindication is doubtful, resting in rigid codes of decisive action in many spheres of life: as husband, father, lover, provider, warrior. A restricted status, there are always men who fail the test.[4]

The character in Shakespeare who exposes this dynamic most dramatically is probably Caius Martius, the hero of *Coriolanus*. He achieves manhood near the start of the play in a symbolic act of rebirth as he emerges, covered in blood, from the gates of the city of Corioles, earning in that deed the name Coriolanus that gives Shakespeare's play its title. Just as decisively Caius Martius loses his masculine identity when he is vanquished at the end of the play by his Volscian rival Aufidius, who taunts him as 'thou boy of tears'. The very violence of Martius's reaction shows just how fragile his masculine identity is:

> Cut me to pieces, Volsces. Men and lads,
> Stain all your edges on me. 'Boy'! False hound,
> If you have writ your annals true, 'tis there
> That, like an eagle in a dove-cote, I
> Fluttered your Volscians in Corioles.
> Alone I did it. 'Boy'!
>
> (5.6.112–17)

The hero of Corioles rankles at his demotion—chronological, social, sexual—to the status of 'boy'. A protagonist in an equally precarious position is Macbeth. His masculinity is constantly on the line. 'I do fear thy nature,' says Lady Macbeth as she reflects over Macbeth's letter announcing the witches' prophecy, 'It is too full o'th' milk of human kindness | To catch the nearest way' (1.5.15–17). 'Are you a man?' she asks her husband aside when the ghost of Banquo interrupts the feast in Act 3, Scene 4 (3.4.57). Such scenes of anxiety about male identity should make us hear with fresh ears the lines of an irresolute son who declares, 'To be, or not to be; that is the question' (*Hamlet*, 3.1.58).

Shakespeare's comedies often invite the conclusion that masculinity is more like a suit of clothes that can be put on and taken off at will than a matter of biological destiny. All the complications in *The Two Gentlemen of Verona* follow from the decision of Proteus's father to make a man of his youthful son: 'he cannot be a perfect man', the father tells a friend, 'Not being tried and tutored in the world'. Therefore, he will follow the course taken by many fathers in early modern England and send his son to someone else's household for finishing off—in this case, to the emperor's court at Milan (1.3.20–1). Proteus's mistress Julia, when she decides to follow her lover there, becomes the first in a long line of Shakespeare's comic heroines who don men's clothes and, for the nonce, take on masculine identity. The discrepancy in such escapades between assumed social swagger and missing biological equipment is pointed up in the teasing of Julia's maid. Julia will have to wear breeches, the maid tells her, and 'You must needs have them with a codpiece, madam'. 'Out, out, Lucetta,' Julia exclaims (2.7.53–4). *Out*, indeed. However temporary such cross-dressing may be, it serves to remind audiences that masculinity is a matter of appearances. That holds true, whatever happens to be behind the codpiece, as both a physically biological male (Sir Andrew Aguecheek) and a fictionally biological female (Viola-as-'Cesario') attest in *Twelfth Night*. Egging on a reluctant Sir Andrew to challenge 'Cesario' to a sword fight, Sir Toby advises, 'as thou drawest, swear horrible, for it comes to pass oft that a terrible oath, with a swaggering accent sharply twanged off, gives manhood more approbation than ever proof itself would have earned him' (3.4.175–9). 'Cesario', for his/her part, is even more acutely aware that manhood in such situations is a matter of performance on the part of the actor and of 'imagination' on the part of the observer. When Antonio stumbles onto the fight and takes 'Cesario' to be Sebastian, Viola exclaims in an aside, 'Prove true, imagination, O prove true, | That I, dear brother, be now ta'en for you!' (3.4.367–8). When it comes to imagination, Orsino's is particularly active. He persists in calling Viola 'Cesario', even after Viola's female identity has been revealed, until 'in other habits you are seen' (5.1.383). 'Habits' in early seventeenth-century usage could mean both clothing (*Oxford English Dictionary*, 'habit' I.1–2) and patterns of behaviour ('habit' III.8–10).

Masculinity in all these instances is a matter of contingency, of circumstances, of performance. Shakespeare is not alone in having recognized that state of affairs. Indeed, early modern writers seem to have responded to the situation, emotionally at least, in ways remarkably similar to one another. In Lynn Enterline's interpretation, *The Comedy of Errors* and *The Merchant of Venice* share with works by Torquato Tasso, Andrew Marvell, and John Webster a curious sense of self-love combined with loss, typified in the lines with which Antonio opens *The Merchant of Venice*: 'In sooth, I know not why I am so sad' (1.1.1).[5] Where Enterline finds self-love and loss Mark Breitenberg finds a pervasive sense of anxiety. Breitenberg approaches the male protagonists in *The Rape of Lucrece*, *Love's Labour's Lost*, and *Othello* via the *Anatomy of Melancholy* and Robert Burton's epic attempt to maintain masculine rationality in the face of effeminating passion—the very predicament in which Lear finds himself *vis-à-vis* his daughters. Constantly in fear of losing their masculine self-posses-sion, Shakespeare's protagonists, like Burton, are caught up in an endless, ultimately hopeless situation. They must keep *talking* about anxiety in a futile attempt to *contain* anxiety. In particular, they must keep talking about their anxieties about women.[6]

Narcissism, melancholy, and anxiety fail to exhaust, however, the variety of emotional responses to the existential challenge 'Be a man' or the variety of stratagems Shakespeare and his contemporaries devised to meet that challenge. To understand how Shakespeare represents early modern masculinity in its full perplexity, we need to consider the subject not just from *one* critical vantage-point, like deconstruction or psychoanalytical theory, but from *several* critical vantage-points, as if we were the observers in Fig. 1 and were contemplating the statue of Hercules first from this angle, then from that, now from over here, then from over there. The result should be a rounded view of the subject. Each of the five chapters of *Shakespeare and Masculinity* pursues a different approach, drawing in each case on the entire range of Shakespeare's texts and looking out for change and development in the course of Shakespeare's career. Chapter 1, 'Persons', reads early modern medical and ethical texts alongside Shakespeare's scripts to explore what it was like in 1600 to inhabit a biologically male body. Chapter 2, 'Ideals', turns to conduct books for evidence of what early modern writers thought masculinity *ought* to be, and looks for evid-ence of those ideals in Shakespeare's plays and poems. How early modern males negotiated the life changes from boyhood to adoles-cence to maturity to old age—or at least how Shakespeare *represents* them as doing so—is the subject of Chapter 3, 'Passages'. It is only after considering the historical evidence in the first three chapters that Chapter 4 assumes the deconstructionist stance taken by most recent gender critics and considers the various 'Others' against which mas-culinity in Shakespeare's works is defined and maintained. In an attempt to move beyond the deconstructionist model of gender Chap-ter 5, 'Coalescences', invites you to consider the performance of mas-culinity in the theatre as an experiment in which self and others, past and present, one culture's ideals and those of another, present realities and future possibilities converge in potentially liberating ways.

2a. (*left*) The Veins of the Body, from Helkiah Crooke, *Microcosmographia, A Description of the Body of Man* (1618). **2b.** (*right*) Velvet Hose, from Robert Greene, *A Quip for an Upstart Courtier* (1592).

Persons

One signal difficulty in talking about masculine identity in Shakespeare's England is the fact that many of the words we use today to talk about self-consciousness did not exist then, or at least not with the meanings we assume. Early modern English provided no 'ego', no 'psyche', no 'personality', not even 'individual' in the sense of an inward perception about who one is. The word 'self' still carried its originary force as a way of saying 'that very one' (*Oxford English Dictionary* A.1), as in the report made to Caesar that Antony's wound to the heart has been inflicted by 'that self hand | Which writ his honour in the acts it did' (*Antony and Cleopatra*, 5.1.21–2) or as a synonym for 'one and the same' (*OED* B.1), as in Regan's assertion 'I am made of that self mettle as my sister' (*Tragedy of King Lear*, 1.1.69). When characters in Shakespeare's plays speak reflexively of 'self' (*OED* C.1), they do so via a kind of synecdoche in which the body stands for one's entire being, past, present, and future. Cressida is speaking in distinctly physical terms when she confesses to Troilus, 'I have a kind of self resides with you— | And an unkind self, that itself will leave | To be another's fool' (*Troilus and Cressida*, 3.2.144–6). Cressida uses the word 'self' here in just the way most of Shakespeare's characters do: as a place-marker. 'Self' as 'a permanent subject of successive and varying states of consciousness' (*OED* C.3) dates only from the late seventeenth century.

The True Knowledge of a Man's Own Self (1602), as inscribed by Philippe de Mornay and translated by Anthony Munday, turns out to be *physiological* knowledge. Like a mirror, the pocket-sized book promises to show the reader not only his external appearance but 'the inward parts of the body, from the very hour of conception, to the latest minute of life'.[1] For Helkiah Crooke, in his huge tome

Microcosmographia: A Description of the Body of Man (1618), this
amounts to knowing the entire universe, since 'Man is a Little world,
and contains in himself the seeds of all those things which are contained in the most spacious and ample bosom of this whole Universe,
Stars, Meteors, Metals, Minerals, Vegetables, Animals, and Spirits'.
In the last analysis, says Crooke, to know one's 'self' is to know God:
'he which is well read in his own body, shall see in all even the least
operations of his mind or actions of his body a lively Impression and
infallible mark of Divinity.'[2] If the body is a text, the reader of that text
is the soul. *Nosce teipsum* ('know thyself'): when a man educated under
principles of Christian humanism heeded Socrates' advice, what he
was expected to discover was a soul-in-a-body.[3] Such a discovery was
hardly calculated to make him feel unique.

In their centrifugal spiral away from the individual reader toward *all*
human bodies, toward the cosmos, toward God Himself statements
like Crooke's are a far cry from the centripetal post-Romantic 'ego' we
are likely to assume as the subject of self-knowledge. Even someone
like Montaigne, so insistent on testing supposedly universal precepts
against his own experience, arrives, not at self-knowledge in the post-
seventeenth-century sense of the word, but at scepticism that a soul-in-
a-body can ever know much for sure. For us, then, 'self' in Shakespeare's
scripts is a highly misleading word. The words and phrases that early
modern English did provide for what we would understand as interiority—'individual' (in the sense of being undividable), 'the closet of the
heart', 'secrets', a distinction between 'inward' behaviour and 'outward'
behaviour—all lack, as Anne Ferry has pointed out, a sense of con-
tinuous inner consciousness.[4] What they imply instead is something
much more physical. For an early modern Englishman, to know oneself
was to be 'well read in his own body'. Such knowledge prompted him to
speak, not of 'myself', but of 'my *self*'.

A suggestive synonym for 'self' emerges in the anxious, politically
charged exchange in *2 Henry IV,* between the newly proclaimed Henry
V and his former antagonist the Lord Chief Justice. How, Harry asks,
can I forget all the indignities you laid on me when I was a prince? You
even sent me to prison! The Lord Chief Justice's reply is carefully
calculated: 'I then did use the person of your father. | The image of his
power lay then in me'. Consider, he goes on, how you would feel now if
your decrees were flouted by *your* son:

> After this cold considerance, sentence me;
> And, as you are a king, speak in your state
> What I have done that misbecame my place,
> My person, or my liege's sovereignty.
>
> (5.2.72–3, 97–100)

The word 'person' functions here in at least three senses: as agent (*OED* II.2.a, 'An individual human being.... In earliest use, The human being acting in some capacity'), as personage (*OED* II.2.b, 'A man or woman of distinction or importance'), and as actor (*OED* I.1, 'A character sustained or assumed in a drama or the like, or in actual life'). The Lord Chief Justice has acted as an agent of Harry's father, temporarily assuming his identity as king. It is the third of these senses that explains the other two: in Latin, *persona* designated the mask that actors wore on the stage, a mask that was often equipped with a megaphone for projecting the voice, hence *per-sona* or 'through-sounding'. Also implicit in the Lord Chief Justice's choice of 'person' is a fourth sense of the word as physical body (*OED* III.4, 'The living body of a human being'). It is, after all, a threat of physical punishment, incarceration at the least, that animates the Lord Chief Justice's apology. As a prince, Harry was not afraid to box the justice's ears (*2 Henry IV*, 1.2.194–6). Antonio seems to have this bodily sense of the word in mind when he pledges to Bassanio 'My purse, my person, my extremest means' (*Merchant of Venice*, 1.1.138). The adjectival form 'personal' in Shakespeare's plays and poems almost always carries a sense of 'person' as a body. Hotspur complains that Bolingbroke rose to power by beheading the lords left behind as deputies while Richard II 'was personal in the Irish war' (*1 Henry IV*, 4.3.90). 'And everything lies level to our wish', the dying Henry IV tells his lords; 'Only we want a little personal strength' (*2 Henry IV*, 4.3.7–8). Physical body, agent, personage, actor on-stage: the word 'person' offers us a way of getting at masculine identity on terms that Shakespeare himself would have understood. Let us consider masculinity according to each of the word's four meanings in turn.

Physical Body

The bodily basis of identity becomes stunningly clear in a story that George Trosse (b. 1631) tells about himself in his spiritual autobiography. In his youth in Exeter it was typical for Trosse to drink himself into a stupor and ride home drunk. Coming home one night in such a condition, he hears what he takes to be the voice of God. 'Who art thou?' the voice asks. Locking himself in an 'Inner-Room'—the kind of space Anne Ferry associates with inwardness in Renaissance poetry—Trosse proceeds to strip off his clothes, first his stockings, then his hose, then his doublet.

> As I was thus unclothing myself, I had a strong internal impression, that all was well done, and a full compliance with the design of the voice. In answer likewise to this call, I would bow my body as low as possibly I could, with a great deal of pain, and this I often repeated: but all I could do was not low enough, nor humble enough. At last, observing that there was an hole in the planking of the room, I lay my self down flat upon the ground, and thrust my head there as far as I could; but because I could not fully do it, I put my hand into the hole, and took out earth and dust, and sprinkled it on my head. . . .[5]

'Who art thou?' In effect, Trosse answers the voice's question thus: I am my naked body. In this real-life enactment of Lear's loss of identity—'Off, off, you lendings!' (*Tragedy of King Lear*, 3.4.102)—we encounter a perception that might at first seem quite modern, a sense that articles of clothing figure as so many external signifiers. When, after several weeks of treatment at a physician's house, Trosse attempts to dress himself, he feels the weight of his fine clothes: 'My buttons, gold, silver and silk upon my sleeves lay very heavy on my conscience, as an intolerable burden, as weighty as a world' (96). The body beneath those clothes, however, is not the body given to us by modern medicine. We encounter in Trosse's story and in Lear's speeches a sense of the body as vile, abhorrent, alien from the speaker even as he uses that body to speak. Trosse's body, like Lear's, 'smells of mortality' (4.5.129). Instructed by early modern anatomists like Crooke, we should expect to find in Shakespeare's male protagonists a sense of physical person quite different from our own.

In early modern English the word 'masculinity' was, indeed, primarily a biological concept, the equivalent of what we in modern English would call 'maleness' (*OED* 'masculine' 1).[6] When Thersites in *Troilus and Cressida* taunts Patroclus as Achilles' 'masculine whore' (5.1.17), it is body parts that he has in mind. Even Viola, in disguise as 'Cesario', is thinking in bodily terms when she is reunited with her brother Sebastian and calls his attention to her 'masculine usurped attire' (*Twelfth Night*, 5.1.248). Both speakers might also be thinking of grammar, since 'gender' in early modern English had more to do with the declension of masculine, feminine, and neuter nouns in Latin (*OED* 'gender' 2, 'masculine' 3) than it did with human behaviour (*OED* 'gender' 3). By the laws of Latin grammar, Patroclus as *meretrix* ('whore') ought to be feminine; Viola's clothing, like an adjective agreeing with a noun, ought to match her person in feminine gender. Only in the 1620s, after Shakespeare's writing career was over, did 'masculinity' begin to acquire our sense of the word as describing attributes and actions seen as appropriate to males (*OED* 'masculine' 5). Shakespeare's own word for such attributes and actions is 'manliness'. Troilus is described by Ulysses as being 'Manly as Hector but more dangerous' (*Troilus and Cressida*, 4.6.107). To one way of thinking, then, this book ought to be entitled *Shakespeare and Manliness*. On the other hand, 'masculinity' stands as a useful reminder that male identity was then, and is now, sited in the body.

When Shakespeare's characters say they are speaking from the heart, we think we understand them. 'But goes thy heart with this?' Lear asks Cordelia. 'Ay, my good lord' (*Tragedy of King Lear*, 1.1.104–5). When Shakespeare's characters say they are speaking from the stomach or the liver or the spleen, we are apt to sit up and take notice. Titus Andronicus, seeing the mutilated body of Lavinia, finds the sources of his voice much deeper in his own body than modern listeners are likely to imagine:

> . . . my bowels cannot hide her woes,
> But like a drunkard must I vomit them.
> Then give me leave, for losers will have leave
> To ease their stomachs with their bitter tongues.
>
> (*Titus Andronicus*, 3.1.229–32)

Present in Titus's outcry is a now obsolete sense of the word 'stomach': 'the inward seat of passion, emotion, secret thoughts, affections, or feelings' (*OED* 6.a). 'To utter (the bottom of) one's stomach' was thus 'to disclose one's inmost thoughts' (*OED* 6.b). In *The Tempest* Ferdinand cites other bodily parts to assure Prospero of his self-restraint: 'I warrant you, sir, | The white cold virgin snow upon my heart | Abates the ardour of my liver' (4.1.54–6). In *Love's Labour's Lost* Don Armado berates the clown Costard for making him lose his melancholy cool: 'By virtue, thou enforcest laughter—thy silly thought my spleen. The heaving of my lungs provokes me to ridiculous smiling' (3.1.73–5). Such speeches, for us, are metaphors. For Titus, Ferdinand, Don Armado, the actors who played those roles, and the audiences who listened, they were physiological facts of personhood. In his autobiography Simonds D'Ewes (b. 1602) includes an account of the post-mortem anatomy of King James, an account that assumes personal identity to be a function of body parts:

> Being embowelled, his heart was found to be very great, which argued him to be as very considerate, so extraordinary fearful, which hindered him from attempting any great actions. His liver was as fresh as if he had been a young man; one of his kidneys sound, the other shrunk and two little stones found in it; his lights and gall almost black, which proceeded doubtless from excessive care and melancholy. The semitures of his skull were so strong and firm as they could scarcely be broken open with a saw or chisel; and the pia mater so full of brains, as they could scarcely be kept from spilling.[7]

Big heart, black lungs and gall bladder, huge brain: hence fearful, melancholy, intelligent.

The key to all these citations of the human body is to be found in Galen's second-century treatises on the body's parts and functions and in the medical writings of his ancient, medieval, and early modern disciples. Accounts of Galenic medicine in early modern culture by J. B. Bamborough, Nancy G. Siraisi, Thomas Laqueur, Gail Kern Paster, and others have demonstrated the tenacity of ancient ideas, even as contradictory evidence kept turning up on the dissecting tables of sixteenth- and seventeenth-century anatomists.[8] In the 1618 and 1631 editions of *Microcosmographia* Crooke scrupulously considers, for each body part, both received opinion and recent evidence, usually finding some way of accommodating what modern anatomists were seeing to what the old books said. In some ways, Galenic medicine might seem to anticipate our own ideas about genetic inheritance and body chemistry as explanations for the differences between one individual and another, but the differences from our conceptions of masculine identity are profound.

'If the dull substance of my flesh were thought, | Injurious distance should not stop my way', the speaker of Shakespeare's Sonnet 44 writes to his lover, separated from him by land and sea. But, alas, 'so much of earth and water wrought, | I must attend time's leisure with my moan' (44.1–2, 11–12). The ensuing sonnet extends earth and water to include 'the other two, slight air and purging fire', both of which attend on the absent lover, the first as the writer's thought, the second as his desire.

> For when these quicker elements are gone
> In tender embassy of love to thee,
> My life, being made of four, with two alone
> Sinks down to death, oppressed with melancholy,
> Until life's composition be recured
> By those swift messengers returned from thee....
>
> (45.1–2, 5–10)

Earth, water, air, and fire are the physical 'elements' in which the writer locates his 'life's composition'. The heavier of the four, earth and water, tend downward; the lighter or 'quicker' of the two, air and fire, tend upward and outward. Left only with earth and water, the writer falls into melancholy, as naturally he would, considering that melancholy is a product of earth. As Galen and his followers imagined the human body, each of the four elements forms the basis of a body fluid or 'humour': fire the basis of yellow bile or choler, air of blood, water of phlegm, and earth of black bile or melancholy. Each fluid is imagined to reside in a particular organ. After being 'concocted' (i.e. 'cooked') by the liver out of ingested food, the four fluids are dispersed and stored separately: choler in the gall bladder, blood in the heart, phlegm in the stomach (some say the brain), melancholy in the spleen. The fluid that oozes from the body in a wound is called just what we would call it, blood, but it is imagined to be a mixture of choler, elemental blood, phlegm, and black bile, each of which will settle into a discrete layer or evaporate if the fluid is collected in a glass and allowed to stand. It is this mixture of all four humours that circulates throughout the body via the veins (Siraisi 104–9). (See Crooke's representation of the veins in Figure 2a.) The particular combination of humours in a given person at a given time produces a particular 'complexion' in the sense of the Latin word *complexio* as 'connection' or 'combination'. As with Titus citing his stomach, Ferdinand his heart and liver, and Don Armado his spleen, Galenic ideas about personhood make it hard to know in Sonnets 44 and 45 just where metaphor leaves off and physiological self-knowledge begins. Galenic medicine invited an early modern man to experience his *self* in terms of body fluids and body organs.

As a man given to melancholy, Orsino ('That strain again, it had a dying fall' (*Twelfth Night*, 1.1.4)) reads Olivia's body in just such terms. If she can immure herself in tears during 'seven years' heat' for the death of her brother, how intensely will she love 'when liver, brain, and heart, | Those sovereign thrones, are all supplied, and filled | Her sweet perfections with one self king' (1.1.25, 36–8)—namely, *him*. Liver, brain, and heart are invoked in similarly paradigmatic terms by Cymbeline, as he thanks Belarius, Guiderius, and Arviragus for rescuing him in battle and laments that the fourth rescuer (Innogen in disguise) cannot be found anywhere:

> To my grief I am
> The heir of his reward, which I will add
> To you, the liver, heart, and brain of Britain,
> By whom I grant she lives.

> (5.6.12–15)

Both Orsino and Cymbeline assume Galenic medicine's division of the body into three regions or 'ventricles', each of which is associated with a particular organ and with a particular 'spirit' that carries out specialized body functions. The inferior ventricle, centred on the liver, contains the body's 'natural' or 'vegetative' members, the organs devoted to nutrition, growth and reproduction, activities which are executed by the 'natural' or 'vegetative' spirit. 'Vital' activities of respiration and pulse are performed by the heart and other organs of the middle ventricle, assisted by 'vital' spirit. *Anima*, the Latin word for soul, provides the name for the 'animal' members of the superior ventricle, centred on the brain and performing, via 'animal' spirit, the activities of sensation and locomotion that modern medicine attributes to the nervous system. Such a division into lower, middle, and upper helps to explain the sense of estrangement with which many early modern witnesses regard the lower parts of their bodies. Lear's '*Histerica passio* down...; | Thy element's below' (*Tragedy of King Lear*, 2.2.232–3) has its physiological basis. The hierarchical human body is very much in Henry V's mind even when he goes in disguise as a commoner among his soldiers and tries to level his body with theirs.

A king is but a man, he tells them. 'All his senses have but human conditions. His ceremonies laid by, in his nakedness he appears but a man, and though his affections are higher mounted than ours, yet when they stoop, they stoop with the like wing' (4.1.103–7). The site of those 'affections', in the body natural as in the body politic, is the superior ventricle.

With respect to masculine identity, the most important implication of the elements/humours/organs system is that masculinity is a function of body chemistry. In particular, it is a function of the two 'higher' elements, air and fire, and the two 'hotter' humours compounded of those elements, blood and choler. Crooke in *Microcosmographia* gives careful consideration to the question whether men's bodies are hotter than women's or the other way around. After considering the principles of generation (men as producers of seed, women as receptacles), gestation in womb, the 'habit' of the whole body (musculature and skin), the structure of parts, the manner and order of life, and 'the final cause of creation', Crooke decides in favour of received opinion. The final cause is, to Crooke, the most telling: 'It behoved therefore that man should be hotter, because his body was made to endure labour and travail, as also that his mind should be stout and invincible to undergo dangers, the only hearing whereof will drive a woman as we say out of her little wits' (274).

It is the condition of greater hotness that explains why men's sexual organs extend outside the body, while women's are contained within. Thomas Laqueur has given renewed currency to the ancient idea that men and women share one set of sexual organs, the vagina corresponding to the penis, the ovaries to the testicles. To consider the physical evidence thus is, as Laqueur points out, to see *one* sex, where we see two, and to deprive gender of any 'natural', physiological foundation (8). Despite some reported cases of women working up a heat and turning into men, despite the suggestiveness of the one-sex model for characters like Rosalind and Viola, as early as 1618 Helkiah Crooke was carefully weighing the evidence—and deciding on two sexes, not one (149–50). However one interprets the organs themselves, the difference between external placement of genitals and internal prompted early modern men to contrast the vaginal openness of women's bodies and the foreskinned closedness of their own. The effect was to turn women into the 'leaky vessels' that Gail Kern Paster has found in figures like Olivia (32–3). 'These be her very c's, her u's, and her t's', spells Malvolio as he reads Olivia's body in the evidence of her hand, 'and thus she makes her great P's' (*Twelfth Night*, 2.5.85–6). The extension of the open/closed distinction to other orifices besides the urethra and the vagina explains why women were thought to be more voluble than men. It is a contrast between open and closed bodies that prompts love-struck Troilus to describe himself as being 'weaker than a woman's tear' (1.1.9) and Coriolanus to imagine his stabbing death at the hands of the Volsces as an act of emasculation.[9]

Women possess bodies that are colder and moister than men's are; hence, melancholy and phlegm are less manly humours than blood and choler. Hamlet makes that circumstance painfully apparent. In terms of Galenic medicine, Hamlet is animated by black bile. Levinus Lemnius in *The Touchstone of Complexions* (English translation, 1576) regards melancholy as the worst possible complexion because its qualities of coldness and dryness are the very opposite of the life-sustaining qualities of heat and moisture. Indeed, death is the end toward which coldness and dryness tend: 'For we see in the whole course of Nature, and in all things within the universal world, plants, herbs, all creatures endued with life, men and all that live by breath, when they be once deprived, or lack heat and moisture, quickly to decay, and grow unto destruction.'[10] In not one guise but two Hamlet makes it onto Lemnius's list of the people most subject to melancholy: students, 'which at unseasonable times sit at their books and studies', and grievers over the death of a parent (135, 143ᵛ). For his part, Hamlet repeatedly expresses a wish to turn melancholy into blood: 'blest are those | Whose blood and judgement are so well commingled | That they are not a pipe for Fortune's finger | To sound what stop she please', 'Now could I drink hot blood, | And do such bitter business as the day | Would quake to look on', 'O, from this time forth | My thoughts be bloody or be nothing worth' (3.2.66–9, 3.2.379–81, Q2 4.4.56–7). Whether Hamlet ever succeeds in such wishes is debatable. Laertes, receiving news of his father's murder, has only to wish once: 'That drop of blood that's calm proclaims me bastard' (4.5.116).

Hamlet, well read in his own body, interprets melancholy as a pathological state. Melancholy can overwhelm a man, Lemnius points out, if the spleen has no way of ridding itself of excess black bile. Thus people can fall into melancholy 'by the staying of their hemorrhoids and stopping of their purgations' (143). The very name of Jaques in *As You Like It* (probably pronounced 'jakes', early modern slang for 'toilet') locates his mental disposition just where Lemnius would place it: in the spleen. Lacking a jakes, Jaques has no other orifice for purging melancholy than his mouth. High on Lemnius's list of cures for melancholy is a good laxative (152^v). Don John in *Much Ado about Nothing* exemplifies the potentially tragic results of such a blockage. An excess of phlegm is likewise unmanly: witness flaccid Falstaff. *The History of Henry the Fourth... With the humorous conceits of Sir John Falstaff* (as the 1598 quarto is titled) suggests just how Shakespeare's spectators read the old knight's body. 'That trunk of humours, that bolting-hutch of beastliness, that swollen parcel of dropsies, that huge bombard of sack, that stuffed cloak-bag of guts...' begins Harry's taunting description when he and Falstaff take turns adopting the persona of Harry's father (*1 Henry IV*, 2.5.454–7). Guts loom large in Harry's description because Falstaff's dominant humour is phlegm: cold and moist like the moon ('minions of the moon' Falstaff styles himself and his fellow 'squires of the [k]night's body'), seated in the stomach ('What a devil hast thou to do with the time of day?' Harry asks. 'Unless hours were cups of sack, and minutes capons'), conducive to laziness and cowardice (of Death Sir John declares, 'What need I be so forward with him that calls not on me?') (1.2.24–6, 1.2.6–7, 5.1.128–9). Mistress Ford in *The Merry Wives of Windsor* lights on cold, moist images when she lampoons Falstaff as 'this unwholesome humidity, this gross watery pumpkin' (3.3.37–8). His metamorphosis into a woman is altogether appropriate.

Though constitutive of masculinity, blood and choler are equally undesirable in excess. When the Duchess of York brands Richard III a creature of blood, she has in mind not only the blood on Richard's hands but the blood in his heart and brain: 'Bloody thou art, bloody will be thy end' (4.4.195). Earlier, Lady Anne has countered Richard's claim that he was provoked by the queen's own 'sland'rous tongue' to pull a sword against Margaret: 'Thou wast provokèd by thy bloody mind, | That never dream'st on aught but butcheries' (1.2.99–100). Richmond's summation of Richard's character before the battle of Bosworth Field seems just in every way: 'A bloody tyrant and a homicide; | One raised in blood, and one in blood established' (5.5.200–1). To judge by Lemnius' opinion in *The Secret Miracles of*

Nature (English translation 1658), Richard's outward person manifests his inward nature. Physical deformities affect the organ to which they are closest, Lemnius observes. In Richard's case that organ is the seat of blood, the heart:

> where there is an error about some principal part, there the mind partakes of some inconvenience, and cannot perfectly perform her offices. So they that are deformed with a bunch-back, so it be a natural infirmity, and not accidental, nor come by any fall or blow, are commonly wicked and malicious; because the deprivation is communicated to the heart, that is the fountain and beginning of life.[11]

Excessive choler is even less to be preferred than excessive blood. In moderation, says Lemnius in *The Touchstone of Complexions*, choler or yellow bile makes a man bold, valiant, warlike, rash, ambitious, quarrelsome. In excess it transforms body and mind into a boiling cauldron:

> For choler is of that nature that yieldeth out a fiery force, whose motion (as it were a fire brand) stirreth up and incenseth our minds to hasty moods and furious rages. And for this cause anger is defined to be a heat and certain boiling of the blood about the heart, wherewith the brain also being excited by choler, is set in a heat and testiness, desirous of revenge, whensoever any injury is offered.   (128)

Choler is Coriolanus' making as the hero of Corioles; choler is his undoing as a politician and as a defector to the Volsces. Incensed by Aufidius' insults, Coriolanus rages, virtually begging his own violent death: 'Cut me to pieces, Volsces. Men and lads, | Stain all your edges on me' (5.6.112–13). And so they do.

Radical changes in body chemistry make for radical changes in one's physical person. 'Romeo! Humours! Madman! Passion! Lover!': Mercutio's invocation of his love-struck friend registers how drastically the sight of Juliet has changed Romeo's very person, in this case by rousing his blood (*Romeo and Juliet*, 2.1.7). If Mercutio's five exclamations are heard as five synonyms, Romeo has been reduced to his dominant humour. As its traditional association with Mars as well as Venus attests, amorous passion was not the only thing an excess of blood produced. Mercutio in his duel with Tybalt stands as a case in point. So does Richard III. The regimes of Mars and Venus come together in the blood of Othello. Lemnius' characterization of a sanguine man in *The Touchstone of Complexions* would make us expect just such a combination of martial valour and venereal passion as Othello manifests in the opening scenes of the play—or at least just such a combination as Othello's Venetian employers *expect* him to manifest. Othello himself carefully denies lust as a motive for seconding Desdemona's request to join him on his military mission to Cyprus:

> I therefor beg it not
> To please the palate of my appetite,
> Nor to comply with heat—the young affects
> In me defunct—and proper satisfaction,
> But to be free and bounteous to her mind....
>
> (1.3.261–5)

When Othello leaves Venice for Cyprus, the isle of Venus's birth, the composure that he loses there is, to his own sense of himself, *physiological*. 'Now, by heaven, | My blood begins my safer guides to rule', he warns the duelling Cassio and Montano (2.3.197–8). Iago's insinuations only exacerbate Othello's susceptibility to the sway of blood. When Iago tells of seeing Cassio wipe his beard with the lost handkerchief, Othello's response is single-minded: 'O blood, blood, blood!' Patience, counsels Iago. Never, cries Othello. Like the sea raging through the Hellespont,

> Even so my bloody thoughts with violent pace
> Shall ne'er look back, ne'er ebb to humble love,
> Till that a capable and wide revenge
> Swallow them up.
>
> (3.3.455, 460–3)

In that torrent of blood is swallowed up Othello's very self.

To physicians in their surgeries, if not to spectators at the Globe, such perturbations of the spirit were pathological conditions. What is desirable for the human body, according to Galenic medicine, is a balance or *temperament* of humours. 'Keep me in temper,' Lear pleads. 'I would not be mad' (*Tragedy of King Lear*, 1.5.46). The 'touchstone' of complexions in Lemnius' title, the one against which all others can be judged as aberrations, is a perfect balance of all the humours. A 'perfectly and exactly temperate' body is 'the pattern of virtue' (25ᵛ). In outward person such a complexion produces a man who is tall, well-proportioned, fair of face, golden-haired, and blue-eyed, with a gentle, noble expression, a majestic gait, a commanding glance, and a harmonious voice. In inward person it produces just such a man as Antony invokes in his epitaph on Brutus, 'the noblest Roman of them all':

> His life was gentle, and the elements
> So mixed in him that nature might stand up
> And say to all the world 'This was a man'.
>
> (*Julius Caesar*, 5.5.67, 72–4)

Brutus's tragedy is to be a temperate man in an intemperate world. To describe the workings of a temperate complexion Lemnius turns to music:

as in musical instruments there is perceived a certain accord of tunes and a sweet agreeable harmony in striking the strings, that no unpleasant discord or bungling jar, dislike the curious ear of the hearer: so likewise in a temperate habit of the body, there is an apt and convenient mixture and temperature of the elements and qualities, insomuch that no one quality can by itself be showed, but a constant, absolute and perfect composition, & mingling of the qualities and elements all together. (*Touchstone*, 32)

The music that is ordered to cure Lear of his madness is an attempt to realize this metaphor in physical, physiological fact. Less grandly, Lemnius goes on to compare a well-balanced temperament to well mixed salads, sauces, and medicines.

Whatever Antony may say about Brutus, Lemnius concedes that perfect temperament is an ideal rarely if ever achieved. Perhaps, indeed, among all living persons only Jesus Christ has possessed perfect temperament (*Touchstone*, 33–33ᵛ). If perfect temperament is not achievable, then second best is for blood to dominate the other humours. Indeed, blood is the humour that makes men *men*. 'Such is the force and power of blood in man's body', Lemnius concludes,

specially when through access of age it groweth to heat, and daily more and more increaseth in vital spirit, that it causeth a promptness of mind, quickness in device, and sharpness in practice, which by daily use and exercise attaineth in th'end to wisdom, knowledge and experience of many things. And thus by the benefit of nature and good bringing up, it is brought to pass that they be garnished with many excellent gifts of the mind, and through a ready utterance in the discourse of matters, be to their country a great stay and ornament. (*Touchstone*, 99–99ᵛ)

For all that, there is present in man's bloody inheritance an inherent contradiction. When Crooke contrasts man's stout mind and woman's 'little wit', he is paying tribute to man's supposedly greater reasonableness. Yet blood, with which man is better endowed, is also an enemy to reason. Leave it to a woman to observe as much. 'The brain may devise laws for the blood', Portia tells Nerissa, 'but a hot temper leaps o'er a cold decree' (*The Merchant of Venice*, 1.2.17–18). The dying Henry IV dreads to imagine Harry on the throne, 'When rage and hot blood are his counsellors' (*2 Henry IV*, 4.3.63). 'The reasons you allege do more conduce | To the hot passion of distempered blood | Than to make up a free determination | 'Twixt right and wrong,' Hector tells Paris during the Trojans' war council in *Troilus and Cressida* (2.2.167–70). Since a man's body gradually warms through childhood, then cools off with age, blood is particularly suasive in youth. In his very person, therefore, an early modern man was subject to conflicting physiological imperatives: on the one hand, accept the promptings of blood that make you a man; on the other, be reasonable.

That double challenge is precisely what Prince Harry learns to negotiate in the two parts of *Henry IV*. Several critics have suggested that, among all Shakespeare's plays, the two parts of *Henry IV*, along with *The Merry Wives of Windsor*, are the ones most obviously governed by the humours.[12] The Dauphin in *Henry V*, unaware of Harry's reformation, describes him as 'a vain, giddy, shallow, humorous youth' (2.4.28). The unreformed Harry would claim no less: 'I am now of all humours that have showed themselves humours since the old days of goodman Adam to the pupil age of this present twelve o'clock at midnight' (*1 Henry IV*, 2.5.93–6). In promising to join the battle against Hotspur and the other rebels, Harry hopes that his father may 'salve | The long-grown wounds of my intemperature' (*1 Henry IV*, 3.2.155–6). By turns sanguine (in his love of adventure), phlegmatic (in his laziness), choleric (in throwing at Falstaff the bottle he has found in his scabbard), even melancholy (in his meditation on the crown), the passionate prince has become the stable sovereign by the time he marches to his coronation and dismisses Falstaff: 'Presume not that I am the thing I was. . . . I have turned away my former self' (*2 Henry IV*, 5.5.56-8). Understanding the word 'self' in Mornay's terms, as physical person, invites us to read Harry's transformation as physiological in nature.

In dismissing Falstaff he tempers phlegm. His former boon companion is ordered 'Not to come near our person by ten mile' (*2 Henry IV*, 5.5.65). In vanquishing Hotspur he tempers choler. Percy's very name ('hot' + 'spur') identifies him as the creature of choler he repeatedly demonstrates himself to be. 'What, drunk with choler?' Northumberland interrupts Hotspur in the rebels' council scene. 'Stay and pause awhile' (*1 Henry IV*, 1.3.127). Later in the same scene Hotspur speaks a Galenist's language when he identifies yellow bile as his operative humour and locates it in the organ of its manufacture: 'All studies here I solemnly defy, | Save how to gall and pinch this Bolingbroke' (*1.3.226–7*). It is precisely in a fit of gall that Hotspur dies. 'I can no longer brook thy vanities': the line he hurls at Harry as he takes up the sword fairly bursts with rage (5.4.73). To reduce Hotspur to a creature of choler is to miss, however, the way in which he, as Harry's arch rival, is given to *multiple* humours. Worcester excuses his nephew's behaviour through an appeal to 'youth and heat of blood': 'A hare-brained Hotspur', he calls him, 'governed by a spleen' (*1 Henry IV*, 5.2.17, 19). In Part 2, Lady Percy remembers her husband in similar terms: 'In military rules, humours of blood, | He was the mark and glass, copy and book, | That fashioned others' (2.3.30–2). What Harry achieves that Hotspur does not is a temperate complexion. Whether that is something he has possessed all along ('I know you all, and will a while uphold | The unyoked humour of your idleness' (*1 Henry IV*, 1.2.192–3)) or has acquired only by degrees is a question for debate.

For less apt patients than Harry there were medical therapies for achieving the same end: prime among them were blood-letting and other sorts of purges. The idea in all such cases is to return the body to a state of temperament by ridding it of excess humours. Seen in light of Galenic medicine, the on-stage deaths of Richard III, Hamlet, Othello, Coriolanus, and Hotspur present themselves as therapies of a sort. In each case a spokesman steps forward, someone possessed of greater equanimity than the protagonist who has just bled to death in the audience's view. Richmond takes command of the stage from Richard III, Fortinbras from Hamlet, Lodovico from Othello, Aufidius from Coriolanus, Harry from Hotspur. A sense of blood-letting as a purge seems to inform King John's response when the pope's emissary has disrupted the just-concluded peace between France and England. John's promise of revenge is viscerally physical:

France, I am burned up with inflaming wrath,
A rage whose heat hath this condition:
That nothing can allay, nothing but blood,
The blood, and dearest-valued blood, of France.

(3.1.266–9)

The bloody consummation that John promises is a physiological consummation, in which excess choler is discharged through the spilling of blood.

The purge that comes about in comedy is not one of blood but of melancholy. If the spleen is doing its work, Lemnius explains, 'and do exactly drink up the drossy feculency of the blood, it maketh a man thereupon wonderful merry and jocund' (*Touchstone*, 138ᵛ). He goes on to specify jovial company as an antidote to black bile. Boyet seems to have such advice in mind when he describes how Navarre and his lords disport themselves when they discover that all of them, against their solemn oaths, have fallen in love:

With that they all did tumble on the ground
With such a zealous laughter, so profound,
That in this spleen ridiculous appears,
To check their folly, passion's solemn tears.

(*Love's Labour's Lost*, 5.2.115–18)

Tears are only one form of the body's purge in laughter. Laurent Joubert in his *Traité du Ris* (1579) specifies several others in his chapter on 'Whence it comes that one pisses, shits, and sweats by dint of laughing'. The reasons are physiological. First of all, alternate expansions and contractions of the heart in laughter cause a man to lose control of his sphincter muscles. As for sweat,

It is caused by the agitation and general commotion, which excite the humours and dilate the pores of the skin, neither more nor less than does hard labour. But the face especially sweats profusely from a big laugh because of the moisture in this part of the body, which is adjacent to the brain, and because of the softness and sparseness of its skin, with the affluence of the spirits and sanguine vapour that rise up into it and are able to make a lot of water, either on their own or with the humours.[13]

According to Galenic physiology, tragedy and comedy are differing sorts of designs on a man's physical person.

Agent

The word 'person' as agent (*OED* II.2.a) would seem to be closer to our own sense of self-identity. Yet 'person' in this sense entails, not jumping up and saying 'I've gotta be *me*', but performing one or another social role. When the Lord Chief Justice tells Harry, 'I then did use the person of your father', he is referring to Henry IV, not as a unique psychological being, but precisely as a father. In asking Harry to consider whether he did anything that 'misbecame my place, | My person, or my liege's sovereignty', he speaks of his own identity with the same specificity: as Lord Chief Justice (*2 Henry IV*, 5.2.72, 99–100). What the Lord Chief Justice may 'really' be, apart from these roles, is not at issue. The role-playing essence of person-as-agent is emphasized in the Duke of Vienna's disguise in *Measure for Measure*. 'Instruct me | How I may formally in person bear | Like a true friar', the Duke asks the friar whose robes he is borrowing (1.3.46–48). When the Duke appears in his own person at the end of the play, Escalus puts Lucio on the spot about his slanders of the Duke-as-friar: 'Signor Lucio, did not you say you knew that Friar Lodowick to be a dishonest person?' (5.1.258–9). Indeed I did, says Lucio—and tries to prove it when the Duke returns to the stage once again in disguise. You slandered the Duke, Lucio baits the Duke-as-friar. 'You must, sir, change persons with me ere you make that my report,' replies his disguised interlocutor (5.1.333–4). In all these exchanges 'person' functions as a social role, something that can be put on and taken off along with a costume.

For all that, early modern men do testify to a central essence in personhood, to something that they feel makes them unique. They call that something 'soul'.[14] 'Poor soul, the centre of my sinful earth,' begins Sonnet 146 and proceeds to draw out an extended image of outward ostentation and inward depravity: 'Why dost thou pine within and suffer dearth, | Painting thy outward walls so costly gay?' (146.1, 3–4). Like 'ego' or 'psyche', 'soul' seems to exist 'in here'. Its relationship to the world round about, however, is rather different. Within the co-ordinates of empirical science, we tend to locate ourselves in perspective space. We see ourselves *against* the space around us. Within the coordinates of Platonic philosophy and Christian theology, early modern men tend to see themselves within a series of concentric circles. They see themselves as *coincident* with the space around them. Hamlet captures this dimensionality in his encomium on 'what a piece of work is a man': 'How *noble* [i.e. *elevated*] in reason, how *infinite* in faculty' (*Hamlet*, 2.2.305–6, emphasis added). The soul can be experienced as the centre of *my* earth because, in a sense, it is also the centre of *the* earth. Sir Walter Ralegh begins *The History of the World* (published 1614) by locating that history in his own self and in the selves of his readers. History begins with the creation of man in his physical person:

Man, thus compounded and formed by God, was an abstract or model, or brief story of the universal. . . . And whereas God created three sorts of living natures, (to wit) angelical, rational, and brutal; giving to angels an intellectual, and to beasts a sensual nature, he vouchsafed unto man, both the intellectual of angels, the sensitive of beasts, and the proper rational belonging unto man; . . . and because in the little frame of man's body there is a representation of the universal, and (by allusion) a kind of participation of all the parts thereof, therefore was man called *microcosmos*, or the little world.[15]

Not *a* little world, but *the* little world. 'Abstract' or 'model' may suggest a mere analogy between the world of the self and the world at large; 'story' entails active participation. It presumes a plot in which 'I' as an actor move through the world, not as a finite entity, but as the very centre of that world.

The nature of the experiencing 'I' in this configuration of body and space is spiritual; its relationship to my physical person is ambiguous. On the one hand, Platonic philosophy invites me to consider 'I' as something quite separate from my body. 'Though the substance of the Soul is thought to contract no stain or fault from the body', Lemnius observes in *The Secret Miracles of Nature*, 'yet as a thick cloud darkeneth the sun beams, and as the eye by looking through a glass of divers colours, sees things otherwise than they are, as red, yellow, green, blue; so intemperance of the body shadows and darkens the light of reason and the mind, and causeth the actions of these to be worse performed' (36–7). The soul, Lemnius continues, has two ways to operate: *through* the organs of the body and *apart from* the organs of the body. For its 'vegetative' functions of controlling growth, nutrition, and reproduction and for its 'sensible' functions of perception and locomotion, the soul certainly needs the body. For its 'rational' functions of knowing and willing, however, the soul can operate quite independently:

when the soul is bent on the contemplation of things, when it remembereth things past, and meditates of things to come, and joins things present with them, when it discourseth and searcheth out hidden things, when it is ravished, and carried aloft, as Paul was, and is made partaker of hidden mysteries, it useth its inbred force, received from God, and needs no bodily help, unless it would act something thereby.   (40)

Whatever the promptings of Platonic philosophy, however, Galenic physiology reminds me that my 'I' operates most of the time as part and parcel of my body. Where, then, does it reside? Modern imagination is apt to locate the soul in the heart; early modern medicine disperses it throughout the body in the form of 'animal' spirits that communicate between the brain and the rest of the body. Prince Henry speaks for an alternative tradition when he describes his dying father's ravings as proceeding from 'his pure brain, | Which some suppose the soul's frail dwelling house' (*King John*, 5.7.2–3). Dispersed through the body or sited in the brain, 'animal' spirits are the means by which the soul comes to know the world, through the communication of sense experience to the brain, as well as the means by which the soul contrives to act in the world, through the communication of the brain's commands to tongue, hands, and feet. *Wit* to know and *will* to do: these are the soul's rational functions. It is the susceptibility of both these functions to the power of fiction-made-of-words that Sir Philip Sidney celebrates in *A Defence of Poesy*. 'The highest end of the mistress-knowledge', Sidney says, 'stands (as I think) in the knowledge of a man's self, in the ethic and politic consideration, with the end of well-doing and not of well-knowing only.'[16] In Sidney's formulation, 'poesy' can be understood as a form of soul-speech. A play in performance is *sensed* by the eyes and the ears, but it is *understood* by the soul.

When Shakespeare's protagonists refer to other people as 'souls' ('Poor souls, they perished', exclaims Miranda after seeing the shipwreck engineered by Prospero (*Tempest*, 1.2.9)); indeed, when they speak of *themselves* as 'souls' ('It goes on, I see, | As my soul prompts it', Prospero observes (*Tempest*, 1.2.422–3))—they are speaking, not just of metonymy, but synecdoche. The soul is related to the body, not only as cause for effect, but as part for whole. So insistent is the idea of soul as the *centre* of selfhood, Leeds Barroll has argued, that our primary guide to early modern men's sense of themselves should not be Galenic physiology but what Barroll calls 'Renaissance transcendentalism'. If a man's essence is the soul with which he was endowed at creation, then 'the desideratum for the human personality' must be, not the integration of soul and body, but their separation. What that might mean in practice is precisely the opposite of our modern sense of individuality as 'self-actualization':

by this logic, any thought system not oriented toward Supreme Being was, by definition, 'apart'. Self-differentiation merely isolated man from that Supreme Unity which he was not supposed to be able to attain by himself in the first place. If he aspired solely to what we might now regard as the conditions of his own identity, a man was not 'whole': he was isolated, alone, 'nothing'.[17]

Fulke Greville catches the duality of both systems of self-knowledge, the physiological and the transcendental, when he laments,

> Oh wearisome condition of humanity!
> Born under one law, to another bound;
> Vainly begot, and yet forbidden vanity,
> Created sick, commanded to be sound. . . .[18]

To act as a person was to act under two regimes at once, the body's and the soul's. Hamlet, for one, chafes under that duality. He concludes his encomium of man's infinite faculty and god-like apprehension with an anguished turn: 'And yet to me what is this quintessence of dust?' (*Hamlet*, 2.2.309–10).

Personage

A conspicuously important instance of transcendentalism is the doctrine of 'the king's two bodies'.[19] In effect, a king was deemed to be not one person (his physical self) but two (his physical self plus the embodiment of the idea of king). Or, rather, he was three persons: as physical body and the embodier of kingship he became a *personage*. Shakespeare's kings and those who speak to them give frequent testimony to this third sense of 'person' as 'a man or woman of distinction or importance'. The separation between the king's person-as-body and his person-as-agent—and the amalgamation of the two in his person-as-personage—are pointed up by, once again, the Lord Chief Justice when he defends himself to Harry. How would Harry feel if his own son were to rebel and 'blunt the sword | That guards the peace and safety of your person, | Nay, more, to spurn at your most royal image, | And mock your workings in a second body?' (*2 Henry IV*, 5.2.86–9). At least three senses of 'person' come into play here. 'Your person' carries the physical force it usually does in early modern English, at the same time that it positions Harry as an agent, as king and hypothetical father. The physical force of 'person' is underscored by the Justice's reference to Harry as 'a second body', while the opposition between that 'second body' and the 'royal image' it rejects points up the former separateness of Harry as a physical person and the personage that he, as newly crowned king, has become. Earlier Henry IV has invoked the same three senses in telling Harry how careful he has been to tend his own image: 'Thus did I keep my person fresh and new, | My presence like a robe pontifical—| Ne'er seen but wondered at' (*1 Henry IV*, 3.2.55–7). In his own eyes Henry IV *impersonates* (literally, 'puts in person') the king according to the doctrine of the king's two bodies. In Douglas's eyes he impersonates the king according to the conventions of the playhouse: 'What art thou', Douglas asks Henry IV on the battlefield, 'That counterfeit'st the person of a king?' (*1 Henry IV*, 5.4.26-7). A knack for impersonation, in both senses of the word, runs in the Plantagenet family. Once Harry has assumed the crown, he speaks of himself in just the terms of triple personhood his father has used. To Canterbury in the council scene of *Henry V* he cautions, 'take heed how you impawn our person' (1.2.21). 'You have conspired against our royal person,' he says to Grey and Scrope as he sentences them for their treason. 'Touching our person seek we no revenge, | But we our kingdom's safety must so tender,| ... that to her laws | We do deliver you' (2.2.163, 171–4). '*Our* royal person': if Henry V succeeds as king, it is because he understands, accepts, and exploits the coincidence of *my* body and the *king's* body in 'personage'.

'Person' in this third sense of the word is very much a matter of external signifiers. Traditionally the monarch-to-be spent the night before his coronation in fasting and prayer and arrived for the ceremony itself dressed only in a penitent's plain robe. In the course of the ceremony the penitent lay prostrate before the altar—Elizabeth opted only to kneel—and was raised to kingship, not by receiving the crown, but by being christened by the Archbishop of Canterbury or (in the politically complicated case of Elizabeth) by a willing substitute. Then came the external signs of kingship. Vestments, sword, bracelets, mantle, crown, ring, gloves, sceptre, rod: the monarch was invested with these properties, in this precise order, one by one.[20] Henry IV is perhaps remembering his assumption of the personage of a king when he identifies 'my presence' with 'a robe pontifical'. Feeling the weight of buttons, gold, silver, and silk sleeves upon his body, George Trosse plays out a humbler version of the process whereby person-as-body and person-as-agent present themselves to the world as a personage.

To understand the construction of masculinity in Shakespeare's plays and poems we must learn to read these visible signs of person-hood. By law, clothing in early modern England was supposed to be an index to the wearer's social status. Three statutes dating from the reigns of Henry VIII (1533 and 1542) and Philip and Mary (1555) were reaffirmed, extended, and brought up to date with changing fashions and escalating prices in no fewer than nine royal proclamations issued during Elizabeth's reign. Attempts at government control of apparel ended in 1604, but only because Parliament rejected bills that would have given power of regulation solely to the crown.[21] The Act of 1533 divides the people of the realm into twelve ranks, each distinguished from the next by precisely graded fabrics, yardage, colours, and adorn-ments.[22] The social engineering implicit in the parliamentary statutes becomes ever more explicit in the royal proclamations. The penulti-mate of these proclamations (1597) attributes to the extravagant dress of 'the better sort' nothing less than 'the decay and lack of hospital-ity... principally occasioned by the immeasurable charges and expenses which they are put to in superfluous apparelling of their wives, chil-dren, and families'. The hospitality of England's traditional feudal economy, in which social betters reaffirm their status by obliging their social inferiors, is being replaced by an open market in which social status can be purchased for cash. The result is 'the confusion also of degrees in all places, ... where the meanest are as richly apparelled as their betters'. Indeed, 'the pride that such inferior persons take in their garments' drives many of them 'to robbing and stealing by the high-way'.[23] The increasingly loose connection between sartorial signs and social substance in the course of the sixteenth and seventeenth cen-turies can be witnessed in George Trosse's silk sleeves and gold and silver buttons—articles that had once been reserved for nobility.

Robert Greene's satiric pamphlet *A Quip for an Upstart Courtier* (1592) addresses this slippage as Velvet Britches and Cloth Britches debate who has the stronger claim to 'frank tenement', the right to dwell, in England. Velvet Britches—or at least half of him—appears in Figure 2b in all his Italianate splendour. Outrageously large breeches, or 'hose' as they were generally called in early modern English, were singled out for special attention in the proclamation of 1562, and protection of English-produced goods against imports had been part of the laws' inspiration from the very beginning (Hooper 439). Dressed unostentatiously in the simple, English-made clothing of his ancestors, Cloth Britches reminds Velvet Britches, 'though you be never so richly daubed with gold and powdered with pearl, yet you are but a case for the buttocks, and a cover for the basest part of a man's body no more than I'.[24] Velvet Britches takes an altogether more capitalistic view of the matter. Everyone, he claims, aspires to dress upscale:

What drives merchants to seek foreign marts, to venture their goods and hazard their lives? Not, if still the end of their travail were a pair of cloth britches. No, velvet, costly attire, curious and quaint apparel is the spur that pricks them forward to attempt such a danger. Doth not the soldier fight to be brave, the lawyer study to countenance himself with cost? The artificer takes pains only for my sake, that wearing me he may brag it amongst the best. What credit carries he nowadays that goes pinned up in a cloth britch? Who will keep him company that thinks well of himself, unless he use the simple slave to make clean his shoes? The world is changed, and men are grown to more wit, and their minds to aspire after more honourable thoughts.

In sum, 'what is the end of service to a man, but to countenance himself and credit his master with brave suits?' (11.230–1). In the view of Velvet Britches, the world is full of persons wanting to be personages. Against such claims Cloth Britches affirms the traditional value of clothing as a marker of the class, nation, and gender to which a man is born. Despite the occasions when Shakespeare shares Greene's disdain for clothes without a body—'Dost know this water-fly?' Hamlet asks Horatio when 'young Osric, a courtier', brings news of the intended match with Laertes (*Hamlet*, 5.2.83–4)—costume remains a major way of establishing personage in the theatre. 'What is thy name?' Henry V asks Mountjoy, arriving as envoy from the French court. 'I know thy quality' (3.6.137). He knows that quality from the personage Mountjoy shows himself to be in dress and deportment.

Perhaps the most tangible pieces of evidence we have of what made up a personage in early modern England are painted portraits. Across

the period covered by Roy Strong's catalogue *The English Icon: Elizabethan and Jacobean Portraiture* there were of course changes in fashion
and, to some degree, in the conventions of painting, but during the
twenty years from 1590 to 1610 the clothing and accoutrements in full-
length portraits of men tend to accentuate the same features of the
male body: a head set off from the rest of the body by a ruff, a fairly
slender upper chest, an ample lower torso emphasized by the cut and
the bulk of the subject's jacket, exaggerated thighs, elongated calves,
small feet. In effect, these portraits define three focal centres: head,
groin, and thighs. Velvet Britches, in all his vanity, can stand as an
instance (see Figure 2b). Philip Stubbes in his *Anatomy of Abuses* (1583)
leaves no doubt about where the viewer's eye is drawn after he has
noticed another man's head. Stubbes's spokesman Philoponus
describes to his interlocutor the outrageous clothing of the inhabitants
of 'Ailgna' (alias Anglia)—their ruffs, their hose, above all their jackets
or doublets, stuffed full of padding: 'certain I am there was never any
kind of apparel ever invented that could more disproportion the body
of man than these doublets with great bellies hanging down beneath
their pudenda...and stuffed with four, five, or six pound of bombast
at the least'.[25] Helping to draw the viewer's eye to the codpiece were
chains, girdles, or straps for scabbards. It should come as no surprise
that ruffs, breeches, and swords are the very articles of apparel most
often singled out for surveillance in the proclamations of 1562 and 1580
(Hooper 440, 444–5). Head, groin, and thighs are each distinguished
by conspicuous markers of masculinity.

On the head the essential sign is a beard. Except for the Dutch,
Lemnius observes, 'other nations think, that such as are smooth and
want beards, are not so strong for Venus-sports, and fit to get children,
that many men are unwilling to marry their daughters to them'
(*Miracles*, 282–3). Beatrice reads male bodies in just this way: 'He
that hath a beard is more than a youth', she quips, 'and he that hath
no beard is less than a man' (*Much Ado about Nothing*, 2.1.30–3). In
boasting to Hotspur, Douglas stakes his very manhood on his beard:
'No man so potent breathes upon the ground | But I will beard him'
(*1 Henry IV*, 4.1.11–12). Thighs and groin signify in even more palpable
terms. Where earlier fashion had favoured a codpiece—'A round hose,
madam, now's not worth a pin | Unless you have a codpiece to stick
pins on,' Lucetta advises Julia in *The Two Gentlemen of Verona*

(2.7.55–6)—turn-of-the-century fashion accentuated the dagger or rapier that most men in early modern England carried with them whenever they left the security of home. Difference in social rank was measured by the permitted length of this weapon and by its adornment. The proclamation of 1562 lays down specific limitations:

Her Majesty's pleasure is that no man shall after ten days next following this proclamation wear any sword, rapier, or any weapon in their stead passing the length of one yard and half a quarter of blade at the uppermost: neither any dagger above the length of twelve inches in blade: neither any buckler with a sharp point or with any point above two inches of length ....

The penalty imposed is forfeiture of the weapon, imprisonment, and a fine.[26] In many painted portraits the masculine subject is shown grasping his rapier by the hand. The weapon in Cornelius Ketel's 1577 portrait of Sir Martin Frobisher, now in the Bodleian Library, Oxford, is a pistol that the subject brandishes just inches from his penis.[27] The concealed anatomical counterpart to such ostentatiously *un*concealed weapons is exposed in *Twelfth Night* when 'Cesario', who, truth to tell, can advance no physiological claims to a sword, tries to get out of a match with Sir Andrew. Impossible, counters Sir Toby: 'Therefore on, or strip your sword stark naked, for meddle you must, that's certain, or forswear to wear iron about you' (3.4.243–5). The jokes bandied by thrust-happy Samson with his Capulet mate Gregory at the beginning of *Romeo and Juliet*—'I will show myself a tyrant: when I have fought with the men I will be civil with maids—I will cut off their [maiden]heads' (1.1.20–2)—point up how handy a sword is in turning a person into a personage. As devices for violating the persons of other people, rapiers function as the ultimate extension of the male body into social space.

Actor

The list of 'Names of the *Actors*' appended to *The Tempest* in the 1623 folio contains, not what we might expect, the names of the performers who originally played the roles in the theatre, but the names of the characters in the fiction.[28] The *dramatis personae*, the 'persons of the play', are first and foremost persons-as-agents. Peter Quince the carpenter may not get all the words quite right, but he knows what 'person' means in a play. Let one of his fellow players come in with a lantern, he suggests, 'and say he comes to disfigure, or to present, the person of Moonshine' (*A Midsummer Night's Dream*, 3.1.55–6). Malvolio reveals an acquaintance with the vocabulary of the theatre—surprising in one so opposed to mirth—when he upbraids Sir Toby Belch and crew during their midnight revels: 'My masters, are you mad?.... Is there no respect of place, persons, nor time in you?' (*Twelfth Night*, 2.3.83, 88–9).

In a play as performed, it is not just persons-as-agents that are implicated in the *dramatis personae* but persons-as-personages. A 1598 inventory of costumes and props owned by the Admiral's Men includes items restricted by the sumptuary laws to royalty and nobility:

one pair of French hose, cloth of gold
one pair of cloth-of-gold hose with silver panes [i.e., infolded panels]
one pair of cloth-of-silver hose with satin and silver panes
Tamburlaine's coat with copper lace.

Also included in the inventory are assorted properties out of Elizabethan and Jacobean portraiture: a globe and golden sceptre, a copper target, and six foils, armour, a gilt spear, and a long sword.[29] What these trunks of costumes and racks of weapons made possible is a radical split between signifier and signified. The signs of personage were real; the persons displaying those signs were not what they seemed. What the acting troupes bought were not specially made costumes but the cast-off clothes of actual people, particularly of noblemen. Thomas Platter, a Swiss traveller who saw *Julius Caesar* at the newly built Globe in 1599, found this custom worthy of record in his journal: 'it is the English usage for eminent lords or knights at their decease to bequeath and leave almost the best of their clothes to their serving men, which it is unseemly for the latter to wear, so that they offer them then for sale for a small sum to the actors.'[30]

Dressed in such clothes, a commoner could become a king. By that possibility the literal-minded among the monarch's subjects were made decidedly uncomfortable. When a player and a dancing master show up as possible jurors in the quarrel between Velvet Britches and Cloth Britches, Velvet Britches is all for them: 'The player and the usher of the dancing school are plain, honest, humble men, that for a penny or an old-cast suit of apparel [will do anything].' Cloth Britches is less enthusiastic: 'of the two I hold the Player to be the better Christian, although in his own imagination too full of self-liking and self-love and is unfit to be of the Jury though I hide and conceal his faults and fopperies, in that I have been merry at his sports.' Cloth Britches will concede his enjoyment, even *if* the players always present the social likes of him as a clown or a fool (Greene II: 291–2). Where does the player's inflated sense of 'self' come from? 'Fopperies' suggests an answer: from his clothes. Stephen Gosson in *The School of Abuse* (1579) complains that 'the very hirelings of some of our players . . . jet under gentlemen's noses in suits of silk, exercising themselves to prating on the stage, and common scoffing when they come abroad, where they look askance over the shoulder at every man, of whom the Sunday before they begged an alms'.[31] It is worth noting that in the same season Platter saw *Julius Caesar* Shakespeare's company was also mounting a now-lost play entitled *Cloth Breeches and Velvet Hose*.[32]

Richard Burbage playing Richard II presents a striking instance of the actor as exultant self. To person-as-role and person-as-agent Richard B. as Richard Two added person-as-personage when he performed in the prison scene the character's longest soliloquy in the play: 'Thus play I in one person many people, | And none contented.' The arrival of Richard II's appointed murderers brought to a close what must have been one of Burbage's greatest moments onstage, but Richard/'Richard' maintained the same complicated sense of personhood to the end: 'That hand shall burn in never-quenching fire,' Richard warns his killers, 'That staggers thus my person' (*Richard II*, 5.5.31–2, 108–9). The larger-than-life personages of *Henry VIII*—or *All Is True*, to give the play the title by which some contemporaries knew it—are revealed in the Prologue to be theatrical illusions:

> Think ye see
> The very persons of our noble story
> As they were living; think you see them great,
> And followed with the general throng and sweat
> Of thousand friends; then, in a moment, see
> How soon this mightiness meets misery.
>
> (Pro. 25–30)

Only Henry VIII escapes the *un*making of personhood along with the making. The christening of Princess Elizabeth prompts his final speech in the play: 'O lord Archbishop,' he affirms, 'Thou hast made me now a man. Never before | This happy child did I get anything' (5.4.63–5). The word 'person' occurs more often in this highly metatheatrical script than in any other play by Shakespeare. What the audience is invited to witness, in Henry's words as well as the Prologue's, is manhood being made before one's very eyes.

To person-as-agent and person-as-personage Rosalind-as-*persona* joins a playful insistence on person-as-body. The mock-wooing that Rosalind-as-'Ganymede' stages with Orlando in Act 4 of *As You Like It* is designed to test Orlando's resourcefulness as a suitor—in effect, to throw him off, to put him out. 'What, of my suit?,' Orlando exclaims. 'Not out of your apparel,' Rosalind/'Ganymede' replies—with at least a verbal glance at Orlando's person—'and yet out of your suit.' But hold: 'Am not I your Rosalind?' I enjoy saying you are, Orlando admits.

> ROSALIND Well, in her person I say I will not have you.
> ORLANDO Then in mine own person I die.
> ROSALIND No, faith; die by attorney. The poor world is almost six thousand years old, and in all this time there was not any man died in his own person, videlicet, in a love-cause..... Men have died from time to time, and worms have eaten them, but not for love.
>
> (4.1.81–3, 86–101)

The word-play here on 'person' (as theatrical role, as legal agent, as physical body) is quite as dizzying as the word-play on 'die' (as departing from life, as reaching sexual climax). In such a moment masculinity is shown to be very much a theatrical effect, an illusion produced by *personae*.

That illusion remains grounded, however, in persons-as-bodies. As Joseph R. Roach has demonstrated, early modern remarks about the actor's craft assume early modern ideas about the actor's body—and the bodies of his customers.[33] When Hamlet marvels how his friend the travelling player can 'in a dream of passion' turn pale, weep, look about distractedly, and speak in a broken voice (2.2.554), he is using the word 'passion' in a specifically Galenic sense, as a perturbation of the actor's bodily person, brought on by something he has apprehended with his soul. The player has, in physical fact, breathed in the very spirit of Hecuba. 'Is it not monstrous', Hamlet wonders,

> that this player here,
> But in a fiction, in a dream of passion,
> Could force his soul so to his whole conceit
> That from her working all his visage wanned....
>
> (2.2.553–6)

'Her' in the last line may as well refer to Hecuba as to the player's soul. For in the player's heart, where in-breathed air is mixed with blood, Hecuba's *anima* has taken possession of his own 'animal' spirits, transforming his physical person. What's Hecuba to him? A spirit. Or he to Hecuba? A body. In such a situation '*im*personation' is more than a metaphor. The actor, having giving up his person to the spirit of someone else, imparts that spirit through projected breath and projected eye-beams to the persons of his audience. The actor's art consists in being able to discipline and control what would otherwise be an act of self-annihilation.

In the course of his treatise on the humoral body Lemnius describes one particular temperament that seems ideally suited for actors. Out of a combination of two parts blood and one part choler mixed with melancholy

proceedeth such a complexion and bodily habit, as produceth sundry motions, affections, and inclinations of the mind, and which doth inwardly dispose, fashion and frame their natures and dispositions (yea before they break out into words) enabling them fit and meet to discharge and execute the part of any person, that we either of ourselves take in hand, or which by nature and public function is to us assigned.

And to clinch the point he quotes some lines on natural aptitude from Horace's *Ars Poetica* (*Touchstone*, 100–100ᵛ). Although cowardly, slow-moving phlegm is conspicuously absent from Lemnius's blood-dominated formula for stage success, he suggests elsewhere in *The Touchstone of Complexions* that actors affect a perfect balance among *all* the humours, particularly in copying the perfectly tempered man's upright deportment and comely motion (36ᵛ). Visual elements compose only one aspect of an actor's *persona*: sound constitutes the other. In voice as well as in visage the warm-bloodedness of masculinity proves to be an advantage. The pseudonymous astrologer 'Arcandam' in a book translated into English in 1592 describes how different humours produce different qualities of voice, phlegm generating a feeble voice, choler a harsh voice. Best of all is a voice dominated by blood (Bamborough 38–9). 'They therefore that have hot bodies', Lemnius observes, 'are also of nature variable, and changeable, ready, prompt, lively, lusty and appliable: of tongue, trowling, perfect, and persuasive: delivering their words distinctly, plainly and pleasantly, with a voice thereto not squeaking and slender, but strainable, comely and audible' (*Touchstone*, 45ᵛ). The very qualities of body that produce good exemplars of masculinity are those that produce good actors.

If gender is a performance, in Shakespeare's plays as in early modern culture as a whole, it is a performance carried out by what Shakespeare and his contemporaries understood as 'persons'. Within the fictions themselves, numerous characters testify to an experience of gender that is sited in their *physical* persons. In Galenic physiology, masculinity consists not, as modern psychoanalytical theory would have it, in the possession of a penis, but in the possession of the hot, moist complexion of which the penis is but one sign. In the social roles they play—father, son, justice, king—Shakespeare's male characters attest that masculinity is also a function of persons as *agents*. In describing their inner essence as a 'soul', they act under the aegis of transcendental imperatives as well as the promptings of their humoral bodies. Physical persons and persons-as-agents are manifested in painted portraits as *personages*. Personages are, indeed, just what spectators at the Globe paid to see. Stage performances of masculinity entail all four senses of 'person'. As *personae*, as agents, as personages, as physical persons Shakespeare and his fellow actors replicated within the small space of the Globe's wooden O the very processes whereby masculine identity was performed in the world of early modern England at large.

Vertues honor, Wisdomes valure, Graces seruaunt, Mercies loue,
Gods elected, Truths beloued, Heauens affected: Doe, a proue

3. T. Cockson, *The Right Honourable Robert Devereux, Earl of Essex* (c.1595–8).

Ideals

If 'manners maketh man', Shakespeare and his contemporaries had plenty of places to turn for advice. First of all, to proverbs. 'As the man is so is his talk.' 'One man is no man.' 'A man is weal or woe as he thinks himself so.' 'Wise men have their mouth in their heart, fools their heart in their mouth.'¹ | 'Give thy thoughts no tongue, | Nor any unproportioned thought his act.' | 'Be thou familiar but by no means vulgar.' 'Neither a borrower nor a lender be.' Polonius may be a lord, but he draws his precepts from a treasury that was open to all men (*Hamlet*, 1.3.59–61, 75). For men who could read printed books (statistics based on the ability to sign one's name suggest such men made up about a quarter of the male population), further resources were to be found in the booksellers' stalls of St Paul's Churchyard. Ranged against the total output of Europe's printing presses between 1500 and 1650, the scores of conduct books published then would probably take up just as much space, relatively speaking, as the self-help section in any bookstore today. Baldasar Castiglione's *Il Libro del Cortegiano* (1528, English translation as *The Book of the Courtier* 1588) is only the most famous in a series that includes Giovanni della Casa's *Galateo... Or rather a treatise of the manners and behaviours it behoveth a man to use and eschew in his familiar conversation* (1558, English translation 1576), Stephano Guazzo's *Civil Conversation* (1574, English translation 1581), and Pierre de la Primaudaye's *The French Academy* (1577, English translation 1586), as well as distinctively English productions like Henry Peacham's *The Complete Gentleman* (1622) and Richard Brathwait's *The English Gentleman* (1630), not to mention, further down the social scale, books like Robert Cleaver's *A Godly Form of Household Government* (1598), the *Haven of Pleasure: Containing a freeman's felicity and a true direction of how to live well* (1596) by one I.T. (or perhaps J.T.), and William Gouge's *Of Domestical Duties* (1622). The very existence of such books—and in such numbers—stands as testimony that masculine identity was understood to be a social construction long before post-structuralist theory made an issue of the fact.

In addition to proverbs and conduct books, a man trying to shape himself to the expectations of his peers might turn also to the theatre. In defending stage plays against moral detractors, the actor and playwright Thomas Heywood falls back on the assumption, as old as Cicero, that the fundamental purpose of all kinds of fiction is to teach ethics by offering positive examples to be emulated and negative examples to be rejected. Thomas Nashe in his satirical pamphlet *Piers Penniless* (1592) cites history plays in particular for depicting 'forefathers' valiant acts' and singles out for particular praise Lord Talbot in *1 Henry VI*: 'How would it have joyed brave Talbot, the terror of the French, to think that after he had lain two hundred years in his tomb he should triumph again on the stage, and have his bones new-embalmed with the tears of ten thousand spectators at least.'[2] Nashe presumably has in mind scenes like those in which Talbot fights Joan of Arc single-handedly (1.7) or inspires the flagging English army to storm the walls of Orléans (2.1). The soldiers' rallying cry is 'A Talbot! A Talbot!' One of them reads out the moral of the staged exemplum for the spectators' benefit: 'The cry of "Talbot" serves me for a sword, | For I have loaden me with many spoils, | Using no other weapon but his name' (2.1.79, 81–3). When Talbot reappears in the next scene he assumes the definite article: 'Here is the Talbot,' he tells the French messenger. 'Who would speak with him?' (2.2.37). Such scenes, at least as Nashe reads them, offer men in the audience ideals on which to model their own behaviour: 'So bewitching a thing is lively and well spirited action, that it hath power to new mold the hearts of the spectators and fashion them to the shape of any notable attempt' (B4). Richard III, by contrast, would stand as an example to be shunned. 'If we present a Tragedy', Heywood assures readers of his *An Apology for Actors* (1612), 'we include the fatal and abortive ends of such as commit notorious murders, which is aggravated and acted with all the Art that may be, to terrify men from the like abhorred practices' (F3[v]).[3]

Enemies of the theatre weren't so sure. The anonymous I.G. (or J.G.) who published *A Refutation of the Apology for Actors* three years after Heywood's *Apology* assumes, along with Philip Stubbes in *The Anatomy of Abuses,* that playgoers will be incited to perform the very deeds of lust and violence that Heywood claims they will learn to despise. Contemporary controversy over sex and violence on film and television suggests that the issues here have by no means been settled. Heywood's testimony that audiences were disposed to respond to plays in terms of ethical ideals is borne out by first-hand accounts like those of Simon Forman, who saw three of Shakespeare's plays in 1611 and recorded his impressions on paper. Forman makes no comment on Hermione's statue coming to life at the end of *The Winter's Tale*, but Autolycus' clowning exploits earlier in the play inspire this conclusion: 'Beware of trusting feigned beggars or fawning fellows.'[4] Heywood's idealistic premises run exactly counter to the assumption of new-historicist critics that stage plays offer evidence of how writers, actors, and audiences actually lived their lives. The truth must lie somewhere in between. The relationship between dramatic fictions and social realities was, and is, a *reciprocal* matter: Shakespeare's plays represent masculine identity in ways that must have been recognizable from everyday life even as they set up models of action and eloquence that a man might want to imitate.

It is often in closing moments that Shakespeare's scripts take an idealistic turn. Antony's praise of Brutus is a case in point. 'This was the noblest Roman of them all,' he declares to Octavius, Messala, Lucillius, the assembled army—and the assembled audience at the Globe.

> All the conspirators save only he
> Did that they did in envy of great Caesar.
> He only in a general honest thought
> And common good to all made one of them.
> His life was gentle, and the elements
> So mixed in him that nature might stand up
> And say to all the world 'This was a man'.
>
> (*Julius Caesar*, 5.5.68–74)

If, as Jacques Lacan argues, a person's self-identity is made out of language, it is worth noting the key words that are made synonymous here with 'man.' Such words may tell us a lot about the construction of masculinity in Elizabethan culture at large. The controlling words in Antony's speech are 'noble', 'honest', and 'gentle'. Two other words have been attached to Brutus since Cassius first broached the subject of conspiracy to him in Act 1. 'What is it that you would impart to me?' Brutus answers Cassius's insinuations.

> If it be aught toward the general good,
> Set honour in one eye and death i'th'other,
> And I will look on both indifferently;
> For let the gods so speed me as I love
> The name of honour more than I fear death.

Cassius's reply is assured: 'I know that virtue to be in you, Brutus, | As well as I do know your outward favour' (1.2.86–93). Nobility, honesty, gentleness, honour, virtue: in the world of *Julius Caesar* these are the qualities that make a man a man. A good argument can be made that they are the very qualities that define ideal manhood in early modern England as well.

In a sermon on chivalry preached before the Artillery Company of London in 1626 William Gouge laments that the English language, unlike Latin, has no way of distinguishing 'man' as a term for just any male (*homo*) from 'man' as the embodiment of virtue and prowess (*vir*):

Our English is herein penurious: it wanteth fit words to express this difference. We call all, whether mighty or mean *men*, yet sometimes this word *men* in our tongue hath his emphasis, as in these and such like phrases: 'They have played the *men*,' 'They have showed themselves *men*,' 'They are *men* indeed.' Thus in the English translation of the scripture it is used (1 Corinthians 16: 13): 'Quit you like *men*' and (2 Samuel 10: 12) 'Let us play the *men*.'[5]

The fact that *virtue* is derived from *vir* establishes a fundamental connection between masculinity and conformity to ethical ideals. The link between the two consists in the root sense of *virtue* as inherent power or efficacy, whether in a supernatural or divine being (*OED* I.1), in a mortal person (*OED* I.6), or in physical entities like plants, minerals, and drugs (*OED* II.9, 11). Cassius professes to read this inner quality in Brutus's 'outward favour.' Honesty is one way of describing the congruity of outer show with inner truth. Considerations rather less metaphysical inform nobility, gentleness, and honour. All three words refer to distinctions that are social as well as ethical. William Harrison in his *Description of England* (1577) distinguishes four 'sorts' or 'orders' of people: (1) nobility and other gentlemen whose wealth is in land, (2) inhabitants of cities and towns who earn their living by practising a profession or plying a trade, (3) yeomen farmers who own or lease the land they work, and (4) labourers who own nothing themselves and sell their services to others.[6] Nobility, gentleness, and honour are part and parcel of this social hierarchy. 'Noble' may describe a man's deeds, but in the first instance nobility is a fact of birth. Anyone can cultivate 'gentle' behaviour, but that behaviour is the sort expected of men who do not have to work for a living. The very idea of honour—'high respect, esteem, or reverence, accorded to exalted worth or rank' (*OED* 1)—implies a separation of higher from lower. In an exhaustive study of scripts written for the stage between 1591 and 1640 C. L. Barber has demonstrated that the most frequent uses of the word 'honour' in connection with men have to do with social rank, specifically with the behaviour of characters belonging to the gentry. Honourableness as a mark of moral character becomes frequent only later in the seventeenth century.[7] Any discussion of ideals of masculinity in early modern England must take into account, then, differences in social rank.

Sir William Segar in his treatise on *Honour Military and Civil* (1602) takes the radical position that 'there are but two arenas of action for men, business and honour':

The principal marks whereat every man's endeavour in this life aimeth are either profit or honour, th'one proper to vulgar people and men of inferior fortune, the other due to persons of better birth and generous disposition. For as the former by pains and parsimony do only labour to become rich, so th'other by military skill or knowledge in civil government aspire to honour and human glory.[8]

Segar's book is ostensibly addressed to men of the latter sort. However, the very fact that he should write such a book—full of definitions of ranks, lists of duties, and tables of precedence—suggests that traditional ideas of honour needed defending, implicitly against trespassers from the arena of commerce. In effect, Segar is acknowledging the existence of two distinct economic systems in England of the 1590s, the older feudal system based on land and the newer capitalist system based on money—but he is granting legitimacy only to the former.[9] Conflict between the two systems is played out in *The Merry Wives of Windsor*. Justice Shallow enters the play full of indignation that Falstaff has poached deer from his land—and stands ready to carry his case to the royal court of Star Chamber (1.1.1–3). In the traditional feudal value system deer *signified*. By law of the realm, venison could not be bought or sold in England; it could only be given away by landowners as a sign of their largesse.[10] As a sign of status, deer belonged to the arena of honour, not to the arena of commerce. Shallow's sense of personal violation is appropriate to a play in which honour and commerce are comically confused as *Sir* John Falstaff joins members of the cash-hungry local gentry in pursuing a townsman's daughter's dowry. For all its economic plausibility, however, Segar's recognition of just two codes of manhood in the England of his day overlooks the variety of competing ideals to be found in proverbs, conduct books, and plays. At least five ideal types offer themselves for emulation in Shakespeare's scripts: the chivalrous knight, the Herculean hero, the humanist man of moderation, the merchant prince, and the saucy jack. Let us examine those five types one by one.

Chivalrous Knight

In an age of gunpowder, chivalry was already something of an anachronism. Long after the mounted knight with a lance had been replaced in actual warfare by a soldier with a gun, noblemen and gentlemen in Renaissance England still liked to have their portraits painted with all the accoutrements of chivalry: helmet, breastplate, sword, lance. Sir Martin Frobisher, whose portrait by Cornelius Ketel we noted in Chapter 1, is unusual in being shown with a pistol. At the annual celebration of her accession to the throne, Queen Elizabeth's male courtiers delighted in staging a tournament in which they assumed roles out of romantic fiction: The Shepherd Knight, the Frozen Knight, the Black Knight, the Unknown Knight stood ready to defend their sovereign lady's honour against all challengers. Gentlemen-in-training at the inns of court followed suit, turning their Christmas festivities into entertainments for the pleasure of a mock-prince, complete with knights who went off on quests. The first recorded performance of *The Comedy of Errors*, for example, took place in 1594 at Gray's Inn before 'The Prince of Purpool' (*alias* Henry Helmes, one of the law students), who sent off various of his knights on missions to the land of the Tartars and to Russia.[11] The chivalric knights who figure in Shakespeare's scripts bring with them a similar aura of aesthetic anachronism.

It has been often remarked, for example, how *Richard II* begins in a ceremonial feudal world and ends in the world of practical politics that Shakespeare and his contemporaries inhabited. '*Old* John of Gaunt, *time-honoured* Lancaster...': Richard's very first words stress the passedness of the England over which he presides (1.1.1, emphasis added). Bolingbroke's formal challenge to Mowbray in the first scene— Bolingbroke throws down his gage in the presence of the king— locates the play solidly within Segar's arena of honour. Richard's decision to decide the issue in a trial by combat confirms that impression. The trial itself is a ceremonial affair in which trumpets signal the approach of each combatant and the Lord Marshal, as if coached by Segar, speaks in precise formulas. No better illustration than Bolingbroke could be found to support Richard McCoy's argument that the cult of chivalry in late sixteenth-century England served to negotiate some central conflicts for men under Elizabeth's government: obedience versus honour, deference versus aggression, royal sovereignty versus aristocratic self-assertion.[12] The consummate courtier, as Castiglione's Count Ludovico argues, is first of all a warrior, but a *faithful* warrior: 'I judge the principal and true profession of a Courtier ought to be in feats of arms, the which above all I will have him practise lively, and to be known among other of his hardiness, for his achieving of enterprises, and for his fidelity toward him whom he serveth.' In affairs other than arms, however, the courtier should be 'lowly, sober, and circumspect, fleeing above all things bragging and unshameful praising of himself.'[13]

In his very first words Henry Bolingbroke pointedly addresses the tensions in the role of knight: 'Many years of happy days befall | My gracious sovereign, my most loving liege!' (*Richard II*, 1.1.20–1). Mowbray speaks briefly to the same effect. When Bolingbroke proceeds to explain his grievance, he is careful once again to show due deference ('First—heaven be the record to my speech— | In the devotion of a subject's love, | ... | Come I appellant to this princely presence') (1.1.30–1, 34) before he thrusts at Mowbray words that are sharpened with a sense of honour, energized by aggression, and deployed to assert his aristocratic selfhood: 'what I speak | My body shall make good upon this earth, | Or my divine soul answer it in heaven. | Thou art a traitor and a miscreant...' (1.1.30–4, 36–9). The king's interruption of the combat, his decision to banish both contestants, frees Bolingbroke to forgo obedience, deference, and acknowledgement of royal sovereignty and to pursue honour, aggression, and his personal rights. Bolingbroke's eventual success in deposing Richard puts the seal on his transformation from chivalric knight to Machiavellian politician.

The Bolingbroke of Shakespeare's stage found a real-life counterpart in the Essex of Elizabeth's court. In popular imagination the second Earl of Essex figured as the ideal knight. A broadside image published by T. Cockson in the late 1590s shows the Earl on horseback against scenes of his military victories: Cadiz, Rouen, the Treceras Islands, and Ireland (see Figure 3). The caption at the bottom leaves no ideal trait unattributed: Essex is lauded as 'Virtue's honour, Wisdom's valour, Grace's servant, Mercy's love, God's elected, Truth's beloved, Heaven's affected.' In his physical person and in the text that describes him, Essex embodies Segar's prescription of the ideal knight. *Honour Military and Civil* demands that a knight 'be of good constitution and convenient strength to endure travail in actions appertaining to soldiers'. Note in Cockson's image the military campaigns won by Virtue's honour and Wisdom's valour. 'He should be well favoured of face and comely. He should be of bold aspect, rather inclined to severity than softness.' The Earl's lips and eyes are a study in affable dignity. 'He should be sober and discreet, not inclined to vain delights or effeminate pleasures, obedient, vigilant and patient, faithful and loyal, constant and resolute.' The perhaps questionable hat may, to late sixteenth-century taste, have been seen as appropriate for Grace's servant. Note, too, the Earl Marshal's staff, Essex's badge of office under Elizabeth, in his right hand. 'He should be charitable, because wars are not taken in hand for the destruction of countries and towns but the defence of laws and people.' A precept certainly honoured by Mercy's love. 'Lastly, he should be fortunate, since Fortune is the Lady of Arms and showeth her power in nothing more than in the adventures of war' (Segar 49–50). End of comparison: Essex was executed for an attempt to depose Elizabeth, his response to her punishment for his unsuccessful attempt to wage war in Ireland in his own right. Perhaps as a cover, perhaps as inspiration, the conspirators had hired the Lord Chamberlain's Men to revive an old play the day before the attempted rebellion. The play they chose was *Richard II*. Essex, like Bolingbroke, lost his balance: the chivalrous knight became the devious rebel. Several details in Cockson's image confirm that what a viewer sees is an ideal type, not the sixteenth-century equivalent of a photograph. Essex's dress, complete with currently fashionable hat rather than serviceable helmet, is ceremonial. The battle in the middle distance is being fought with lances, not guns. The image hovers somewhere in between romantic fiction and empirical possibility.

Bolingbroke belongs to that space, as do such other knightly heroes in Shakespeare's scripts as Troilus, Hector, Pericles, Palamon, and Arcite. All of them embody virtue, honour, honesty, nobility, and gentleness to a superlative degree, even as they are distanced from the sixteenth- and seventeenth-century men who watched their exploits in the theatre. Honesty is perhaps the trait that distances them the most. 'Why should I war without the walls of Troy | That find such cruel battle here within?' (*Troilus and Cressida*, 1.1.2–3): in his opening speech Troilus distinguishes himself among the chivalrous Trojans for wearing his heart on his sleeve. 'As true as Troilus' becomes his badge of honour. The scene in which Cressida reviews the Trojan warriors returning from the battlefield as Pandarus describes them one by one (1.2.173–267) plays very much like the opening procession to one of Queen Elizabeth's Accession Day tilts. When an actual trial by combat is arranged later in the play, the Trojans' champion is Hector. As with Troilus, the trait that crowns Hector's virtue, honour, nobility, and gentleness is his honesty. In council Hector candidly admits to his brothers that Helen is not worth defending—and yet capitulates on a point of honour: 'For 'tis a cause that hath no mean dependence | Upon our joint and several dignities' (2.2.191–2). At King Simonides' court Pericles figures in a pageant-like sequence very much like the one that opens *Troilus and Cressida*. Once again a feminine spectator, in this case Thaisa, is invited to take stock of the knights who might serve her while King Simonides reads out the motto with which each has chosen to emblazon himself. Pericles, in rusty armour, bearing a withered branch green only at the top, wins Thaisa's hand by displaying the very lack of presumption that Castiglione recommends (*Pericles* scenes 6 and 7). Palamon and Arcite in *The Two Noble Kinsmen* betray a hyperbolic courtliness that borders on naivety as they try to sequester themselves against the temptations of the world and yet promptly fall in love with the same woman. By 1613, when the play was likely first performed, the tournament in which the two knights decide the issue between them (5.5) had become an object of nostalgia, a theatrical set piece appropriate to an outworn code of masculinity that belonged to Chaucer's time, not King James's. In Richard McCoy's view, chivalry died with Prince Henry in 1612.

Herculean Hero

To a different order of morality entirely belongs the Herculean hero. In a study that ranges from Sophocles to Seneca to Shakespeare to Dryden, Eugene M. Waith finds the Herculean hero to be 'a warrior of great stature who is guilty of striking departures from the morality of the society in which he lives.'[14] The key word here is guilt: where the chivalrous knight exemplifies the highest masculine ideals of his society, the Herculean hero behaves according to a code of ethics that is all his own. In narratives produced in ancient Greece and Rome, Hercules is a demi-god, part mortal, part divine. He plays out on a colossal scale the conflict between heroic valour and the social values that govern the behaviour of ordinary men. As signal instances in Shakespeare's plays, Waith cites Antony and Coriolanus. Equally worthy of attention, especially in contrast to Hector, is Achilles in *Troilus and Cressida*. Achilles' difference from the other Greeks, his refusal to join them in battle against the Trojans, is the very subject of the Greeks' council in Act 1, Scene 3. In Ulysses' summation, 'The great Achilles, whom opinion crowns | The sinew and the forehand of our host, | Having his ear full of his airy fame | Grows dainty of his worth, and in his tent | Lies mocking our designs' (1.3.142–6). The fact that Achilles has a male lover, Patroclus, who joins him in his mocking may also set him apart from his peers. When the slaying of Patroclus spurs Achilles into action, he fights with a superhuman ferocity—and kills the unarmed Hector in an act of brutality totally against the laws of chivalry. In the combat of Hector with Achilles we witness the clash of two quite distinct ethical ideals.

Antony and Coriolanus join Achilles as Herculean heroes who stand aloft from the crowd, rather as the Farnese statue of Hercules does in Goltzius's engraving (see Fig. 1). All three of Shakespeare's Herculean heroes display their formidable physical prowess from an ethical platform that puts them, shoulders and *head*, above other men. Described in Philo's opening speech as 'the triple pillar of the world', Antony joins in the love of Cleopatra with a passion no less great than the passion with which he is wont to join battle. Where conventional ethics sees a breach ('Nay, but this dotage of our General's | O'erflows the measure' (1.1.1–2)) Antony sees continuity ('The nobleness of life | Is to do thus. . . . | We stand up peerless' (1.1.38–9, 42)). Antony's death may come as an ultimate vindication of the Roman position—but not before the audience has surrendered to the rhetoric of Antony's and Cleopatra's speeches. Coriolanus likewise operates from an ethical imperative that is shown to be untenable. His bravery in battle is coupled with a personal pride that dooms him to isolation and tragic death. Unlike the chivalric hero in most other respects, the Herculean hero is no less distant in space and time from audiences on the South Bank. Hamlet gauges that distance when he compares Claudius' likeness to that of his murdered father and pronounces it 'no more like my father | Than I to Hercules' (1.2.152–3).

Humanist Man of Moderation

Brutus may exemplify all the definitive ideals of early modern masculinity—nobility, honesty, gentleness, honour, virtue—but, as Antony points out, it is the distinctive *combination* of those elements that might prompt Nature to stand up and declare, 'This was a man.' What Brutus possesses that the Herculean hero does not is a tempering of masculine traits, an equanimity of spirit that enables him to face wisely and confidently whatever challenges the world brings his way. Roger Ascham describes just such a man as the goal of his educational programme in *The Schoolmaster* (1570): 'nobility governed by learning and wisdom is indeed most like a fair ship, having tide and wind at will, under the rule of a skilful master, when contrariwise a ship carried, yea, with the highest tide and greatest wind, lacking a skilful master, most commonly doth either sink itself upon sands or break itself upon rocks.'[15] Brutus figures as a third ideal type: the man of moderation advocated by humanist education. As such, he speaks to the audience in soliloquy and reveals a subjectivity that Achilles, Antony, and

Coriolanus lack—and he does so alone at night, in the orchard near his private study. Ordering his servant Lucius to light a taper in his closet, Brutus remains in the orchard to consider the likelihood that Caesar, having once been crowned as king, will abuse his power. Brutus's soliloquy is full of a philosopher's apothegms: 'Th'abuse of greatness is when it disjoins | Remorse from power' (2.1.18–19). His hesitancy to act, and his acute awareness of what such an act would entail, is far indeed from the valour of the knight or the forthrightness of the Herculean hero. In his conclusions Brutus recalls, in fact, that other product of humanistic learning, Hamlet: 'Between the acting of a dreadful thing | And the first motion, all the interim is | Like a phantasma or a hideous dream' (2.1.63–5).

Ascham grounds his vision of ideal masculinity in classical antiquity, specifically in the Athens of Plato and Aristotle. Let any language—Italian, Spanish, French, Dutch, English, even Latin—boast its greatest authors (Cicero and one or two other Latin authors excepted); 'they all be patched clouts and rags in comparison of fair-woven broadcloths' produced by 'those worthy wits of Athens.' The precepts of classical Greek authors stand as worthy guides to modern English young men: 'The remembrance of such a commonwealth, using such discipline and order for youth, and thereby bringing forth to their praise, and leaving to us for our example, such captains for war, such counsellors for peace and matchless masters of all kind of learning, is pleasant for me to recite and not irksome, I trust for other to hear, except it be such as make neither count of virtue nor learning' (Ascham 48–9). 'Virtue' and 'learning' are all but made synonymous. A particularly learned and virtuous exemplar of Ascham's ideal is Sir Thomas More in the contributions that Shakespeare almost certainly made to the collaborative play bearing the hero's name. By sheer force of reason More is able to reduce the London mob to peace and obedience in Addition II.D. In a later scene (Addition III) he speaks in soliloquy and shows the same self-consciousness that distinguishes Brutus and Hamlet. Moderation remains his guiding principle to the end: 'let this be thy maxim', he concludes: 'to be great | Is, when the thread of hazard is once spun, | A bottom great wound up, greatly undone' (Add.III.19–21). The man of learning, of virtue, of caution, of moderation is to be found, too, in Duke Vincentio of *Measure for Measure* and in Prospero of *The Tempest*. Both of them relinquish the duties of active leadership for purposes of contemplation. Both use their position of detachment as a staging ground for reforming the political worlds they have left behind. Both show remarkable forbearance toward their enemies.

Merchant Prince

The move from chivalrous knight and Herculean hero to humanist man of moderation was, for the men in Shakespeare's audience, a move closer to the world of empirical possibility. Closer still was a fourth ideal type, the merchant prince. Prescriptions of how such a man should act are to be found, not in Castiglione, but in homely productions like Robert Cleaver's *A Godly Form of Household Government*, which went through six printings between 1598 and 1612 before John Dod expanded it in editions of 1614, 1621, and 1624. Everyone cannot be king of the realm, but he *can* be king of his own house. 'A household is as it were a little commonwealth', Cleaver explains, 'by the good government whereof, God's glory may be advanced, and the Commonwealth which standest of several Families benefitted; and all that live in that Family receive much comfort and commodity.'[16] In Cleaver's view every man has a calling or vocation. For men who live off the labours of others (by William Harrison's definition, this would include most gentlemen) Cleaver has nothing but contempt:

These be they for whose maintenance in their jollity, a number are fain to toil very hardly, fare meanly, and spend their strength to the very skin and bones, and yet can get but a slender recompense, through their unmerciful exactions. But enough of them: to return. The good government of a house must be none of these; but he must have a calling that is good, honest, and lawful, not only gainful to himself, but also holy and profitable to the society of mankind: For thus much doth Saint Paul comprehend within the compass of his words (Ephesians 24: 28), 'But let him labour the thing that is good.'

'Good, honest, and lawful': to these ideal characteristics Cleaver is quick to add diligence. Numerous quotations from the Bible support Cleaver's exhortation to determined, steady work. As Proverbs 22: 29 has it, 'Thou seest that a diligent man in his business standeth before Kings' (D7^v–D8^v). Also to be desired is prudence. Cleaver's advice on not living beyond one's means is cast in images of voyaging: a man should be wary of hoisting higher sails than his abilities warrant, lest he crash on the rocks. Nonetheless, 'when a man spieth an opportunity of honest gain and commodity, he is to follow that while the time serveth' (E_4^v–E_5^v). Shrewdness may be the merchant prince's definitive trait.

For examples of such a man Shakespeare's audience had no need for recourse to the pages of Chaucer or Plutarch; they could simply look about them as they made their way to the theatre. On the stage itself, however, they might have had trouble finding a clear exemplar of Cleaver's ideal. *The Merry Wives of Windsor* is the closest Shakespeare comes to portraying the kind of merchant-hero celebrated in novellas like Thomas Deloney's *Jack of Newbury* or in plays like Thomas Heywood's *The Four Prentices of London, together with the conquest of Jerusalem*. Master George Page and Master Frank Ford are cut from Cleaver's sturdy cloth: they both can boast a certain economic success, they extend hospitality to their neighbours, they have spirited but faithful wives, they are nothing if not honest. For all that, Shakespeare presents them with an edge of amused irony that the audience is invited to share. Convinced that his wife has arranged an assignation with Falstaff, Master Ford sets up an equation among wife, money, and reputation that seems all too predictable for a man of his social type: 'See the hell of having a false woman! My bed shall be abused, my coffers ransacked, my reputation gnawn at...' (2.2.281–3). Master Page, confident of his own wife's fidelity, is nonetheless duped by his dowered daughter. In the face of their mistakes both men assume a congenial humility. The moral, as Master Ford sees it, turns on a confusion of emotional goods for material goods: 'Here is no remedy,' he consoles his friend Page. 'In love the heavens themselves do guide the state; | Money buys lands, and wives are sold by fate' (5.5.223–5). The merchant princes of Windsor, it turns out, rule over a rather small territory. Shakespeare, unlike Heywood, never confuses Cheapside with Jerusalem.

The irony that sets off the merchant prince is even sharper with Baptista, Lucentio, and Petruccio in *The Taming of the Shrew*. For one thing, they are actors in a play-within-the-play and hence close to caricature. More than that, all three bring to the marriage market precisely those traits of prudence and (ironically enough in this case) shrewdness that Cleaver praises. Lucentio, who speaks first, sets the standard by locating himself proudly among William Harrison's citizen-sort: 'Pisa, renownèd for grave citizens, | Gave me my being, and my father first— | A merchant of great traffic through the world' (1.1.10–12). Petruccio, for his part, tells his friend Hortensio that he has recently lost his father and needs a rich wife: 'I come to wive it wealthily in Padua; | If wealthily, then happily in Padua' (1.2.74–5). Kate is Hortensio's recommendation. Once a match has been struck, Kate's father Baptista makes no bones about his own motives in the business:

> GREMIO   Was ever match clapped up so suddenly?
> BAPTISTA Faith, gentlemen, now I play a merchant's part,
>   And venture madly on a desperate mart.
> TRANIO   'Twas a commodity lay fretting by you.
>   'Twill bring you gain, or perish on the seas.
>
>   (2.1.321–5)

Kate as commodity, Baptista as seller, Petruccio as buyer: the situation is never so crass in Shakespeare's later plays, but images of voyaging and venturing often figure as metaphors for courtship. Even Troilus, that consummate *chevalier*, can say of Cressida, 'Between our Ilium and where she resides | Let it be called the wild and wand'ring flood, | Ourself the merchant, and this sailing Pandar | Our doubtful hope, our convoy, and our barque' (*Troilus and Cressida*, 1.1.101–4). Helen, in Troilus's eyes, is 'a pearl | Whose price hath launched above a thousand ships | And turned crowned kings to merchants' (2.2.80–82). As a prince indeed Troilus can speak figuratively as a merchant, but Bassanio speaks as a merchant who would be a prince when he describes Portia's hair as 'a golden fleece, | Which makes her seat of Belmont Colchis' strand'—and asks Antonio for a loan to outfit his argosy thither (*The Merchant of Venice*, 1.1.170–1). The amorous swains who play the suitor in Shakespeare's comedies may not be so dissimilar to Petruccio as they present themselves. Demetrius and Lysander in *A Midsummer Night's Dream*, Sebastian in *Twelfth Night*, Claudio in *Measure for Measure*: who *are* these young men? Are they noblemen's sons or wealthy merchant's sons? Shakespeare leaves their exact social status ambiguous. All that we learn about Sebastian's origins, for example, is his statement to Antonio that his father 'was that Sebastian of Messaline whom I know you have heard of' (2.1.15–16). To Olivia's question 'What is your parentage?' his sister, in

disguise as 'Cesario', replies, 'Above my fortunes, yet my state is well. |
I am a gentleman' (1.5.267–9). With enough money to back him up, the
title of 'gentleman' could be appropriated by a man in the arena of
commerce. Whatever their economic origins, the protagonists in
Shakespeare's comedies lay hazard for marriages that turn out to be
good investments. To an ambitious man like Bassanio the merchant-
adventurer's code of ethics offered a means for insinuating himself into
the arena of honour.

Saucy Jack

Furthest of all from Castiglione's courtier, but closest perhaps to the
hearts of Shakespeare's audience, is the saucy jack. When the speaker
in sonnet 128, addressing the dark lady, professes his envy of the 'saucy
jacks' who 'kiss the tender inward of thy hand' (128.13, 6), he has in
mind not just the string-pluckers that pop up and down as she plays
the virginals (*OED* 'jack' II.14) but the upstart knaves who steal kisses
that should be his (*OED* 'saucy' 2, 'jack' I.2). On the stage, as in this
sonnet, the saucy jack is resourceful but suave, calculating but ingra-
tiating, resolute but jaunty. His code of ethics comes not from books
but from ballads; he shows his mettle not in a tournament but in a jig.
'This was the noblest Roman of them all' (*Julius Caesar*, 5.5.67)—with
those words still ringing in his head Thomas Platter describes what
came last in a performance of *Julius Caesar* at the Globe in September
1599: 'When the play was over, they danced very marvellously and
gracefully together as is their wont, two dressed as men and two as
women.'[7] At least through the 1590s jigs customarily concluded plays
at the South Bank theatres, tragedies and comedies alike. Platter does
not specify just which jig followed Antony's encomium of the greatest
Roman of them all, but it might have concerned the exploits of Row-
land or Simpkin, tricksters who dance their way in and out of amorous
intrigues in a number of surviving jigs.

   In 'Singing Simpkin', for example, the hero takes advantage of an
old husband's momentary absence from home to court the husband's
lusty young wife. When another would-be seducer shows up in the
person of Bluster, the wife puts Simpkin in a chest, giving him a
perfect opportunity to cut down his bragging rival in asides to the
audience:

BLUSTER	Yet in the bloody war full oft,
	My courage I did try.
WIFE	I know you have killed many a man.
SIMPKIN (*aside*)	You lie, you slut, you lie.
BLUSTER	I never came before a foe,
	By night nor yet by day,
	But that I stoutly roused myself,
SIMPKIN (*aside*)	And nimbly ran away.

The old husband suddenly returns home, but the wife manages to convince him that Bluster has broken into the house in pursuit of an innocent man (*alias* Simpkin), whom she has protected by locking him in the chest. Described by the wife as 'a goodly handsome sweet young man | As e'er was seen with eye', Simpkin finally gets the chance to take the wife in hand while the old husband chases Bluster away.[18] The chivalrous knight could hardly find a sharper rival than the saucy jack: while the one vies for honour with his valour, the other wins the day with his wit.

There is something of the saucy jack in most of Shakespeare's clowns, but four exemplars call particular attention to themselves: Tranio in *The Taming of the Shrew*, Bottom in *A Midsummer Night's Dream*, Lancelot Gobbo in *The Merchant of Venice*, and Autolycus in *The Winter's Tale*. All four of them play out parodies of serious models of masculinity. Tranio more than rises to the occasion when his master Lucentio suggests that they exchange costumes and identities for the better wooing of Baptista's other daughter, Bianca. '*Enter Tranio, brave*' reads the stage direction as the sometime servant, now a wealthy merchant's son, joins Bianca's other suitors (*The Taming of the Shrew*, 1.2.217 s.d.). Bottom, through no other means than being in the right place at the right time, plays the royal consort to Titania, Queen of the Fairies. Lancelot Gobbo's name might suggest a parody of knighthood, but Shylock's underfed servant is content to pose as a merchant-prince. Lancelot's blind father, not recognizing his son, inquires the way to Shylock's house and asks whether 'one Lancelot' dwells there or not:

> LANCELOT Talk you of young Master Lancelot?
> GOBBO No master, sir, but a poor man's son. His father,
>   though I say't, is an honest exceeding poor man, and,
>   God be thanked, well to live.

> LANCELOT Well, let his father be what a will, we talk of
>   young Master Lancelot.
> GOBBO Your worship's friend, and Lancelot, sir.
>
>   (*The Merchant of Venice*, 2.2.42–3, 46–51)

Lancelot, a bleeder of humours, may even be holding the humanist man of learning up for laughs as he finally reveals himself to his father and kneels to ask his blessing in a parody of Jacob stealing Esau's birthright (Gen. 27). Esau's hairiness, a key element in the biblical story, is recalled when blind old Gobbo feels Lancelot's head and exclaims, 'Lord worshipped might he be, what a beard hast thou got!' (2.2.88–9). Autolycus, a self-described 'snapper up of unconsidered trifles', parodies the parable of the Good Samaritan (Luke 10: 30–7) when he pretends to have been robbed and beaten as a way of relieving the clown of his purse (*The Winter's Tale*, 4.3.25–6, 49–117). Later he dupes the shepherds again as he outdoes Castiglione and plays the courtier:

> OLD SHEPHERD Are you a courtier, an't like you, sir?
> AUTOLYCUS Whether it like me or no, I am a courtier.
>   Seest thou not the air of the court in these enfoldings?
>   Hath not my gait in it the measure of the court?
>   Receives not thy nose court-odour from me? Reflect I
>   not on thy baseness court-contempt?
>
>   (4.4.729–33)

The effect of all these parodies is to empty the masculine ideals in question of their content, to expose them as only so much posing.

As saucy jacks, Tranio, Bottom, Lancelot, and Autolycus are likewise smooth of tongue. 'What, this gentleman will out-talk us all!' is Gremio's response when Tranio introduces himself to his rivals for Bianca's hand (*The Taming of the Shrew*, 1.2.248). Bottom may get some of the words in the wrong places, but his stupendous description of his no less stupendous dream ('The eye of man hath not heard, the ear of man hath not seen...') is one of the great set pieces in Shakespeare's plays (*A Midsummer Night's Dream*, 4.1.208–9). Lancelot's verbal virtuosity causes Lorenzo to exclaim, 'Goodly Lord, what a wit-snapper are you!' (*The Merchant of Venice*, 3.5.46). As ballad monger and con artist, Autolycus uses words as his stock-in-trade. Like their counterparts in stage jigs, at least two of Shakespeare's saucy jacks, Bottom and Lancelot, are apparently great lovers. The occasion for Lancelot's cleverest sleight-of-hand is Lorenzo's accusation that Lancelot has impregnated a certain Moor. Some dizzying puns on 'Moor' and 'more' give Lancelot the escape clause he needs: 'It is much that the Moor should be more than reason, but if she be less than an honest woman, she is indeed more than I took her for' (*The Merchant of Venice*, 3.5.38–40). Finally, all four saucy jacks manage to achieve their ends by flouting conventional codes of ethics. Through extravagant lying—he even invents the financial settlement—Tranio succeeds in securing Bianca for Lucentio. Bottom gets to spend time on top. Lancelot never has to answer for his dalliance with the Moor. In the most extravagant triumph of all, Autolycus earns a reputation as a brave and sober man. Practising to be gentlemen (their reward for returning Perdita to Leontes and Florizel to Polixines), the Old Shepherd and the Clown resolve to make Autolycus one, too—at least by repute. Says the Clown to the 'courtier' who once contemned them, 'I'll swear to the Prince thou art a tall fellow of thy hands and that thou wilt not be drunk; but I know thou art no tall fellow of thy hands and thou wilt be drunk; but I'll swear it, and I would thou wouldst be a tall fellow of thy hands' (*The Winter's Tale*, 5.2.161–6). To judge by Shakespeare's saucy jacks, a man is no more but what a man swears he is.

Gentleman

The chivalrous knight, the Herculean hero, the humanist man of moderation, the merchant prince, the saucy jack: it might be possible to isolate other ideal types in Shakespeare's plays, but the general picture is clear enough. For different social groups in early modern England there were different masculinities, and Shakespeare portrays them in all their variety. The degree of attention he gives to one ideal over another, however, suggests that Segar was quite right to declare that there are but two arenas of action open to a man, honour and commerce. In Shakespeare's plays, shades of the chivalric knight and solidities of the merchant prince far outnumber other ideals of masculinity. What is more, shades and solidities are frequently confused. Bassanio's portrayal of himself as Jason in quest for the golden fleece and Troilus's celebration of beauty that can turn crowned kings to merchants represent a fusion of the courtly and the commercial that goes back to Shakespeare's earliest plays. *The Comedy of Errors*, for example, has its origins in Plautus' citizen comedy *Menaechmi*, but the occasion for its first recorded performance, as we have seen, was a fantasy of chivalry during the Gray's Inn Christmas revels of 1594. 'Merchant of Syracusa, plead no more' (1.1.3): the play may begin with references to shipping, traffic, marts, fairs, confiscated goods, and ransom payments, but it ends in a convergence of completed quests. After years of voyaging over the eastern Mediterranean a father finds his sons, the sons find each other, they all find the lady who has waited like Penelope for their quests to end. Plautus' merchants become, in Shakespeare's play, romantic adventurers. Such a fusion of masculine ideals would have had particular appeal in a society that was made up of temporally distinct cultures, each fostering a different set of values. Raymond Williams's claim that all but the most isolated societies include residual, dominant, and emergent elements finds an especially clear example in early modern England, where money-based capitalism (the emergent culture) was replacing land-based feudalism (the residual culture).[19] The dominant culture needed some compromise between the two economic systems and the two models of masculine identity they entailed.

William Gouge's sermon on 'The Dignity of Chivalry', preached before the Artillery Company of London in 1626, demonstrates one such compromise. To speak of chivalry to such a group was in itself a challenge. Gouge's listeners were citizens, not noblemen; they used guns, not swords; their purpose was domestic defence, not crusades against the infidel. All quite homely. Gouge attacks the problem of social status head on by making chivalric ideals achievable by any man who is good enough at what he does: 'Of old, the best of a nation, best in blood and birth, as kings, princes, nobles, their children and kindred: best in stature and properness of body, as the three tall, proper sons of Isaiah: best in courage, valour, and strength, as they whom Saul chose to follow him: best any other way, "They were men of war"' (12–13). In Gouge's reformulation, blood and birth alone do not a nobleman make. To socially diverse audiences at the Globe, Shakespeare's scripts offered similar compromises.

The knight and the merchant prince converge in the gentleman. The two 'gentlemen' of Verona in what may be Shakespeare's earliest play seem to be the sons of merchants, but both of them are sent for finishing to the Duke's court in Milan. A gentleman, or so the play implies, is made, not born. When Valentine's resourcefulness finally persuades the Duke to dismiss Sir Thurio, the titled suitor to his daughter, Silvia, and reward her instead to Valentine, the merchant's son suddenly becomes a gentleman. 'I do applaud thy spirit', says the Duke. 'Sir Valentine, | Thou art a gentleman, and well derived. | Take thou thy Silvia, for thou hast deserved her' (5.4.138, 143–5). If Valentine was not a gentleman before, he is now. For advice on how to achieve that status, young men of a later generation could turn to books like Henry Peacham's *The Complete Gentleman* (1622) and Richard Brathwait's *The English Gentleman* (1630). The publishing dates are significant: both books sum up fifty years of revisionist thinking while England was being transformed from a feudal society into a capitalist society. Peacham insists that nobility is an achievement and not a fact of birth. Titles alone do not confer honour: 'nobility, being inherent and natural, can have, as the diamond, the lustre but only from itself. Honours and titles externally conferred are but attendant upon desert and are but as apparel and the drapery to a beautiful body.'[20] After listing the great men of history who had but humble births, Peacham proceeds to consider various ways of making a living and whether they qualify a man for the status of gentleman. Lawyers and physicians both pass muster. Merchants present a harder case, since trade has been reckoned 'base and much derogating from nobility' since the time of Aristotle. Nonetheless, Peacham finds room for merchants in the arena of honour—but only because, like knights, they venture their means and their persons in remote places: 'I cannot, by the leave of so reverend judgments, but account the honest merchant among the number of benefactors to his country while he exposeth as well his life as goods to the hazard of infinite dangers' (21–2). Absolutely not to be admitted as gentlemen are practitioners of 'mechanical arts' like 'painters, stageplayers, tumblers, ordinary fiddlers, innkeepers, fencers, jugglers, dancers, mountebanks, bear-wards, and the like . . . because their bodies are spent with labour and travail' (23). (Let it be noted that Shakespeare's claim to a gentleman's coat of arms after 1596 was based on his father's status, not his.) Brathwait, whose book is addressed to 'every gentleman of selecter rank and quality', is less concerned with economic considerations than with moral precepts. He insists that a gentleman has a calling or vocation just as other men do: 'of all other degrees, none are less exempted from a calling than great men, who, set like high peers or mounts, should so over-view others as their lives may be lines of direction unto others.'[21] The precise guidelines that Brathwait has in mind are those defining the humanist man of moderation. The Theophrastian character of 'A Gentleman' that concludes Brathwait's book celebrates generosity, learning, self-control, moderation, perfection, virtue, and humility (3N1–3N2^v). In Peacham's and Brathwait's handbooks, as in Shakespeare's scripts, 'gentleman' is a status to which many men could aspire—or at least could *imagine* themselves aspiring.

Commonalities and Conflicts

As different as they may be in other respects, all of the ideal types we have surveyed—chivalrous knight, Herculean hero, humanist man of moderation, merchant prince, saucy jack, gentleman—share a few basic similarities. First is the recognition that masculine identity of whatever kind is something men give to each other. It is not achieved in isolation. 'A solitary man is either a beast or an angel': this common proverb (Tilley M388) is the starting-point for Sir Francis Bacon's essay 'Of Friendship'. As usual, Bacon takes a thoroughly practical view of the matter. Men *need* friends, Bacon observes, for discharging passions, for counsel, for carrying out things they cannot do by themselves. The third of these 'fruits of friendship' is, in Bacon's account, strictly a matter of political utility:

A man hath a body and that body is confined to a place, but where friendship is, all offices of life are, as it were, granted to him and his deputy. For he may exercise them by his friend. How many things are there which a man cannot, with any face or comeliness, say or do himself? A man can scarce allege his own merits with modesty, much less extol them. A man cannot sometimes brook to supplicate or beg. And a number of such like. But all these things are graceful in a friend's mouth which are blushing in a man's own.[22]

Bacon's essay takes its place in a philosophical tradition that goes back to Aristotle's *Nicomachean Ethics*. For Aristotle, and for his successors Cicero, Montaigne, and Bacon, friendship between men who are

social equals constitutes the most important human bond there is.
Aristotle, like Bacon, understands male friendship in fundamentally
political terms: 'One can see also in one's travels how near and dear a
thing every man is to every other. Friendship also seems to be the bond
that holds communities together, and lawgivers seem to attach more
importance to it than justice.'[23] Concord is the aim of lawmaking, and
where friendship exists there is already concord. Aristotle differs from
Bacon in insisting that true friendship is possible only between men
who do not otherwise need something from one another—i.e.
between social equals. Hence the idealization of male friendship in
Cicero's *De Amicitia* and in Montaigne's essay 'Of Friendship' (1.27).
Hence, too, Montaigne's reluctant conclusion that friendship is no
more possible between a husband and a wife than between a master
and a servant or between a father and a son. Male friendship as
Montaigne imagines it is a tight knot that women's minds are not
strong enough to endure.

And truly, if without that, such a genuine and voluntary acquaintance might be
contracted, where not only minds had this entire jovissance but also bodies a
share of the alliance, and where a man might be wholly engaged, it is certain
that friendship would thereby be more complete and full. But this sex could
never yet by any example attain unto it and is by ancient schools rejected
thence.[24]

Shakespeare's plays are full of testimonials to the primacy of male
friendship. The very first speeches in what may be Shakespeare's very
first play are devoted to it. Proteus begs his friend Valentine not to go
off to the duke's court in Milan:

> Wilt thou be gone? Sweet Valentine, adieu.
> Think on thy Proteus when thou haply seest
> Some rare noteworthy object in thy travel.
> Wish me partaker in thy happiness
> When thou dost meet good hap; and in thy danger—
> If ever danger do environ thee—
> Commend thy grievance to my holy prayers;
> For I will be thy beadsman, Valentine.

Valentine's reply is barbed: 'And on a love-book pray for my success?'
(*The Two Gentlemen of Verona*, 1.1.11–18). Proteus is staying behind
because of his love for Julia. When he falls precipitately in love with

Proteus's mistress Silvia, the comedy finds its complication: 'To leave my Julia shall I be forsworn? | To love fair Silvia shall I be forsworn? | To wrong my friend I shall be *much* forsworn' (2.6.1–3, punctuation altered, emphasis added). *The Two Gentlemen of Verona* inaugurates a series of conflicts between male bonds and marriage that continues right to the end of Shakespeare's career in *The Two Noble Kinsmen*. Among the stratagems Shakespeare tries to resolve that standoff are a communal living arrangement among the two friends and their wives (*The Two Gentlemen of Verona*), postponement of marriage (*Love's Labour's Lost*), the convenient death of the groom's friend (*Romeo and Juliet*), the wife's buying-out of the friend (*The Merchant of Venice*), a temporary change of gender on the part of the wife-to-be (*As You Like It*), the husband's murder of the wife (*Othello*), the wife's tricking the reluctant husband into thinking he is sleeping with a whore and the public discrediting of his friend (*All's Well That Ends Well*), the insanity and death of the wife who has come between the husband and his political allies (*Macbeth*), the suicides of both husband and wife (*Antony and Cleopatra*), reconciliation of husband, wife, and friend in old age (*The Winter's Tale*), and ritualized killing of one friend by the other (*The Two Noble Kinsmen*). Suffice it to say, the conflict between male bonds and love for women admits of no easy solution.

A second factor common to all the ideal types of masculinity is their reversibility. Even the saucy jack can be parodied. The chivalrous knight is carried to an absurd extreme in Don Adriano de Armado in *Love's Labour's Lost*. Every knight needs a lady. Don Armado finds his in a country wench. As if instructed by Castiglione on all points but humility, Don Armado presents himself as a compleat courtier and special friend to the King of Navarre. He boasts to the local school-master Holofernes, 'Some certain special honours it pleaseth his greatness to impart to Armado, a soldier, a man of travel, that hath seen the world' (5.1.100–2). Chief among these honours is the king's commission that Don Armado produce some courtly entertainment for the Princess of France and her ladies. Holofernes, himself a parody of the humanist man of learning, suggests a Pageant of the Nine Worthies. If, in Mote's *mot juste*, Don Armado and Holofernes 'have been at a great feast of languages and stolen the scraps' (5.1.36–7), Holofernes surely has the fuller sack. On the selection of afternoon as the time for the pageant he provides Don Armado with a humanist scholar's learned gloss: 'The posterior of the day, most generous sir, is liable, congruent, and measurable for the afternoon. The word is well culled, choice, sweet, and apt, I do assure you, sir, I do assure' (5.1.86–9). Among the nine worthies to be presented is Hercules—played by little Mote. The Herculean hero is likewise parodied in Ajax, all brawn and no brain, in *Troilus and Cressida*. According to Thersites, the foil to Achilles 'wears his wit in his belly and his guts in his head' (2.1.75–6). A nightmare version of the merchant prince takes the stage in Shylock. He possesses, in the extreme, all the qualities that Cleaver lauds in *A Godly Form of Household Government*: diligence, prudence, shrewdness, even lawfulness and honesty. What he lacks, to the Venetians' view, are any of the saving graces of the Christian gentleman: 'We all expect a *gentle* answer, Jew,' charges the Duke (*The Merchant of Venice*, 4.1.33, emphasis added). In Lucio's antics in *Measure for Measure* the saucy jack fails, for once, to operate outside law and custom to the end. Lucio (likely pronounced '*loose*-io') displays all the rhetorical, libidinous, and ethical agility of Tranio, Bottom, Lancelot Gobbo, and Autolycus, but, unlike them, he gets caught. He even has to marry his whore— enough to dilute any man's sauce.

Also common to the masculine ideals is their very ideality. In proverbs, in conduct books, on the stage ideals remain ideals: models of what a man *might be*, not copies of what he *is*. 'No man living all things can' goes one proverb (Tilley M315). 'No man so stout but another may be as stout as he' goes another (M343). 'A man must not roam above his reach' counsels a third (M282). Thomas North translated Plutarch's *Lives of the Noble Grecians and Romans Compared Together* (1579) precisely to set up ancient paragons of virtue against which modern men might pattern their own behaviour. North's dedicatory epistle to Queen Elizabeth declares that the book is addressed to 'the common sort of your subjects': 'For among all the profane books that are in reputation at this day there is none, your highness best knows, that teacheth so much honour, love, obedience, reverence, zeal, and devotion to princes as these lives of Plutarch do.' North trusts that by 'adding the encouragement of these examples to the forwardness of their own dispositions' the book's readers will perform for the queen deeds of service in war and honour in peace.[25] For all his optimism, North recognizes that 'examples' are one thing and individual 'dispositions' something else again. In the theatre the distance between ideals and realities can be measured in feet and inches. In everyday life men do not speak in verse, their companions do not feed them great lines, the choices they face seldom seem to be life-defining, the shape of the lives they lead is not so legible as that of lives compressed within the two hours' traffic of the stage. The turn to ideals at the ends of Shakespeare's plays serves to enhance the spectators' sense of distance. In all of the plays that Elizabeth's common subject William Shakespeare found in North's Plutarch, the deaths of the principals are framed by a survivor and held up for viewing. Antony's tribute to 'the noblest Roman of them all' serves that function in *Julius Caesar* (5.5.67). Caesar takes charge of the story in *Antony and Cleopatra*—and interprets it to reflect his own glory as the man responsible for the protagonists' downfall:

> High events as these
> Strike those that make them, and their story is
> No less in pity than his glory which
> Brought them to be lamented.
>
> (5.2.354-7)

In effect, Caesar invites spectators to step back from the emblem of the two dead bodies they see onstage and to accept the caption he provides: Antony in the embrace of Cleopatra becomes an object of pity, an example of masculine ideals betrayed. Aufidius distances Coriolanus in a similar way by turning the just dead hero into 'a noble memory' in the play's last line (*Coriolanus*, 5.6.154).

All of the masculine ideals, finally, entail certain fundamental conflicts. First is the simple fact that the ideals contradict each other. A man cannot be the chivalrous knight and the saucy jack or the Herculean hero and the merchant prince at the same time—or at least he cannot comfortably be so. Paul Smith's general observation about identity formation seems particularly apt for men in an evolving society like early modern England: an individual possesses not just one identity but several. He stands at the intersection of several different social roles.[26] Bassanio is a signal example. Situated economically among Harrison's citizen-sort (for whom diligence, lawfulness, honesty, prudence, and shrewdness are ethical ideals), Bassanio in his quest for Portia takes on traits of the chivalrous knight (whose guiding principle is honour). The two roles are reconciled, as much as they can be, in the gentleman that Bassanio becomes by marrying Portia and forsaking the Rialto for Belmont.

Prince Harry presents an even more complicated case. Born into the arena of honour, he seems to be more comfortable in the arena of commerce—and along the shadowy margins of the arena, at that, among men whose *un*godly government would drive Robert Cleaver to apoplexy. In the course of *1* and *2 Henry IV*, Harry plays the saucy jack on Gad's Hill, the Herculean hero on the battlefield, and the chivalrous knight in his man-to-man combat with Hotspur. Even the merchant comes into Harry's repertoire in his conversation with Poins shortly before becoming king. With some embarrassment Harry confides in Poins that he is weary—and, what's more, that he has a thirst for small beer. 'Indeed,' he confesses, 'these humble considerations make me out of love with my greatness.' What a disgrace, Harry tells Poins, to remember your name. Or to recognize you once I've become king. 'Or to take note how many pair of silk stockings thou hast— videlicet these, and those that were thy peach-coloured ones! Or to bear the inventory of thy shirts—as one for superfluity, and another for use' (*2 Henry IV*, 2.2.1–6, 11–12, 13–14, 14–18). In the context of earlier depictions of monarchs Eric Auerbach thinks it remarkable that a prince should admit to weariness; no less remarkable is a prince who inventories stockings and shirts.[27] In two of Harry's rare reflective soliloquies we perhaps hear the humanist man of moderation. In the first of these Harry shares with the audience his reasoned political philosophy: 'I'll so offend to make offence a skill, | Redeeming time when men think least I will' (*1 Henry IV*, 1.2.213–14). In the second he performs a scholar's turn on the contrast between a crown and a nightcap:

> O polished perturbation, golden care,
> That keep'st the ports of slumber open wide
> To many a watchful night!—Sleep with it now;
> Yet not so sound, and half so deeply sweet,
> As he whose brow with homely biggen bound
> Snores out the watch of night.
>
> (*2 Henry IV*, 4.3.154–9)

Harry presents an extreme instance of a common situation: Shakespeare's male protagonists are apt to find their identities *vis-à-vis* not one ethical ideal but several.

Harry illustrates another conflict involved in the achievement of masculine ideals as he negotiates a tension between affiliation and aggression. If masculine identity is something that men give each other, they do so under a complicated system of rules whereby they alternately abet and oppose one another. Harry's relationship with Hotspur is a case in point. In terms of body chemistry, what we witness in the rivalry between Harry and Hotspur is a contest between Hotspur's choler-driven anger and Harry's calculated reasonableness. In terms of ethical ideals, it is an act of collaboration, an achievement of masculinity in terms of one another's identity. 'The theme of honour's tongue' is how Harry's father describes Hotspur in the first scene of *1 Henry IV*—and wishes aloud that 'some night-tripping fairy' had switched Hotspur in the cradle for his own riotous son (1.1.80, 85–8). It is necessary for Harry, first to identify with Hotspur as the ideal son, and then to kill him in order to achieve his own identity as king-in-the-making. Hotspur, for his part, seems to realize as much. 'O Harry, thou hast robbed me of my youth' are his dying words (5.4.76). Standing above his vanquished adversary, Harry finds in Hotspur the very type of noble manhood: 'This earth that bears thee dead | Bears not alive so stout a gentleman.' One hero *yields* to another, in more ways than one. The entire scene is played out as an exercise in chivalry. 'If thou wert sensible of courtesy,' Harry continues, 'I should not make so dear a show of zeal; | But let my favours hide thy mangled face.' In effect, the noble foes exchange honours as merchants might exchange commodities:

> And even in thy behalf I'll thank myself
> For doing these fair rites of tenderness.
> Adieu, and take thy praise with thee to heaven.
> Thy ignominy sleep with thee in the grave,
> But not remembered in thy epitaph.

(5.4.91–100)

The moment of stasis does not last, however. Harry immediately returns to the gauntlet of challenges that stand between him and kingship. Grounded in different ethical traditions, championed by competing social groups, pursued in acts of affiliation and aggression, masculine ideals in Shakespeare's plays are never lastingly realized.

Passages

For all the fame of books like Castiglione's *The Courtier*, early modern masculinity existed not in print but in persons, in human bodies in their physical quiddity, in their susceptibility to changes from within and without. As Plato would put it, ideals present a state of *being*; realities, a state of *becoming*.[1] Early modern masculinity cannot be considered apart from time. Shakespeare acknowledges as much in one of his most quoted speeches. 'All the world's a stage,' declares Jaques, 'And all the men and women merely players' (*As You Like It*, 2.7.139–40). As is his wont in his other set pieces in this play ('I can suck melancholy out of a song as a weasel sucks eggs', he boasts twelve words into his part (2.5.11–12)), Jaques draws out the proposition with a melancholic's painstaking ingenuity. The 'acts' of the play are seven: first 'the infant, | Mewling and puking in the nurse's arms', then 'the whining schoolboy', then 'the lover, | Sighing like furnace', then 'a soldier | ... | Jealous in honour, sudden, and quick in quarrel', then 'the justice | In fair round belly with good capon lined', then 'the lean and slippered pantaloon, | ... | his big, manly voice, | Turning again toward childish treble', finally 'second childishness and mere oblivion, | Sans teeth, sans eyes, sans taste, sans everything'. Although women are also mentioned as players on the world's stage, Jaques shows himself to be a man of his own time in imagining the representatives of each age beyond infancy as a boy or man. No sooner has Jaques finished than pat arrives a living emblem in the persons of Orlando the sighing lover, bearing his 'venerable burden' Old Adam, the both of them welcomed to Arden by Duke Senior, who if not round-bellied in his pinched present circumstances is nonetheless 'full of wise saws and modern instances' (2.7.139–66). 'Now, my co-mates and brothers in

4. Anonymous, *The Dance and Song of Death* (1569).

exile, | Hath not old custom made this life more sweet | Than that of painted pomp?' have been Duke Senior's sententious first words in the play (2.1.1–3). Old Adam, for his part, specifies his age as 'now almost fourscore' (2.3.72).

What Jaques sets in place is a sense of man's existence as a series of life-*stages*, in every sense of the word. Feste, the clown in *Twelfth Night*, performs his own life as four stages, not seven, in the song that rounds off the last of Shakespeare's romance comedies. Each stage gets a stanza. The discreteness of each stage and each stanza is underscored by the fact that one follows the other, not via 'and' but via 'but': 'When that I was and a little tiny boy...', '*But* when I came to man's estate...', '*But* when I came, alas, to wive...', '*But* when I came unto my beds...' (5.1.385–404, emphasis added). Several of Shakespeare's scripts seem to focus on one of the 'buts' that separate these life-stages. *1 Henry IV*, for example, turns on the 'but' that distinguishes 'man's estate' from youth. Still another 'but', still another conjunction of life-stages, is marked out as the subject of *The Tragedy of King Lear* when the old king reveals his 'darker purpose':

> 'tis our fast intent
> To shake all cares and business from our age,
> Conferring them on younger strengths while we
> Unburdened crawl toward death.
>
> (1.1.36, 38–41)

Perhaps we should say that *King Lear* focuses on *two* particular 'buts', since the closing lines of the play echo Lear's opening distinction between eld and youth, unbuffered until, perhaps, the very end by an intervening stage of manhood: 'The oldest hath borne most. We that are young | Shall never see so much, nor live so long' (5.3.301–2). In a world peopled by young people about to marry and doddering old men it is, perhaps, only Kent who can lay claim throughout the play to 'man's estate'.

In part, then, masculinity in Shakespeare's plays and poems is a function of *time*. Our own ways of reading male identity with respect to time differ markedly from those of Shakespeare and his contemporaries. Sigmund Freud's sequence of psycho-sexual stages of 'development' conceives of male identity in distinctively nineteenth-century terms suggested by evolutionary biology and the laws of physics: the evolving subject passes through a series of phases—oral, anal, genital—in which he learns to deploy the 'energy' of desire so as to arrive at healthy, socially adapted, sexually functional adulthood.[2] Applications of Freud's theory to Shakespeare's plays by Coppélia Kahn in *Man's Estate*, Peter Erickson in *Patriarchal Structures in Shakespeare's Drama*, and Janet Adelman in *Suffocating Mothers* all demonstrate how readily readable Shakespeare's plays are in Freudian terms. Kahn, for example, sees both of the history tetralogies as enactments of various ways in which a male child can attain identity *vis-à-vis* his mother and his father. Separation from the mother and emulation of the father are crucial in each case. In *1, 2,* and *3 Henry VI* and *Richard III* emphasis falls on sons' roles as emulators, avengers, and overthrowers of their fathers. Richard III, despised and rebuked by his mother, can only parody the principles of paternal emulation and sibling rivalry that are played straight by characters like the Talbots, father and son. In *1* and *2 Henry IV* and *Henry V* Prince Harry rejects a surrogate mother-figure in the soft and round person of Falstaff at the same time that he rebels against his father and yet becomes a king in the very image of his father.[3]

Although early versions of Freud's theory closely relate sexual desire and desire for death, the stages of life beyond sexually active adulthood, the passages from early adulthood to old age to death, are largely beyond Freud's purview. Erik H. Erikson addresses this lack in his construct of a 'life-cycle' of seven 'stages', each of which requires the subject to negotiate a different 'crisis'. Thus, in infancy the subject must come to terms with trust versus mistrust, in early childhood with autonomy versus shame and doubt, in play age with initiative versus guilt, in school age with industry versus inferiority, in adolescence with identity versus identity diffusion, in young adulthood with intimacy versus isolation, in adulthood with generativity versus self-absorption, and in mature age with integrity versus disgust and despair.[4] As with Freud, Erikson assumes that the stages he has isolated have universal applicability to people in all cultures, in all periods of history. Thus, with respect to the early childhood crisis of autonomy versus shame and doubt he observes, 'People all over the world seem convinced that to make the right (meaning *their*) kind of human being, one must consistently introduce the senses of shame, doubt, guilt, and fear into a child's life. Only the patterns vary' (74).

Cultural differences assume much larger importance in Jacques Lacan's model of ego development, in which the male subject achieves self-identity by first getting a sense of his physical separateness from his mother's body (thus entering the imaginary order), then endowing that physical body with social identity via language (the symbolic order), and for the rest of his life struggling with the desire to escape language and return to originary wholeness (the real). Death—or at least death as represented in tragedy—becomes, in Lacan's understanding of art, an intimation of that desired wholeness. In representations of death audiences enjoy the fantasy of a state of being *beyond* language if not *before* language.[5] Lacan's language-based theory has been given its subtlest applications to Shakespeare's texts in two books by Joel Fineman, *Shakespeare's Perjured Eye* and *The Subjectivity Effect in Western Literary Tradition*, and in a series of essays by Cynthia Marshall. In her essay 'Wound-Man: *Coriolanus*, Gender, and the Theatrical Construction of Interiority' (1996), for example, Marshall argues that frequent references to Coriolanus's perforated body serve to effeminize the hero in ways that conflict with the early modern rhetoric of manhood.[6] Because language varies from culture to culture, Lacan's theory leaves open the possibility of cultural difference in the formation of masculine identity. Hence its attractiveness to text-based critics like Fineman and Marshall. It assumes, nevertheless, that identity formation, always and everywhere, is a three-part process and that it moves toward the same goal of existential awareness.

Ages of Man

As suggestive as these contemporary models may be, early modern men and women had their own typologies for understanding how masculine identity is achieved, maintained, and sometimes lost across time—typologies with different intellectual origins from our own, differently calibrated experiences of time, and a different sense of the end to which these passages lead. Encouragement to think of a man's life as a sequence of 'ages' came from the Greeks. J. A. Burrow in *The Ages of Man: A Study in Medieval Writing and Thought* (1986) has demonstrated that there were four such conceptions current in ancient, medieval, and early modern thought: one based on Ptolemaic astrology, one on Aristotelian biology, one on Galenic medicine, and one on Christian theology. Aristotle in his treatise *On the Soul* (*De Anima*) plots out three phases of human life: growth, maturity, and decay. Christian theology drew correspondences between the course of a man's life and the six historical ages of the world. In distinguishing seven 'acts' in the drama of a man's life Jaques is speaking for a typology conceived within the other two schemes: Ptolemaic astrology and Galenic medicine. Ptolemy's model of the universe, in which earth occupies the centre, invited early modern men and women to think of their lives as circumscribed by the orbits of the planets. As there were seven planets moving around the earth, so a human life was imagined to move through seven ages, each corresponding to a planet and sharing that planet's mythical traits. The first age corresponded to the moon, closest to the earth; the other ages moved, by degrees, toward Saturn, furthest from the earth:

Planet	Age	Shared traits
moon	infancy	chastity and purity
Mercury	childhood	learning and eloquence
Venus	adolescence	softness and sensuality
sun } Mars	young manhood	power and substance
Jupiter	manhood	anger and ferocity
Saturn	old age	heaviness and gravity

Galen's idea of the human body, still current in Shakespeare's lifetime, suggested four passages of life, each dominated by one of the body's four humours and each corresponding with one of the four basic elements and one of the four seasons of the year:

Fluid	Age	Element	Characteristics	Season
blood	infancy	air	hot, moist	spring
choler	youth	fire	hot, dry	summer
black bile	maturity	earth	cold, dry	autumn
phlegm	old age	water	cold, moist	winter[7]

Jaques gives voice to Ptolemy's scheme; Feste, to Galen's. In practice it was the two schemes in combination that gave early modern men such an acute sense of the changeableness of their bodies and their dispositions across time. Sir Walter Ralegh in his *History of the World* understands the whole concept as one of the ways in which the body of a man epitomizes the whole universe, so that 'the four complexions resemble the four elements, and the seven ages of man the seven planets'. Thus,

our infancy is compared to the moon, in which we seem only to live and grow as plants; the second age to Mercury, wherein we are taught and instructed; our third age to Venus, the days of love, desire, and vanity; the fourth to the sun, the strong, flourishing, and beautiful age of man's life; the fifth to Mars, in which we seek honour and victory, and in which our thoughts travail to ambitious ends; the sixth age is ascribed to Jupiter, in which we begin to take accompt of our times, judge of ourselves, and grow to the perfection of our understanding; the last and seventh to Saturn, wherein our days are sad and overcast, and in which we find by dear and lamentable experience, and by the loss which can never be repaired, that of all our vain passions and affections past, the sorrow only abideth . . . .[8]

Whatever the explanation for these changes, however many stages or phases a life might be imagined to pass through, no one mistook the inevitable end of it all: not socially adapted, sexually functional adulthood, as classic psychoanalytical theory would have it, but death and 'mere oblivion'. 'The Dance and Song of Death', a printed broadside put into circulation when Shakespeare was 5 years old, gives physical immediacy to this understanding (see Figure 4). Henry Cuffe in *The Differences of the Ages of Man's Life* (1607) is primarily concerned with death, with why some people live longer than others. 'Touching the causes of long life,' Cuffe proposes, 'we may thus briefly dichotomize them, for they are either inward or outward.'[9] The outward reasons have to do in part with the planets:

though it be true that the celestial bodies have no direct action either of inclination or constraint upon the reasonable soul of man, which is immaterial, yet is it as true that they have singular and especial operations upon our bodies; for so we see the fruitfulness and barrenness of the earth depends upon the heaven's good and bad aspect; the sea follows the motion and alteration of the moon, the year distinguished into its four parts according to the access or further absence of the sun; and therefore Galen, the father of physicians, counselled his scholars to have especial respect unto the conjunctions of the planets in their signs, whensoever they undertake any cure . . . (107–8)

The inward reasons—and this is what interests Cuffe the most—have to do with the human body. The ages of man are functions of changing body chemistry: 'An age is a period and term of man's life, wherein his natural complexion and temperature naturally and of its own accord is evidently changed. For such is the disposition and nature of our body, that by the continual combat and interchangeable dominion of the ever-jarring elements it often changeth its primary constitution…' Thus, one and the same body is 'diversely tempered' at different times: 'our infancy full of moisture, as the fluid soft substance of our flesh manifestly declareth: our youth bringeth a farther degree of solidity: our riper age ever temperate: thence still our body declineth into cold and dryness, till at length death ceaseth upon our bodies, being the last end and period of our life' (111–12). Combining Aristotle's scheme of three ages with Ptolemy's seven and Galen's four, Cuffe goes on to identify specific ages with specific ranges of years. Childhood (equivalent to Aristotle's growth period) Cuffe reckons to last until age 25, with subdivisions into infancy (through age 3 or 4), boyhood (through age 9 or 10), 'our budding and blossoming age' (years unspecified), and finally 'youth' (until age 25). Manhood (Aristotle's maturity) is subdivided into a second 'youth' ('for so the penury of our English tongue warrenteth me to call it') or 'prime' (age 25 to 35 or 40) and then manhood proper (until age 50). Finally, old age (Aristotle's decay) is also subdivided into parts. During the first part (until age 65) strength and heat are impaired but not too much; during the second, or 'decrepit old age', 'our strength and heat is so far decayed, that not only our ability is taken away, but even all willingness, to the least strength and motion of our body: and this is the conclusion and end of our life, resembling death itself, whose harbinger and forerunner it is' (117–20).

According to Henry Cuffe, then, the passages of a man's life in early modern England looked like this:

birth → infancy → boyhood → budding age → youth → prime
manhood → later manhood → old age → decrepit old age → death

Conventional ideas about old age as a second childhood—'they say an old man is twice a child', Rosencrantz, echoing a popular proverb, sneers to Hamlet behind Polonius's back (2.2.387)—make it possible to see this linear scheme in circular terms (see diagram). In such a scheme life truly is a *cycle*: prime manhood figures as the point at which a man is farthest from the oblivion of before-birth and after-death, while other points on the compass—infancy and decrepit old age, boyhood

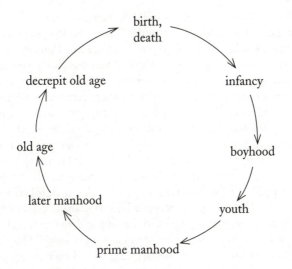

and old age, youth and later manhood—shape up as corresponding opposites. This is precisely the sense of life passages that we see in 'The Dance and Song of Death'. The participants in Death's circle dance are opposites: a beggar and a king, a fool and a wise man, a child and an old man. The design invites the viewer to contemplate not only how one ends as one began but how Death can intervene in the dance at any time.

Whatever connections there may have been between chronological time and the body's four humours, whatever influence the planets may have exerted, there were very good social reasons for Cuffe to demarcate the stages of man's life at precisely the ages he does. The end of infancy was marked by the end of breast-feeding, which advice books and anecdotal evidence suggests to have taken place as late as age 3. Juliet's nurse testifies as much when she reminds Lady Capulet that it has been eleven years since Juliet, now approaching 14, was weaned. Putting wormwood on her breast did the trick (*Romeo and Juliet*, 1.3.22–37). The very fact that Juliet had a wet-nurse marks her elevated social station. At the time the play was first performed, in 1594 or 1595, children of the nobility and the gentry were more likely to be suckled by someone hired for the purpose than by their mothers—and somewhat more likely, as a result, to die from lacking the immunities provided by their own mothers' milk. A change in dress distinguished the second half of childhood from the first. Up to age 7 boys and girls were dressed alike in 'coats' (gowns) and aprons. Putting boys into doublets and hose at age 7—the so-called 'breeching' of boys—marked the beginning of a gendered distinction in child-rearing that might also include removing a boy from his mother's care and consigning his keeping and education to a male authority figure. Bianca in *The Taming of the Shrew* alludes to this practice when she defies her new tutor (the suitor Lucentio in disguise) and lute-master (Hortensio): 'I am no breeching scholar in the schools. | I'll not be tied to hours nor 'pointed times, | But learn my lessons as I please myself' (3.1.18–20). Age 7 was chosen for breeching in part because it signalled a child's arrival at the biblical 'age of accountability' (Romans 14: 12) when he could begin to distinguish right from wrong and, in certain schools of Protestant theology, become responsible for his sins.[10] The decisive importance of breeching in turning ungendered infants into boys is registered in the fact that Cuffe, throughout *The Differences in the Ages of Man's Life*, assumes that his exemplar is male.

A change even more dramatic than breeching came at age 9 or 10, at the end of childhood and the beginning of what Cuffe calls 'our budding and blossoming age', when boys of privileged social station might be sent to continue their education away from home and when boys of working parents would begin to contribute their labour to the family enterprise. In their early to mid-teens boys of all social ranks were likely to be sent away from home to receive the training that would prepare them for adulthood. Cuffe fails to specify the exact year at which 'budding age' begins; perhaps because it varied from one social group to another. In her study of *Adolescence and Youth in Early Modern England* Ilana Ben-Amos calculates from sixteenth- and seventeenth-century documentary records that 13 was the mean age for entering agricultural service, 16 for entering university, and 17.7 for taking up an apprenticeship in a trade or a craft in London. The mean age for beginning apprenticeships elsewhere in the country was lower. Autobiographical writers who include a description of their apprenticeships suggest a mean age of 14.7 (Ben-Amos 62). More variable still was the age at which boys at the top of the social hierarchy might become part of a nobleman's retinue in order to learn the arts of a courtier. Old Adam in *As You Like It* is perhaps suggesting an average

age for entering service of all kinds when he tells young Orlando, 'From seventeen years till now almost fourscore | Here livèd I .... | At seventeen years, many their fortunes seek' (2.3.72–4). Several early modern writers of their own life stories confirm Adam's implication that leaving home was something boys at such an age *wanted* to do. Sydnam Poyntz, for example, declares,

> It is well known to most how near youth and rashness are of affinity, which I may instance in myself, for having no sooner attained to 16 years of age, but I began to harbour these conjectures in myself. To be found an apprentice—that life I deemed little better than a dog's life and base. At last I resolved with myself thus: to live and die a soldier would be as noble in death as life.

And in short order off he went to Dover and to the religious wars on the Continent.[11] Even if a teenage boy did not leave home to learn a trade or a craft, to study for a profession, or to fashion himself as a courtier, he was likely to be hired out as a servant in a household other than the one in which he grew up.

The arrangement that later social historians have called 'life-cycle service' had a number of causes: parents themselves might not be able to offer employment to their children; one or both parents might be deceased; economic difficulties might threaten the household. For boys from such families life-cycle service provided a means of support and a chance to better their social position. For farmers, craftsmen, and tradesmen it provided a ready source of cheap labour. For boys from all social ranks it provided a way of learning an occupation. For all concerned it confirmed the essentially hierarchical structure of early modern society. Although some social historians have seen in the system evidence of emotional distance in parent–child relationships, Ben-Amos insists on life-cycle service as an extension of the family circle rather than a substitution. Usually it was through parental contacts that a boy took up service, apprenticeship, or a university position in the first place, and friends or relatives of the family often looked after a boy in his new location. In each situation a male authority figure—householder, master craftsman, tutor—was supposed to act *in loco parentis* with respect to his charge's welfare.[12] Aside from skittish references to the apprentices who made up a visible and vociferous segment of his audience, Shakespeare's concern with life-service is focused almost exclusively at the top end of the social hierarchy. The youths who offer service to a noble person in Shakespeare's plays—Valentine to the Duke of Milan in *The Two Gentlemen of Verona*, 'Cesario' to Orsino in *Twelfth Night*, Arcite to Theseus in *The Two Noble Kinsmen*—may represent a statistically exclusive group, but they play out one version of a life passage experienced by most men in early modern England.

When the Old Shepherd in *The Winter's Tale* exclaims, 'I would there were no age between ten and three-and-twenty' and complains that 'there is nothing in the between but getting wenches with child, wronging the ancientry, stealing, fighting' (3.3.58–62), he implies that learning a way of making a living and internalizing the hierarchical structure of patriarchal society were not the only things on a young man's mind in 'our budding and blossoming age'. As one proverb had it, 'Youth will have its swing'.[13] Even if the Old Shepherd's estimate of sexual maturity is off by a few years—a contemporary English translation of Aristotle's *Problems* specifies the age as 14, the very age at which a male could legally marry—a lad in early modern England had fourteen or fifteen years to wait until he could marry and enter what Cuffe reckons as the first half of manhood. Unless endowed with a title and a large amount of property, Shakespeare's male contemporaries typically did not marry until age 28 or 29—three or four years later than Cuffe's specified age of 25 for the commencement of manhood. By then they had completed their service, apprenticeship, or other training and had amassed the means to set up their own household. Boys from the nobility and the gentry were likely to be married earlier—and to have their wives chosen for them because the financial and political stakes were so high.[14] Cuffe reads the passage from early youth to later youth as one from Venus's dominion to the Sun's: 'Venus guides our blossoming lustful age: our youthful prime, by the sun's lively operation is lifted up from base delights, to a loftier and more man-like resolution and liveliness' (121). All told, youths between the ages of 10 and 23 occupied a precarious position in the social order. On the one hand, they were expected to defer and submit to parents and masters; on the other, they were encouraged to be independent (Ben-Amos 237). The result was often a confusion of control and licence. Roger Ascham in *The Schoolmaster* will concede that young gentlemen between the ages of 7 and 17 are usually well brought up, but he pronounces ages 17 to 27 'the most dangerous time of all in a man's life and most slippery to stay well in'.[15]

By comparison, the two parts of manhood from ages 25 to 35 or 40 and from 35 or 40 to 50 were more singularly focused on consolidating one's social and economic position through competition and work. Cuffe explains why Mars and Jupiter preside over manhood: 'Mars the stern god of war, hath the precincts of his dominion limited within compass of our man-age, adding courage to our livelihood, and whetting our otherwise dull spirits, unto a more venturous boldness in quarrelling combats' (121). After age 50 came the spectre of death. Or, more likely, *before* age 50: in his statistical study of London in the sixteenth century Steve Rappaport cites a life expectancy at birth of only twenty to twenty-five years in London's poorer parishes, thirty to thirty-five years in wealthier parishes, and up to age 50 outside London, yielding an overall average somewhere in the lower 40s. Because of recurrences of the plague and lack of effective remedies against other diseases, a husband's chances of losing his wife before old age and a child's likelihood of losing one or both parents before he reached adulthood were far higher than today. Death was more likely to come in manhood, even in what Cuffe styles the 'prime' of manhood between ages 25 and 35 or 40, than in old age after 50—just the reverse of what is the case today. Ralph A. Houlbrooke suggests as a rough estimate that at least half of people reaching age 25 had lost a parent, more than likely the father.[16] If average life expectancy across all the factors of geography and social rank was about 40, then most men in early modern England would never experience what Cuffe reckons to be old age. The realities of death in early modern England meant that, in practice, the passages of a man's life were likely to look like this:

birth ⟶ infancy ⟶ boyhood ⟶ budding age

⟶ youth ⟶ prime manhood ⟶ death

Death could come during *any* passage; on average, it came at the very peak of manhood. The designer of 'The Dance and Song of Death' (Figure 4) has given these demographic facts pictographic presence.

Taking Jaques's 'ages of man' speech as a reference point, it is tempting to read *Romeo and Juliet* as a tragedy of youth, *Macbeth* as a tragedy of middle age, and *Lear* as a tragedy of old age. Juliet and Romeo each has a counterpart to point up their extreme youth—the old Nurse for Juliet and Friar Laurence for Romeo. 'Young son,' Friar Laurence greets Romeo in their first exchange:

> it argues a distempered head
> So soon to bid good morrow to thy bed.
> Care keeps his watch in every old man's eye,
> And where care lodges, sleep will never lie,
> But where unbruisèd youth with unstuffed brain
> Doth couch his limbs, there golden sleep doth reign.
>
> (2.2.33–8)

In his sheer ambition Macbeth epitomizes what Ptolemy, Aristotle, Galen, and Christian theology all took male adulthood to be, a time, in Cuffe's words, of 'venturous boldness in quarrelling combats'. For his part, Lear presents himself from the very beginning of the play as an old man, resolved 'to shake all cares and business from our age, | Conferring them on younger strengths' (*The Tragedy of King Lear*, 1.1.39–40). Displaced by his elder daughters, he casts himself near the end of the play as 'a very foolish, fond old man, | Fourscore and upward, | Not an hour more nor less' (4.6.53–5). It is worth observing that the male protagonists in Shakespeare's sequence of tragedies follow the trajectory from youth to middle age to old age in part because Richard Burbage, the actor who played Shakespeare's tragic protagonists, aged from 27 years at the time *Romeo and Juliet* was on the boards in about 1594 to 39 when *Antony and Cleopatra* was first performed in about 1606. By the time he played Prospero in *The Tempest* five years later, Burbage had exceeded the average life expectancy for men in early modern England. He died, aged 52, in 1619.[17]

Whether or not Burbage's advancing age, or even Shakespeare's, accounts for the shift, there does indeed seem to be a general progression of ages in the scripts Shakespeare produced in the course of his career. Youth holds centre stage not only in comedies with youthful protagonists from *The Two Gentlemen of Verona* (late 1580s) through to *Twelfth Night* (1602) but in tragedies like *Romeo and Juliet* (1594), and in history plays like *Richard II*, *1* and *2 Henry IV*, *Henry V*, and *Richard III*, which dramatize the life stories of impetuous young men on the make. As poems about sexual passion, *Venus and Adonis* (1593) and *The Rape of Lucrece* (1594) belong to this youthful group of works. A move from youth to manhood occurs in *Hamlet* (1602), with a protagonist specified by the grave-digger to be 30 years old, despite his being a university student; in *Troilus and Cressida*

(1603), which traces the titular hero's transformation from giddy lover in his first speech ('Why should I war without the walls of Troy | That find such cruel battle here within?' (1.1.2–3)) to bloody-minded warrior in his last ('Let Titan rise as early as he dare, | I'll through and through you!' (5.11.25–6)); in *Measure for Measure* (1604), presided over by a Duke who has ruled Vienna long enough to be notably unsuccessful at the job; in *Othello* (also 1604), in which the protagonist, seasoned in seven years of Venetian wars, protests that he has not married Desdemona 'To please the palate of my appetite, | Nor to comply with heat—the young affects | in me defunct' (1.3.262–4); in *Timon of Athens* (likely also 1604), with its transformation of open-handed generosity into crabbed misanthropy; in *Antony and Cleopatra* (1606), in which the general's languorous 'dotage'—a word associated with old age in *King Lear*—is contrasted in the play's first scene with the fire of 'scarce-bearded Caesar' (1.1.1, 22). (A biographically minded critic might wonder whether Shakespeare underwent some kind of midlife crisis in 1604, at age 40, as he approached the average life expectancy of his peers.) In such plays of Shakespeare's middle period one hears dramatic equivalents of the speaker in certain of the sonnets (printed 1609), who casts himself as 'a decrepit father' who 'takes delight | To see his active child do deeds of youth' (37.1–2) and admits on occasion 'my days are past the best' (138.6).

Old age in the later plays (1608–14) manifests itself most obviously, perhaps, in the parts Burbage is likely to have played: Pericles, who ages more than fourteen years in the course of the play that bears his name, Leontes, who does the same in *The Winter's Tale*, Cymbeline, who emphasizes his years in the first scene by chiding his daughter 'O disloyal thing, | That shouldst repair my youth, thou heap'st | A year's age on me' (1.1.132–4), Prospero, who finishes *The Tempest* by declaring, 'Every third thought shall be my grave' (5.1.315), and Henry VIII, whose chief concern throughout *All Is True* is begetting an heir. A pair of questions considered by Cuffe helps to explain some of the traits these protagonists share in common. 'Whence is it that old men are commonly so jealously suspicious?' Cuffe asks.

The cause is their incredulity and hardness of belief, which itself also proceedeth from their much experience of men's wily practices, according to that, 'The burnt child dreadeth the fire'. For such is the extreme badness of our nature, that still we go from one extreme unto another; and so become of men extremely credulous, in our last age extremely suspicious.

'What is the cause', furthermore, 'why old men are so talkative and full of words?'

Either because nature loves to exercise that part most which is least decayed: or that knowledge, the only thing old age can brag of, cannot be manifested but by utterance: or that old men, the nigher they are to their end, they much more desire to have their memory not only by children and posterity, but even by the speeches and deeds fore-uttered and performed in their life or that wisdom (as all good things naturally communicate their good properties) makes them desirous to profit others.   (131–2)

Prospero in particular embodies the qualities that Cuffe sees as typical of old men.

Age exerts its force also in the figures who assume positions of authorial control over two of the late romances: Gower in *Pericles* ('To sing a song that old was sung | From ashes ancient Gower is come' (scene 1.1–2)) and Time in *The Winter's Tale* ('Let me pass | The same I am ere ancient'st order was | Or what is now received' (4.1.9–11)). It is, indeed, the matter of perspective that marks Shakespeare's late romances most graphically as plays concerned with old age. Youthful passions in these plays—Marina's wanderings in *Pericles*, Posthumus's reunion with Innogen in *Cymbeline*, Florizel's wooing of Perdita in *The Winter's Tale*, Ferdinand's courtship of Miranda in *The Tempest*— are framed and watched by ageing men. Prospero's 'discovery' of Miranda and Ferdinand playing chess for the viewing pleasure of his captive peers (5.1.173 s.d.) epitomizes a framing effect that can be witnessed also in *Pericles, Cymbeline*, and *The Winter's Tale*. The most striking case of all may be that of Posthumus. His very name declares that the son lives in the shadow of a dead father. The change in Posthumus's fortunes near the end of the play is announced in a dream-vision in which '*Sicilius Leonatus (father to Posthumus, an old man), attired like a warrior*' speaks first, followed by '*an ancient matron, his wife, and mother to Posthumus*', by Posthumus's two dead brothers, and finally by Jupiter, associated with the planet that corresponds to mature manhood (*Cymbeline*, 5.5.123 s.d.). All in all, Shakespeare's late plays seem designed to exemplify the early modern proverb 'Old man's counsel and young man's action' (Tilley M616).[18]

Rites of Passage

To say that a play is 'about' one particular life stage, however, is to miss the dynamic character of most of Shakespeare's scripts and the way they focus on the shifts from one life passage to another. Analogies between the sequence of seasons and the sequence of ages in a man's life were given visual, aural, tactile, gustatory, and olfactory substance in the formal rites of passage by which boys became youths, youths became men, and men became corpses. *Seasonal* rites were anciently established features of early modern social life: on May Day morris-dancing, Robin Hood plays, and competitive sports signalled the shift from spring to summer; feasting, drinking, and singing at Harvest Home celebrated the shift from summer to autumn; boy-kings, plays, and feasting at Christmas marked the passage from autumn to winter; wrestling matches, football games, cockfights, and (in London at least) ritualized rudeness by apprentices at Shrovetide gave everyone notice that winter was yielding to spring. In *Shakespeare's Festive Comedies* C. L. Barber has found the pulse of these energies and symbolic enactments of these customs in Shakespeare's comedies, Maynard Mack Jr. in *The Killing of the King* and Naomi Liebler in *Shakespeare's Festive Tragedies* have pointed out similar vestiges in Shakespeare's tragedies, while François Laroque in *Shakespeare's Festive World* has discerned marks of festivity throughout Shakespeare's work in dramatic structure, senses of time, portrayals of society, and verbal imagery.[19] *Life-cycle* rites of passage were no less well established in early modern culture than *seasonal* rites of passage. Formal ceremonies, usually notarized in a written document, underscored the passages from one age of a man's life to another: baptism and an entry in the parish register at the beginning of infancy, breeching at the beginning of the second part of childhood, leaving home or beginning to work at the beginning of boyhood, signing an indenture of apprenticeship or going into service at the beginning of the budding age, getting married (with another entry in the parish register) near the beginning of early manhood, and a funeral (with a final entry in the parish register) at the end of later manhood (Houlbrooke 146–53, 171–8, 202–7; Ben-Amos 208–35).

In common with rites of passage in cultures all over the world, the life-marking ceremonies of early modern England moved through what Victor Turner, following a model first suggested by Arnold Van Gennep, demarcates as three distinct phases: an act of *separation* from the subject's previous existence (proceeding to the parish church for a ceremony, removal from home), a period of *transition* or in-betweenness in which his new identity was conferred, and a time of *reaggregation* or *incorporation* in which that new identity was confirmed and a new order of life begun.[20] In the common culture of Great Britain and North America today only weddings typically retain this complete three-part structure. Bachelor parties and bridesmaids' luncheons do the work of separation, the marriage ceremony itself figures as a state of in-betweenness, reaggregation happens, for friends and family, at a reception or dinner afterwards and, for the groom and bride themselves, on a honeymoon trip. Jewish communities in Britain and North America retain a rite of passage from childhood to youth in bar mitzvahs and bat mitzvahs. Some Christian communities mark the same passage in first communions. With respect to the rites of death, most communities in Britain and North America have substituted a single memorial service of some sort for the protracted three-part period of wake, ceremony, and mourning that once was customary. On the whole, English-speaking cultures today lack the strong communal sense of life passages that characterized early modern England.

For David Cressy, surveying the evidence of liturgy, parish registers, court records, diaries, and literary texts, the three events of birth, marriage, and death stand out as 'the landmarks of the life cycle' in Tudor and Stuart England.[21] In Shakespeare's plays, however, leaving home in early youth assumes an importance that rivals these more obvious occasions. The decision of Proteus's father in *The Two Gentlemen of Verona* to send his son to the Duke's court in Milan is prompted by a friend's observation that other men, even those of lower social rank,

> Put forth their sons to seek preferment out—
> Some to the wars, to try their fortune there,
> Some to discover islands far away,
> Some to the studious universities.

(1.3.7–10)

In Proteus's footsteps follow Bertram in *All's Well That Ends Well* ('to th' wars, my boy, to th' wars! | He wears his honour in a box unseen | That hugs his kicky-wicky here at home', advises Paroles (2.3.275–7)), Palamon and Arcite in *The Two Noble Kinsmen* ('Why am I bound | By any generous bond to follow him | Follows his tailor', Palamon exclaims as he persuades Arcite to seek out noble exemplars beyond the peace-loving men who surround them in Thebes (1.2.49–51))— and Prince Harry in *1 Henry IV*. Harry's life away from the royal palace shapes up as an apprenticeship of sorts, with Falstaff as his master in the 'mystery' of dissolute living. Eastcheap, let it be remembered, was situated in the middle of the City of London, where youths of lower social rank than Harry's were spending their seven years of apprenticeship not always in the workshop but sometimes in taverns and in theatres just outside the city walls.

Perhaps, indeed, we should consider all the moves from court or city to places elsewhere in Shakespeare's comedies and romances as instances of service or apprenticeship, as lessons in living that prepare boys to be men. In *Love's Labour's Lost* the King of Navarre refers to his sequestered court as 'a little academe', as if his fellows were students and he their self-appointed schoolmaster (1.1.13). All the wanderings in the woods outside Athens in *A Midsummer Night's Dream* are occasioned by Lysander's determination to exchange Theseus's authority for that of 'a widow aunt, a dowager | Of great revenue' who lives seven leagues from the city and, lacking children herself, 'respects me as her only son' (1.1.157–60). To Orlando in *As You Like It* the forest of Arden figures as an alternative to the 'good education', the 'exercises as may become a gentleman', that are denied him by his elder brother back at court (1.1.62–70). In *Twelfth Night* 'Cesario', who more than once confesses his birth to be better than his fortunes, takes service with Duke Orsino, just as the son of a gentleman might have done in early modern England. In *Cymbeline* Guiderius and Arviragus, exiled in Wales, are trained by Belarius in hunting skills that were part of a nobleman's accomplishments: the princes' existence may be 'beastly', but Belarius has taught them to be 'subtle as the fox for prey, | Like warlike as the wolf for what we eat' (3.3.40–1). In all these instances of leaving home there is an act of separation that leads to a period of in-betweenness, followed by a gesture toward reaggregation. Of the three stages that Turner finds in all rites of passage, it is the second, in-betweenness, that receives most extended attention in Shakespeare's plays: separation typically happens in the first scene or two; reaggregation, in the last. For actors and audiences, as Victor Turner points out, the theatrical performance itself takes place 'on the threshold' (Latin *limen*), in a state of liminality between life before the play and life after the play.[22] In this sense, *every* theatrical performance is about life passages.

As important as youths' removals from home may be, it is, just as Cressy would predict, rites of marriage and rites of death that Shakespeare dramatizes most often. With good reason. In its own way marriage in early modern England was quite as absolute as death. It brought the long ambiguities of youth to an end. In marriage a man became his own master, the head of his own household, the prospective father to his own children. He changed his seating in church. He could hold local office as juryman, reeve, or warden. He was obligated to pay taxes. In the words of Thomas Ridgeway, writing in 1610, 'none . . . be properly *in* the world till they be married, before which time they only go but *about* the world' (quoted in Cressy 290). Despite the importance of marriage as a passage from youth to adulthood, it is curious that Shakespeare's comedies—*The Taming of the Shrew* and *A Midsummer Night's Dream* are exceptions—typically stop short of the ceremony itself. Going to the church in procession, repeating vows, feasting and dancing, being ritually undressed and escorted to bed, being bombarded with your stockings, drinking the traditional posset of sack and sugar, at last being left alone: these are things Shakespeare's marrying couples never experience. The plays themselves become rites of separation and liminality, with reaggregation postponed until after the fiction is over, after the actors have retired to the tiring house, after the audience have left the theatre and made their ways back into the city, whence (in Philip Stubbes's imagination at least) 'everyone brings another homeward of their way very friendly and in their secret conclaves together they play the sodomites or worse'.[23]

What Shakespeare's marrying couples *do* experience is liminality. It is characteristic of in-betweenness, Turner points out, for the usual rules that govern social life to be suspended or even inverted. The participants move, for a time, in a state of 'flow' not unlike what we experience while playing a game or exercising our bodies in a sport:

action follows action according to an internal logic which seems to need no conscious intervention on our part...we experience it as a unified flowing from one moment to the next, in which we feel in control of our actions, and in which there is little distinction between self and environment; between stimulus and response; or between past, present, and future. (55–6)

Hence the strange fictional worlds in which Shakespeare's husbands-and wives-to-be find one another: the woods somewhere between Verona and Milan (*The Two Gentlemen of Verona*), a play-within-the-play (*The Taming of the Shrew*), an Ephesus famed for sorcerers and magicians (*The Comedy of Errors*), fields outside the King of Navarre's palace (*Love's Labour's Lost*), woods outside Athens (*A Midsummer Night's Dream*), the countryhouse of Belmont (*The Merchant of Venice*), the Forest of Arden (*As You Like It*), Illyria (*Twelfth Night*), a Bohemia that (unlike the real one) has a seacoast (*The Winter's Tale*), an uninhabited island (*The Tempest*), the Athens of ancient legend (*The Two Noble Kinsmen*). The only exceptions would seem to be the Messina of *Much Ado About Nothing*, the Vienna of *Measure for Measure*, and the Rousillon of *All's Well That Ends Well*, but even in these three comedies the fictional setting is invested with liminal qualities: Messina figures as a place of refuge from the just-concluded war and much of the crucial action takes place in a garden, the Duke of Vienna first encounters Isabella in a cloister, and the action of *All's Well* soon shifts to Italy, where, from an English point of view, quite anything is possible. In the liminality of the places where the rites of marriage take place Shakespeare stands apart from professional contemporaries like Ben Jonson and Thomas Middleton, who favour the mercantile realities of London. The closest Shakespeare comes to this mode of comedy is *The Merry Wives of Windsor*, but the main subject there is not, after all, what happens *before* marriage but what happens *after*.

Numerous critics of our own day have charted the varied ways in which the marriages in Shakespeare's comedies negotiate the challenges in moving from boyhood to manhood. In Marilyn L. Williamson's view, the comedies represent a series of attempts to maintain male power: first through fantasies of successfully wooing a powerful woman in the early and mid-career 'comedies of courtship', then through a fresh reassertion of male control in the 'problem comedies', and finally through a celebration of patriarchy as a force working across generations in the late romances.[24] Amid all these variations, what seems distinctive about Shakespeare's portrayals of the passage from boyhood to manhood is a concern with how to reconcile two conflicting ideals: the classically sanctioned valuation of male–male friendship above all other human ties and the more recent, distinctively Protestant ideal of companionate marriage, in which the relationship of husband and wife was one of 'communion'. Against Aristotle's definition of male–male friendship, which we noted in Chapter 2, Shakespeare and his audiences had to weigh William Perkins's celebration of married life between husband and wife as 'an holy kind of rejoicing and solacing themselves each with other in a mutual declaration of the signs and tokens of love and kindness'.[25] The older, patriarchal model of marriage, in which the husband was clearly his wife's superior, was compatible with male friendship; the newer, companionate model made the relationship between friendship and marriage less clear. The all-male institutions of boyhood and youth— schools, apprenticeships, universities, the inns of court—fostered male–male friendship, particularly with one's bed fellows; marriage demanded a change.

The crisis is never more pointedly stated than in *The Merchant of Venice*, when Bassanio declares in a court of law that he values his relationship with Antonio more than that with his wife:

> Antonio, I am married to a wife
> Which is as dear to me as life itself,
> But life itself, my wife, and all the world
> Are not with me esteemed above thy life.
> I would lose all, ay, sacrifice them all
> Here to this devil, to deliver you.

No one is more moved by this declaration than Bassanio's wife herself. Portia, disguised as his attorney, replies, 'Your wife would give you little thanks for that | If she were by to hear you make the offer' (4.1.279–86). In referring to Portia as his 'wife' Bassanio is speaking of a marriage that still awaits sexual consummation. Portia has given her successful suitor permission to attend to his friend's business: 'First go with me to church and call me wife, | And then away to Venice to your friend; | For never shall you lie by Portia's side | With an unquiet soul' (3.2.301–4). For his part Bassanio promises, '. . . till I come again | No bed shall e'er be guilty of my stay' (3.2.322–3). (In deferring sexual consummation Bassanio and Portia are untypical of couples in Shakespeare's England. Perhaps 50 per cent, in Cressy's estimate, followed popular tradition and took 'handfasting' in the presence of witnesses as licence for sexually consummating their match before any church ceremony had taken place (267–81).) For Bassanio's rite of passage from youth to manhood to be completed, then, the conflicting demands of friendship and husbandship must be reconciled. The terms in which that happens are pointedly sexual. Discovering in the play's last scene that the lawyer who saved the day for Antonio was none other than Portia in disguise, and being forced by Portia to admit that he gave away his betrothal ring, Bassanio plays his wife's gender ambiguity to his own advantage: 'Sweet doctor, you shall be my bedfellow. | When I am absent, then lie with my wife' (5.1.284–5). As one and the same person, as both 'Doctor Balthasar' and Bassanio's wife, Portia can, in the terms laid down by Bassanio, never sleep with anyone but him. *He*, however, has it both ways: he can sleep, in imagination at least, with both a male bedfellow appropriate to the living arrangements of youth ('sweet doctor') and a female bedfellow appropriate to the living arrangements of marriage (Portia in her own person).

In working out such a compromise between youth and manhood Bassanio echoes Valentine in *The Two Gentlemen of Verona*, who proposes to share with his friend, his friend's new wife, and his own new wife 'One feast, one house, one mutual happiness' (5.4.171), and anticipates Orsino in *Twelfth Night*, who insists on calling his new wife 'Cesario' as long as she is dressed as a page (5.1.381–2). To the degree that such ambiguities are entertained right to the end, the rites of passage in Shakespeare's comedies from youth to manhood seem to stop just short of completion. In the context of all the earlier comedies, Bertram's reluctance to accept Helena as his wife in *All's Well That Ends Well* does not look like such an anomaly, after all. It is only Henry V's impending marriage to Catherine, perhaps, that passes through the separation of Eastcheap and the liminality of the battlefield to achieve reaggregation in the throne room of France. Even so, *The Life of Henry V*, as the play is styled in the 1623 folio, ends on a dubious note: bringing Prince Harry's *Bildungsroman* to full closure, the Chorus reminds the audience of the king's eventual death and sets in motion yet another sequence of life passages by mentioning his son Henry VI, 'in infant bands crowned king | Of France and England' (Ep. 9–10). Under his rule—or rather under the rule of those who governed on his behalf—all that Henry V achieved in France was lost.

Unlike marriage, which 80–90 per cent of Shakespeare's audience experienced at least once, death was something all of them could look forward to.[26] The historical Henry V died of dysentery at age 35, toward the end of what Cuffe describes as the very 'prime' of manhood. Dramatized deaths in Shakespeare's plays, as more often than not in early modern life, occurred well before the protagonists' passage from manhood into the first half of old age at 65 years or into 'decrepit old age' thereafter. Hence, the *drama* of those deaths, their hold on the imaginations of spectators who might themselves be summoned to join the Dance of Death at any time. The old men who do appear on Shakespeare's stage tend to figure in scenes that contrast the frailness of age with the vigour of youth. Old Adam and Orlando, Lear and his daughters, Gloucester and his sons have their counterparts in Lord Talbot and his son John in *1 Henry VI*, Old Clifford and Young Clifford in *2 Henry VI*, John of Gaunt and the King in *Richard II*, and Prince Harry and his father in *2 Henry IV*. The bravery of Talbot in battle against the French in *1 Henry VI* inspired one of the earliest allusions to Shakespeare's work among his contemporaries; just as affecting must have been the old soldier's on-stage death holding the body of his dying son: 'Soldiers, adieu. I have what I would have, | Now my old arms are young John Talbot's grave' (4.7.31–2). Just as striking in *2 Henry VI* is the stage image of youth and eld formed by the body of Old Clifford, killed in combat by York, as it is discovered by his son. Young Clifford himself captions the emblem:

> Wast thou ordainèd, dear father,
> To lose thy youth in peace, and to achieve
> The silver livery of advisèd age,
> And in thy reverence and thy chair-days, thus
> To die in ruffian battle?

> (5.3.45–9)

Critics who would see in Richard II more a poet than a king might heed the dying speeches of John of Gaunt, who sees more a youth than a man. When Richard is summoned to Gaunt's deathbed, York advises

Gaunt, 'Deal mildly with his youth, | For young hot colts, being reined, do rage the more' (2.1.69–70). Gaunt does anything but that. Richard, in response, dismisses Gaunt as 'a lunatic lean-witted fool' who, 'Presuming on an ague's privilege, | Dar'st with thy frozen admonition | Make pale our cheek' (*Richard II*, 2.1.116–19). Cheek, indeed. The most famous of Shakespeare's juxtapositions of youth and old age is probably that of Prince Harry and his dying father in *2 Henry IV*. Though Holinshed specifies that the king, aged 46, was ill with disease when Harry came to him, not languishing in old age, Shakespeare heightens the sense that spectators are seeing two life passages in the scene: Harry's from youth to manhood and the king's from old age to death. The king laments that he lacks 'personal' (i.e. bodily) strength to make his intended pilgrimage to Jerusalem (4.3.8); he locates himself seasonally when he receives Westmorland with good news from the front as 'a summer bird | Which ever in the haunch of winter sings | The lifting up of day' (4.3.91–3); he remarks on his failing sight and giddy brain (4.3.110); above all, he is disposed to look back over a life nearly completed ('My day is dim' (4.3.229)) and to see in Harry 'the noble image of *my* youth' (4.3.55, emphasis added). The father–son pairings in this series of scenes, particularly that of Harry and Henry IV, suggest that early modern culture recognized another rite of passage just as important as leaving home, marriage, and death: the moment when a son inherits his father's ancestral title, his material goods, and his political capital.

At whatever age, however, death in early modern culture figured as the ultimate rite of passage. Michael Neill has argued that the stage deaths in tragedies by Shakespeare and his contemporaries should be understood as exercises in the 'art' of dying (*ars moriendi*), as existential moments in which a man's interiority is revealed.[27] In undergoing death a man was believed to move from one state of being to another, from earth to heaven or to hell. Richard II's final couplet captures this sense of death as a rite of passage that moves vertically: 'Mount, mount, my soul; thy seat is up on high, | Whilst my gross flesh sinks downward, here to die' (5.5.111–12). In death a man was also believed to move from one state of *knowing* to another. St Paul articulates the difference in his first epistle to the Corinthians: 'For now we see through a glass darkly: but then shall we see face to face. Now I know in part: but then shall I know even as I am known'.[28] Shakespeare's onstage portrayals of death capture this sense of liminality. The dying protagonist in one way or another becomes isolated, not only fictionally, from his former social position, but often dramatically as well, from his fellows onstage. Cut off in battle, roving over the stage in a desperate attempt to find a way out, Richard III turns the disjunction between his former state of being as king and his present placelessness into the twice repeated cry 'A horse! A horse! My kingdom for a horse!' (5.7.7, 13). Richard's death at the hands of Richmond seconds later, in dumbshow to the accompaniment of drums and trumpet blasts (*'Alarum...flourish'* (5.8.1 s.d.)), points up how the liminal moment between life and death figures as a liminal moment between language and no language: 'The rest is silence. | O, O, O, O!' (*Hamlet* 5.2.310–11). Hotspur dies in midsentence 'No, Percy, thou art dust, | And food for—' (*1 Henry IV* 5.4.84–5)). Othello, like Romeo before him, relinquishes language, and his life, in the wordless suspiration of a kiss (*Othello*, 5.2.369, *Romeo and Juliet*, 5.3.120). Lear's last words gesture toward Cordelia's silent lips: 'Look there, look there' (*The Tragedy of King Lear*, 5.3.287). After such glimpses into existence beyond the dark glass of language, the reaggregation that concludes death as a rite of passage comes in the words, the often empty and inadequate words, in which the survivors attempt to make sense of it all. Even Richmond's epitaph on Richard III—'The bloody dog is dead' (5.8.2)—rings hollow after the audience has given its imaginative complicity to Richard's asides and soliloquies. Fortinbras's order to 'Bear Hamlet like a soldier to the stage' (5.2.350) recasts the fallen prince's story in a genre very unlike what the audience has heard from Hamlet himself. Othello and Lear fare better in the measured understatements that follow their deaths: Cassio's admission 'This did I fear... | For he was great of heart' (5.2.370–1) and Edgar's (or is it Albany's?) attempt to round off *King Lear* in a pair of couplets: 'The weight of this sad time we must obey...' (*The Tragedy of King Lear*, 5.3.299–302). If Shakespeare's comedies can be viewed as rites of passage from youth to manhood, his tragedies shape up as rites of passage from youth to death or from manhood to death. Rites of both kinds stop short of full reaggregation, in part because performance of the play itself is, for audience and actors, a rite of passage in itself, a liminal state of affairs between two orders of existence, life before the play and life afterwards.

Other Models

However common the ages of man may have been as a way of under-standing manhood as a factor of time, individual men in early modern England found a variety of other ways of making sense of their lives as a sequence. Any man who sat down to write the story of his own life had perforce to find a pattern in that life. Each of the autobiographies that survive from sixteenth- and seventeenth-century England repres-ents an attempt on the part of the author to *justify* his life, in more than one sense of the word: to judge (*OED* 1), to absolve or acquit from an implicit charge of misconduct (*OED* 4), to make exact, to fit or arrange exactly (*OED* 9). Among the patterns these writers use to make sense of their experience, the seven ages of man is in fact quite rare. The professional musician Thomas Whythorne (b. 1528) is among the few who see their life in this way, titling his manuscript 'A Book of Songs and Sonnets, with Long Discourses Set with Them, of the Child's Life, together with a Young Man's Life, and Entering into the Old Man's Life'. Cued by Thomas Elyot's *Castle of Health*, Whythorne fully expected to discover first-hand that 'Cupid and Venus were and would be very busy to trouble the quiet minds of young folk' and tried hard, during the first half of his youth at least, to avoid Cupid's shafts by reading poetry and moral philosophy and studying music.[29] Writing in his mid-30s, Sir Simonds D'Ewes (b. 1602) takes an altogether practical approach and divides his life into four parts: (1) birth, childhood, and early education (to age 15), (2) later education in university and at one of the inns of court (ages 16–24), (3) courtship and marriage to the death of his father (ages 25–8), and (4) his own adult life to the death of his only son and heir (ages 29–34).[30] D'Ewes's focus on the deaths of his father and of his son as turning points suggests that coming into one's inheritance could indeed be a more important rite of passage than marriage.

Writers of a spiritual bent were likely to divide their lives up according to a third pattern, into a 'before' and an 'after'. In his manuscript 'Confessions' Richard Norwood (b. 1590), for example, is able to specify precisely when, at age 25, he gave up his youthful delight in acting women's parts in plays and his addiction to an unnamed 'master sin' and accepted Christ's offer of salvation. Living on

Bermuda, where he had done surveying work, Norwood was reading
St Augustine's *Tractate upon John* when Christ first spoke to him: 'He
that made all things by his word was graciously pleased to open my
heart to the receiving of his word, and by that living word in my heart
to work a new life in me before ever I was aware or thought of any such
thing.'[31] Rhys Evans (b. 1607?) was a tailor's apprentice at age 9 when
on a mountain-top in Wales he received the first vision that set him on
his career as a prophet.[32] George Trosse (b. 1631) was accustomed to
getting so drunk that he would fall off his horse on the way home;
when coming back one night, 'I perceived a voice (I heard it plainly)
saying unto me, "Who art thou?" Which, knowing it could be the
voice of no mortal, I concluded was the voice of God, and with tears, as
I remember, replied, "I am a very great sinner, Lord!"'[33] Trosse
continued to think of this moment as the turning-point in his life,
despite two relapses into alcoholism. The 'before' and 'after' in the life
of Robert Parsons (b. 1546) were marked by his becoming a Jesuit
priest.[34] It seemed only natural to the posthumous editor of the
miscellaneous autobiographical papers left behind by Richard Baxter
(b. 1615) that the great Presbyterian theologian's life should be divided
into half by two chapters of 'self-analysis and life-review' providing a
41-point summary of the ways in which Baxter's thinking differed in
old age from his thinking in youth.[35]

A fourth way of justifying one's life was provided by models like
Boccaccio's *De Casibus Virorum Illustrium* and the English-language *A
Mirror for Magistrates*, with their cumulatively impressive iterations of
the rise and fall of great men. Men of lesser social station than kings or
princes might also think of their lives in such terms. The master
shipwright Phineas Pett (b. 1570), for example, endured bad times in
his early years that included an abusive stepfather and a selfish elder
brother right out of *As You Like It*. Through patronage of the Lord
High Admiral, however, Pett eventually became ship-builder to
Prince Henry. The prince's early death seemed to Pett to mark a
downturn in his fortunes, as the Lord High Admiral's patronage had
marked an upturn.[36] Still another group of autobiographers accepted
the fact that their lives were episodic, that the sequence of events
lacked a grand design. The Presbyterian preacher Adam Martindale
(b. 1623) fails to specify a dramatic life-altering experience like Norwood's, Evans's, or Trosse's and matter-of-factly writes up his life in

seven-year segments, albeit each of them accompanied by a gloss pointing out instances of God's providence. In his first 'septennium', for example, Martindale recalls an event that happened when he was 'a little boy in coats [i.e. not yet breeched] but so grown that I can well remember it': he fell into a marl pit full of water and almost drowned, saved by his older sister, who looked up from her work just in the nick of time. Martindale's gloss on this event, looking back from the vantage point of later manhood, finds meaning by comparing *his* story to the pre-existing story of Abraham's sacrifice of his son Isaac in Genesis 22: 'God sometimes appears in the mount, as he did to save Isaac when the hand of his father was stretched out to slay him, staying so long as will make the deliverance more admirable, yet not so long as to make endeavours unprofitable.'[37] Thomas Raymond (b. 1610), who spent his career in diplomatic service in Venice, casts his autobiography as 'A Rhapsody', full of digressions and anecdotes.[38] Captain John Smith's autobiography is no less episodic, being titled *The True Travels, Adventures, and Observations of Captain John Smith in Europe, Asia, Africa, and America* and following the third-person hero on one voyage after another.[39]

As schemes for justifying a man's life, at least three of these other autobiographical models have their counterparts in Shakespeare's plays. Ways of reading a life and ways of telling a story both come down to questions of *genre*. Who is the protagonist? What happens *to* him? What happens *with* him? When? Where? Why? How does his story end? What is the relationship of the observer or the listener or the reader to the whole affair? The models that sixteenth- and seventeenth-century men used to write up their own lives match with several of the genres in which Shakespeare exercised his dramatic imagination. The rise and fall pattern traced out by the shipwright Phineas Pett informs the life passages in Shakespeare's history plays and certain of his tragedies. Richard II, who begins his dramatic career, in Gaunt's eyes at least, as a rash youth, finishes that career, not by entering prime manhood, as the 'ages of man' model would lead us to expect, but by falling from his former position of power: 'Down, down I come like glist'ring Phaeton' (3.3.177). Edmund in *King Lear*, having ridden Fortune's wheel to its height, looks back over his own life in the moment of death from a prone position at the feet of his brother: 'The wheel is come full circle,' he tells Edgar. 'I am here' (*The Tragedy of King Lear*, 5.3.165). The most spectacular fall of all is perhaps Richard III's: as the ascent has been the most precipitous, so is the descent. The image of Fortune's wheel in all of these careers suggests a circular scheme of life passages (see diagram).

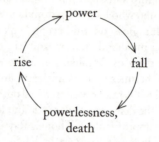

The before-and-after scheme that made most sense to a Jesuit priest like Robert Parsons or to a mystic like Rhys Evans finds its most obvious counterpart, ironically enough, in Shakespeare's comedies, in the scenes of love at first sight that send the protagonists out into the woods beyond Athens or the Forest of Arden or Illyria and eventually into one another's arms in marriage. But the before-and-after model figures even more powerfully in some of the tragedies, especially those in which a single experience changes the protagonist's life for ever. The sight of Juliet at the Capulets' ball inspires Romeo then and there to divide his life into a 'before' and an 'after': 'Did my heart love till now? Forswear it, sight, | For I ne'er saw true beauty till this night' (1.5.51–2). The voice of Old Hamlet's Ghost works the same effect on Young Hamlet as, in retrospect, the voice of God did on Rhys Evans standing atop a mountain in Wales or George Trosse falling home drunk one night: it *rewrites* the listener's sense of his own life. 'Remember me' are Old Hamlet's parting words. 'Remember thee?' Hamlet replies in soliloquy.

> Yea, from the table of my memory
> I'll wipe away all trivial fond records,
> All saws of books, all forms, all pressures past,
> That youth and observation copied there,
> And thy commandment all alone shall live
> Within the book and volume of my brain
>
> (1.5.97–103)

According to this scheme, the passages in Hamlet's life shape up thus:

before ⟶ voice ⟶ after ⟶ death

Of these four segments, death is arguably *not* the most significant. Hamlet's death is, after all, neither a Stoic suicide nor a brutal murder but an ethically confused matter, just as his life has been after hearing the voice of the Ghost. If, as Aristotle proposes, tragedy always involves a turning-point, a moment of *peripeteia*, that moment for Hamlet, as for Romeo, is not the moment of death but the moment in which his life suddenly changes course. Hamlet's charge to Horatio 'Absent thee from felicity a while, | And in this harsh world draw thy breath in pain | To tell my story' (5.2.299–301) is echoed in Othello's request that the Venetians who witness his death should 'speak | Of one that loved not wisely but too well' (5.2.352–3). Both protagonists wish, in the face of death, to justify their lives, in just the ways that sixteenth- and seventeenth-century autobiographers do. For Othello, as for Hamlet, the moment of tragic *peripeteia* is not the moment of death but the moment when his life changes—and when he instantly knows it. Blowing his love out of his open hand, just as Desdemona has let the handkerchief, the token of Othello's love, drop from hers, Othello puts off the identity of lover and takes on the identity of revenger:

> Look here, Iago.
> All my fond love thus do I blow to heaven—'tis gone.
> Arise, black vengeance, from the hollow hell.
> Yield up, O love, thy crown and hearted throne
> To tyrannous hate!
>
> (3.3.449–53)

From the transformation enacted here, half way through the play, Desdemona's death, and Othello's, follow with horrible inevitability.

In the rhapsodic schema, the passages of a man's life appear as a seemingly endless series of episodes:

first this ⟶ then that ⟶ then that ⟶ then that ⟶ etc

If 'but' is the word that joins one passage with another in the ages of man, the before-and-after, and the rise-and-fall models, the operative word here is 'and'. The Shakespeare script that seems most obviously to follow this particular sense of life passages is *Pericles*, a play that roams over the Mediterranean Sea and through at least a decade and a half of the protagonist's life. In their own distinctive ways, however, *The Winter's Tale*, *Cymbeline*, *The Tempest*, *All Is True*, and *The Two Noble Kinsmen* are equally peripatetic in space and wide-ranging in time. Events in *The Winter's Tale* take place in two widely separate places, Sicily and Bohemia, and in two time frames sixteen years apart. *Cymbeline* combines elements of three historical configurations of time and place: classical Rome, ancient Britain, and contemporary Britain. As concentrated as it is in space and time, *The Tempest* nonetheless brings together on one stage, for three hours, men whose life-passages have taken them on a series of voyages and adventures around the Mediterranean Sea and, implicitly at least, across the Atlantic Ocean. With the notable exception of Wolsey's career, the things that come to pass in *All Is True* have little to do with the patterns of rise and fall that dominate Shakespeare's earlier history plays. The Prologue to *The Two Noble Kinsmen*, like Gower's prologue to *Pericles*, presents the events to ensue as an old tale—'Chaucer, of all admired, the story gives: | There constant to eternity it lives' (Pro. 13–14)—but sets up that time-honoured tale with a distinctly seventeenth-century knowingness that compares new plays to maidenheads (Pro. 1). The three queens' petition, Palamon and Arcite's decamping from Thebes to Athens, battles, imprisonment, escapes, the escapades of the Jailer's Daughter and local youths, the tournament in which the two noble kinsmen fight to the death: these disparate events give Shakespeare's last script an episodic quality so extreme that some critics have attributed it to the play's dual authorship.

Among the late romances, *The Two Noble Kinsmen* is the only one to end with the death of a protagonist. By its very episodic structure, rhapsody would seem to defy the inevitability of death—or at least to postpone it—in a way that no other scheme of life-passages can manage. For all that, rhapsody does not escape a sense of purpose and direction. Like Adam Martindale's account of his life in broad seven-year segments, events in Shakespeare's last plays turn out not to be random occurrences but proofs of a mysterious providence. Just as Martindale is able, in retrospect, to see that everything that happened to him at age 7 or age 14 or age 21 was part of a plan he could not have known at the time, so events in Shakespeare's last plays are under the control of a master authority. In *Pericles* that authoritative figure is

Gower: physically and rhetorically he presides over the play. At the end of *Cymbeline* Jupiter himself intervenes to set aright Posthumus's fortunes. Personified Time puts the events of *The Winter's Tale* into a synoptic perspective that none of the characters in the play can appreciate until the end. Dressed in his magic robes, consulting his books, Prospero assumes the mantle of Providence *vis-à-vis* the other characters in *The Tempest*. The birth of the future Queen Elizabeth in *All Is True* figures for Henry VIII as an 'oracle of comfort' (5.4.66) that gives meaning to the whole of the life he has lived in the play. Theseus ends *The Two Noble Kinsmen* in awe at the unseen powers that have been at work in the play's five acts:

> O you heavenly charmers,
> What things you make of us! For what we lack
> We laugh, for what we have, are sorry; still
> Are children in some kind. Let us be thankful
> For that which is, and with you leave dispute
> That are above our question.
>
> (5.6.131–6)

The ages of man, rites of passage, rise and fall, before and after, rhapsody: Shakespeare's plays and poems, like the accounts of their own lives written down by sixteenth- and seventeenth-century men, manifest a variety of ways of understanding masculinity as something that happens in time. Early modern proverbs register this awareness at a popular level: 'Time is the rider that breaks youth', 'A shrewd lad may make a good man', 'Age and wedlock bring a man to his nightcap', 'Old men wish, wise men warn, and young men work', 'Young men think old men fools, but old men know that young men be fools', 'Youth and age will never agree' (Tilley nos. T330, B580, A63, M574, M610, Y43). The result of such thinking was, from yet another point of view, to render masculinity as something inherently unstable, something always in the process of being achieved. Theseus's very last words in *The Two Noble Kinsmen* can stand as a summation of this chapter: 'Let's go off | And bear us like the time' (5.6.136–7).

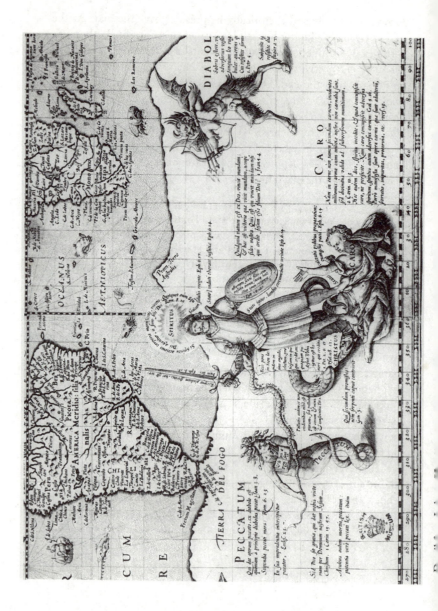

Others

The problem posed by other people in finding and maintaining one's own identity is especially acute in Shakespeare's sonnets. 'Two loves I have, of comfort and despair', declares the speaking persona in sonnet 144,

> Which like two spirits do suggest me still.
> The better angel is a man right fair,
> The worser spirit a woman coloured ill.
>
> (144.1–4)

The word 'suggest' here carries the force of 'prompt' or 'propose', so that the man right fair and the woman coloured ill function as tempter-figures in a morality play, with the persona as the central protagonist. The 'I' who speaks through all the sonnets may seem to enjoy an independent existence, but he is constituted by this 'him' and this 'her'. In poem after poem he defines himself with respect to them. He is quite unimaginable without them. Many of the sonnets address the consequent crisis of 'us'.

In the diptych of sonnets 133 and 134, for example, the persona first imagines himself and the man right fair imprisoned within the ill-coloured woman's 'steel bosom's ward': 'Me from myself thy cruel eye hath taken, | And my next self thou harder hast engrossed' (133.9, 5–6). 'Thy cruel eye' can be heard, if not seen, as 'thy cruel "I"'. 'She' thus subsumes both 'me' and 'him' into *her* overwhelming 'me'. The fact that 'I' and 'he' have exchanged hearts, as lovers in sonnets are wont to do, makes 'her' power as jailer complete. In sonnet 134 these images of imprisonment are given what seems at first a distinctly legalistic turn:

So, now I have confessed that he is thine,
And I myself am mortgaged to thy will,
Myself I'll forfeit, so that other mine
Thou wilt restore to be my comfort still.

(134.1–4)

In the immediately ensuing sonnets 135 and 136, 'will' is going to be sported with as a pun for vagina, so that the fusion of 'me' and 'her', if not of 'me' and 'him', turns out to be a sexual as well as legal 'bond', especially if we take the bawdy hint and interpret 'to write' as 'to prick': 'He learned but surety-like to write for me | Under that bond that him as fast doth bind' (134.7–8). The result, according to the concluding couplet, is an annihilation of masculine identity, both 'mine' and 'his'. For 'whole' in the last line hear 'hole': 'Him have I lost; thou hast both him and me; | He pays the whole, and yet am I not free' (134.13–14).

Sonnets 133 and 134 epitomize the quest in Shakepeare's sonnets for the achievement of masculine identity *vis-à-vis* two opposed others, one gendered male, the other female. The male other is felt, in these particular poems at least, to be 'my next self', an 'other mine'; the female other remains a constant threat to the persona's integrity, even in the sonnets addressed to her directly. Whether the persona ever manages to be 'free' is an open question. In sonnet 126 ('O thou my lovely boy, who in thy power | Dost hold time's fickle glass, his sickle-hour') he seems to be taking leave of his once 'next self'. By sonnet 152 ('In loving thee thou know'st I am forsworn, | But thou art twice forsworn to me love swearing') the speaking 'I' is still very much in thrall to 'her' (152.1–2).

The situatedness of 'I' *vis-à-vis* other people is even more conspicuous in Shakespeare's plays, where no speaking 'I' is ever continuously sustained from start to finish. Other people interrupt: they talk back to the speaking 'me', they carry on conversations with other people when the speaking 'I' is not on stage, they talk about the speaking 'me' behind his back, in soliloquies and asides they can form bonds with the audience that leave the speaking 'me' quite out of the picture. As Bert O. States observes, we think of actors in a play as feeding each other lines; it is more accurate to think of them as feeding each other *character*. Not for nothing do we refer to the persons involved in a play as 'protagonists' and 'antagonists', as 'contestants for' and 'contestants against'. The play as *agon*, or 'contest', might seem to be a function of plot, but the term also captures the onstage relationship of actors with one another. In the theatre as in life, character happens in response to other people: in States's words, it is 'the formation of a response to the stimulus posed by the world. Character is the site of an infinitely delicate self-adjustment as much as it is the site of self-expression."

There comes a moment in *Julius Caesar* when Cassius seems to articulate the situation precisely. Eager to get Brutus to join the conspiracy against Caesar, Cassius has been carefully observing Brutus's behaviour. He takes Brutus aside and tries to find out why Brutus has been so diffident of late. Unsuccessful with direct questions, Cassius at last says, 'Tell me, good Brutus, can you see your face?' 'No, Cassius,' comes the answer, 'for the eye sees not itself | But by reflection, by some other things'. (As in the sonnets, 'eye' can be heard here as 'I'.) Without mirrors, Cassius rejoins, Brutus cannot appreciate the worthiness that other men find in him:

> And since you know you cannot see yourself
> So well as by reflection, I, your glass,
> Will modestly discover to yourself
> That of yourself which you yet know not of.
>
> (1.2.53–5, 69–72)

The stratagem works: Cassius succeeds in winning Brutus's allegiance by appealing to what Brutus thinks other men think of him. The *virtus* of Brutus as a Roman hero resides as much in others as it does in himself.

Deconstructionist theory and Jacques Lacan's version of psychoanalysis both invite us to understand these strategic others as *opposite* selves. If, as Derrida argues, all meanings are made by the marking of binary difference, then 'I' am 'I' because 'I' am not 'you'. At the same time, 'I' need 'you', because, without 'you', 'I' have nothing against which to define my difference. In this double bind Lacan finds a fundamental frustration, an estrangement from the sense of wholeness that human beings enjoy as infants, before they enter into language and learn that there is such a thing as 'I'. In Lacan's view, a person's 'I' is the repository of all the things that have ever been said to that person. 'I' is a function of language, and it exists only in relation to other people. The same double bind is played for all its tragicomic worth in

Samuel Beckett's one-act play 'Not I'.[2] For all that, the sonnet-speaker's reference to the man right fair as 'my next self', even an 'other mine', and Cassius's offer of himself as a mirror to Brutus's worthiness suggest that a man can regard others, not as opposite selves, but as *proximate* selves. That is phenomenologically true if not ontologically so: we can *experience* others as proximate even if they *exist* as quite separate beings. If bodies in perspective space appear to be ranged along a continuum from closer to farther away, might there not be an equivalent continuum in psychic space? To understand masculinity in terms of others, we need to consider two distinct situations: one in which masculinity is defined *vis-à-vis* various opposites and one in which masculinity is experienced as a kind of merging or fusion of self with others. We need to understand, not just the 'not me', but the 'partly me' and the 'other mine'.

David Gilmore's conclusion in *The Making of Masculinity* that manliness is not an essence, that it is not simply *there* in the male body, is based on anthropological observation, but according to Derrida the dubious status of masculinity follows from the nature of language itself. Masculinity, like anything else, is knowable only in terms of the things it is not. In the case of early modern England, we can identify four such points of contrast, each of them involving a major social issue: women, foreigners, persons of lower social rank, and sodomites. With respect to gender, England was ruled until 1603 by a female monarch. The power she enjoyed at the apex of the social hierarchy caused anxieties about male privilege up and down the line. With respect to nationhood, London in 1600 was an international metropolis in which foreigners of various kinds lived in close proximity to people who could claim to be Englishmen by birth. It was not just French refugees from religious oppression, German merchants, Italian bankers, and African servants against whom the men of early modern England defined themselves but immigrants from the countries—Wales, Scotland, and Ireland—that, along with England, made up the emerging nation-state of 'Britain'. With respect to social rank, the theatre was notoriously a venue in which anyone with a penny to spare could claim a place. To this socially diverse audience plays offered models of masculinity that critics of the theatre treated with disdain, suspicion, and fear. With respect to sexuality, England after 1603 was ruled by a king widely rumoured to practise the sin of sodomy. His public behaviour called into question what had been the 'open secret' of homoeroticism as one of the ways in which men in early modern England affirmed their bonds with one another. James's behaviour helped to force the issue of defining *gender* roles *vis-à-vis* *sexual* roles. Out of these four sorts of differences is forged the masculinity on display in Shakespeare's plays and poems.

Women

The importance of women as a defining other can be witnessed on a map of the world published at Amsterdam by Jodocus Hondius in 1597 and dedicated to three English mathematicians. One of them, Edward Wright, had publicized the projectional technique used in the map, a system for turning a sphere into a flat surface originally devised by Gerard Mercator and still known today as 'Mercator projection'. Prominently captioned on Hondius's map are places that had recently been explored by English adventurers: Virginia (1585), the North-West Passage (1585–87), and the island of Novaya Zemlya (1594–95). The ethical ideal that governed these voyages of discovery is emblemized at the bottom in the figure of a Christian Knight who gives the map the name by which it is known today.[3] (See Figure 5.) Outfitted according to St Paul's description in Ephesians 6: 13–17 with the girdle of truth, the breastplate of righteousness, the shoes of the gospel, the shield of faith, the helmet of salvation, and the sword of the spirit, the knight is depicted in triumph over five sorts of evil. Shown in Figure 5 are Flesh at the knight's feet, Sin to his right, and the Devil to his left. Outside the frame to his right is the World; to his left, Death. Flesh, Sin, and the World, let it be noted, are all personified as women; Sin is particularly arresting with her Medusa's head and serpent's tail. In effect, the 'Christian Knight' map of the world combines chivalric ideals with Christian doctrine to provide an epic frame for world-dominion as Europe's destiny. In one glance the viewer's eye is invited to take in all the known world as well as the doctrine that justifies its domination by the viewer and his kind. In this grand scheme the entities to be dominated figure as women.

Tarquin in *The Rape of Lucrece* speaks as a man of the late sixteenth century in imagining the countries of the world as women, as objects there to be *possessed*. Tarquin reads the body of the sleeping Lucrece as a merchant-adventurer might read a map:

> Her breasts like ivory globes circled with blue,
> A pair of maiden worlds unconquerèd,
> Save of their lord no bearing yoke they knew,
> And him by oath they truly honourèd.
> These worlds in Tarquin new ambition bred,
>   Who like a foul usurper went about
> From this fair throne to heave the owner out.
>
>   (407–13)

To possess Lucrece will mean not only to know her sexually (*OED* I.3b) but to seize her (*OED* I.3a), to control her (*OED* I.5a), to own her (*OED* I.2a), to occupy her (*OED* I.1) in the place of her husband Collatine. Something of the same feminine quality characterizes exotic places in Shakespeare's plays like Diana's Ephesus in *The Comedy of Errors* ('There's none but witches do inhabit here' (3.2.162)), Portia's Belmont in *The Merchant of Venice* ('in such a night | Troilus . . . sighed his soul . . . | Where Cressid lay', 'In such a night | Did Thisbe . . .', 'In such a night | Stood Dido . . .', 'In such a night | Medea . . .' (5.1.3–7, 9–10, 12–13)), Venus's Cyprus in *Othello* ('Honey, you shall be well desired in Cyprus, | I have found great love amongst them' (2.1.205–6)), Cleopatra's Egypt in *Antony and Cleopatra* ('She did lie | In her pavilion . . . | O'er-picturing that Venus where we see | The fancy outwork nature' (2.2.205–8)), even Perdita's Bohemia in *The Winter's Tale* ('These your unusual weeds to each part of you | Does give a life; no shepherdess, but Flora | Peering in April's front' (4.4.1–3)). All these places are dangerous to men to the degree that men fail to be conquerors. Their ability to do so is far from a foregone conclusion. '*Histerica passio* down . . . ; | Thy element's below' (*The Tragedy of King Lear*, 2.2.232–3): the unstable nature of a man's physical person, as we observed in Chapter 1, meant that even the most manly of men was susceptible to becoming a woman. Galen's one-sex theory of the human body located masculinity not in the possession of distinctive sexual organs (men's equipment was imagined to be an extruded version of women's) but in behaviour.

To become effeminate was thus an ever-present possibility. As Thomas Gainsford defines the term in *The Rich Cabinet* (1616), effeminateness 'hateth exercise, is an enemy both to strength and wit, when labour perfecteth the understanding and raiseth manhood to full height'.[4] At less than full height an effeminate fool, according to Nicholas Breton in his character book *The Good and the Bad* (1616),

loves nothing but gay, to look in a glass, to keep among wenches, and to play with trifles; to feed on sweetmeats and to be danced in laps, to be embraced in arms, and to be kissed on the cheek; to talk idly, to look demurely, to go nicely, and to laugh continually; to be his mistress' servant, and her maid's master, his father's love and his mother's none-child; to play on a fiddle and sing a love-song; to wear sweet gloves and look on fine things.

So far so bad. In such a catalogue of traits we recognize all too obvious examples in Le Beau in *As You Like It*, Osric in *Hamlet*, Lafeu in *All's Well That Ends Well*, Mardian in *Antony and Cleopatra*. But we can recognize also Orsino in *Twelfth Night*. As Breton goes on, the list of traits continues to get too close for the comfort of satiric distance. An effeminate fool loves also 'to make purposes and write verses, devise riddles and tell lies' (the lords in *Love's Labour's Lost*?), 'to follow plays and study dances' (*Hamlet*?), 'to hear news and buy trifles' (*Richard II*?), 'to sigh for love and weep for kindness' (*Romeo*?), and so on. 'In sum,' says Breton, 'he is a man-child and a woman's man, a gaze of folly, and wisdom's grief.'[5] To love a woman was, or so it could feel, to *become* a woman. Romeo registers that anxiety when he hears of Mercutio's death and declares, 'O sweet Juliet, | Thy beauty hath made me effeminate, | And in my temper softened valour's steel' (3.1.113–15). The final image is telling: the erect penis he gives to Juliet has rendered flaccid the steel sword he *should* be giving to Mercutio's killers. Effeminacy cannot be relegated to a social type. It haunts even the hypermasculine heroes of Shakespeare's Roman plays. Brutus, in Coppélia Kahn's reading, is situated between a public realm of manly 'firmness' and a private realm dominated by 'the melting spirits of women'.[6] Coriolanus's manhood cracks under Volumnia's importuning:

> O mother, mother!
> What have you done? Behold, the heavens do ope,
> The gods look down, and this unnatural scene
> They laugh at.
>
> (5.3.183–6)

Antony's transformation is just as dramatic: 'His captain's heart, | ... |
... | is become the bellows and the fan | To cool a gypsy's lust'
(1.1.6–10). As the repository of all the traits that make a man *not*
a man, women threaten to undermine masculine self-possession
from within. The problem facing a man is, then, a matter of self-
defence.

Luciana in *The Comedy of Errors* offers an account of Ephesus
more satisfactory to male viewers than Antipholus of Syracuse's
description of the place as the haunt of witches. Admonishing her
shrewish sister Adriana, Luciana takes as her text St Paul's advice
in Ephesians 5: 22 that wives should submit themselves to their husbands:

> There's nothing situate under heaven's eye
> But hath his bound in earth, in sea, in sky.
> The beasts, the fishes, and the wingèd fowls
> Are their males' subjects and at their controls.
> Man, more divine, the master of all these,
> Lord of the wide world and wild wat'ry seas,
> Indued with intellectual sense and souls,
> Of more pre-eminence than fish and fowls,
> Are masters to their females, and their lords.
>
> (2.1.16–24)

But then Luciana herself is not married, as Adriana, more knowledge-
able about men, is quick to point out. Let her experience marriage for a
while and *then* preach the doctrine. Women may figure as others in
Shakespeare's plays and poems, but, like Adriana, they by and large
refuse to remain in their oppositional places. Shakespeare's strategies
for dealing with that defiance are several.[7]

Adriana herself is an example of the readiest strategy: defining the
female other in the broadest possible terms and keeping it at a safe
distance. *Vis-à-vis* her husband Adriana plays a type out of a character
book: the Shrewd Wife. Luciana's sermon on submissive wives is
occasioned by Adriana's complaint that her husband, Antipholus of
Ephesus, is late for dinner. Perhaps a merchant has invited him to eat
elsewhere, Luciana reasons. After all, 'A man is master of his liberty.'
Adriana's rejoinder is sharp: 'Why should their liberty than ours be
more?' (*The Comedy of Errors*, 2.1.7, 10). When her husband's twin,

Antipholus of Syracuse, finally shows up, Adriana mistakes him for her husband and berates him up and down: 'Ay, ay, Antipholus, look strange and frown: | Some other mistress hath thy sweet aspects. | I am not Adriana, nor thy wife . . .'. And so on for 34 more scolding lines. Antipholus's astonished or indifferent demeanour all the while is suggested by his curt response: 'Plead you to *me*, fair dame?' (2.2.113–15, 150). The satiric world of *The Comedy of Errors* is womaned with stereotypes: the shrewd wife, the predatory husband-catcher, the calculating courtesan, the lusty fat kitchen wench. Emilia the Abbess, as we shall see, is a signal exception. She walks into the play, not out of Roman comedy, but out of comic romance. Other female others who remain safely true to type are Kate the shrew and Bianca the winsome sister, mine hostess Mistress Quickly, and the resourceful citizen-wives in *The Merry Wives of Windsor*. Mistress Ann Page and Mistress Alice Ford enter into a conspiracy against masculine perfidy in the phlegmatic person of Sir John Falstaff. At the same time, however, they remain true to their husbands. 'Nay, I will consent to act any villainy against him', Mistress Ford declares, 'that may not sully the chariness of our honesty' (2.1.93–5). Unlike their counterparts in satiric comedies by Ben Jonson and Thomas Middleton, *these* citizen-wives are rebelling not against masculinity but against masculinity-*manqué*. Satire offers a way of keeping the female other at arm's length and laughing away its threat.

At his most genial, Shakespeare plays out the contentiousness of men and women as a sport or game. The lords and ladies in *Love's Labour's Lost*, for example, play out rhyming word-games whenever they are together. The ground rules are established in the first encounter of Biron and Rosaline:

> BIRON Your wit's too hot, it speeds too fast, 'twill tire.
> ROSALINE Not till it leave the rider in the mire.
> BIRON What time o'day?
> ROSALINE The hour that fools should ask.
> BIRON Now fair befall your mask.
> ROSALINE Fair fall the face it covers.
> BIRON And send you many lovers.
> ROSALINE Amen, so you be none.
> BIRON Nay, then will I be gone.

(2.1.119–27)

The winner of the game, generally the man, gets the last word by completing the last couplet. The banter of Rosaline and Biron seems like a dress rehearsal for the even more barbed contest of wit between Beatrice and Benedick in *Much Ado About Nothing*. It is Beatrice who begins the match by inserting herself into Benedick's banter with his male friends: 'I wonder that you will still be talking, Signor Benedick. Nobody marks you.' His return-serve does not miss a beat: 'What, my dear Lady Disdain! Are you yet living?' (1.1.110–13) It is Benedick who ends the match by vowing to challenge Claudio to a duel and, in that act, to perform as a man what Beatrice desires as a woman. 'I cannot be a man with wishing,' Beatrice declares, 'therefore I will die a woman with grieving' (4.1.323–4).

Versions of the game between Navarre's lords and the French ladies, between Beatrice and Benedick, are played out also by Portia with Bassanio in the casket scene in *The Merchant of Venice*, by Rosalind with Orlando in the mock-marriage scene in *As You Like It*, by Viola with Orsino in the coy courtship of *Twelfth Night*. Something of the same sportive spirit inspires Helena in the dialogue about virginity she carries on with Paroles in 1.1 of *All's Well That Ends Well*. Tell me what defences a virgin can use against men, Helena asks this *miles gloriosus*, this braggart soldier out of Roman comedy. None, he replies: 'Man, setting down before you, will undermine you and blow you up.' Helena gives as good as she gets: 'Is there no military policy how virgins might blow up men?' (1.1.117–18, 120–1). Desdemona shows herself almost as gamesome in the dialogue about virginity she carries on with Iago, that *miles in*gloriosus, before Othello arrives on Cyprus in 2.1. In these engagements of masculine selves with female others men do not always hold the trump card. The lords in *Love's Labour's Lost* may always complete the couplet, but news of the princess's father's death turns the ending of the play into a stand-off. Benedick's last words are a nervous joke on husbands being cuckolded by their wives, Rosalind has the final move in *As You Like It*, Helena with her bed-trick clearly wins the game over Bertram even if her hold on the prize itself remains insecure. On the whole, however, women in the comedies of Shakespeare's mid-career serve as catalysts in the formation of masculine identity. Comedy enables an amiable *rapprochement* between masculine self and female other.

In the cases of Emilia in *The Comedy of Errors*, Thaisa in *Pericles*, Paulina in *The Winter's Tale*, Innogen in *Cymbeline*, and Princess Elizabeth in *Henry VIII* the female other takes on mythic, quasi-divine qualities appropriate to romance. Emilia, the wife-mother-abbess in *The Comedy of Errors*, seems to fit Northrop Frye's description of 'the sibylline wise mother-figure . . . who sits quietly at home waiting for the hero to finish his wanderings and come back to her' (195). Appropriating images of the Virgin Mary's miraculous conception, Emilia specifies her wait for her wandering husband and sons as having been exactly the span of the life of Christ: 'Thirty-three years have I but gone in travail | Of you, my sons, and till this present hour | My heavy burden ne'er deliverèd'. The ending of the play she casts as 'a gossips' feast', an all-women's gathering that typically followed a christening (5.1.403–5, 408). Innogen is a more active figure than Emilia—she works like a catalyst figure in one of the mid-career comedies as she restores Guiderius and Arviragus to their rightful inheritance and proves her steadfastness as a wife even against her husband's doubts—but her centrality in the play's happy ending exceeds that of Portia, Rosalind, and Viola. Cymbeline himself reaches for a celestial image to describe this circumstance:

> See,
> Posthumus anchors upon Innogen,
> And she, like harmless lightning, throws her eye
> On him, her brothers, me, her master, hitting
> Each object with a joy. The counterchange
> Is severally in all.
>
> (5.6.393–8)

A less obvious instance of the central female other in romance is Miranda. The curtain that is whisked aside in 5.1 discovers Miranda and her husband-to-be at chess, in a masque-like moment that recalls the game-like qualities of male–female relationships in the earlier comedies, Navarre's lord sparring with the Princess of France and her ladies, Portia giving Bassanio the casket test, Rosalind quizzing Orlando about marriage, Viola exchanging veiled body-talk with Orsino:

> MIRANDA   Sweet lord, you play me false.
> FERDINAND   No, my dearest love,
>   I would not for the world.

> MIRANDA   Yes, for a score of kingdoms you should wrangle,
>   An I would call it fair play.

(5.1.174–8)

The 'brave new world' shortly revealed to Miranda by the onlookers to this dramatic emblem opens out into the future. Happiness in that new world, or so Miranda and Ferdinand say to each other, is staked on a game in which the masculine self and its female other play as collaborators, even if playfully antagonistic collaborators. Miranda is accusing her husband-to-be of playing her false, but she does so in a spirit that recalls Portia and Rosalind.

   Among the game-playing women of Shakespeare's plays Desdemona presents a special case. In the banter about virginity she exchanges with Iago in 2.1—such an embarrassment to the actresses who played Desdemona in the later seventeenth century and after—her prose as 'the straight man' offers a somewhat demure contrast to Iago's nimble prose as 'the comic'. 'Come on, come on', Iago teases as he starts this particular skirmish in the battle of the sexes:

> You are pictures out of door,
> Bells in your parlours; wildcats in your kitchens,
> Saints in your injuries; devils being offended,
> Players in your housewifery, and hussies in your beds.

Desdemona rises to the bait: 'O, fie upon thee, slanderer!' (2.1.112–16). And so the game begins. The misogynist quips that follow may be, as Desdemona says, 'old fond paradoxes, to make fools laugh i'th' ale-house' (2.1.140–1), but Iago's jokes about women's faithlessness are turned into dead earnest in the charade he immediately stages: after the comic routine about virginity Desdemona and Cassio are directed to '*talk apart*', while Iago comments on the dumb-show, putting salacious words to the innocent spectacle. Desdemona is turned into a cipher in a jest—and is murdered for playing her part so well. In Iago's eyes Desdemona as female other emasculates Othello: 'Our general's wife is now the general', he tells Cassio (2.3.307–8). One notes the solidarity of male perspective secured by the first-person plural. However innocent she may in fact be, Desdemona is shadowed to the end by the suspicion that she in her erotic otherness is somehow responsible for Othello's destruction. Othello himself seems to acknowledge as much when he tells the witnesses to his suicide, 'Then must you speak | Of one that loved not wisely but too well' (5.2.352–3). Without Desdemona, Othello would still be a respected military hero. Tragedy portrays the female other as a destructive force. With respect to male protagonists Desdemona keeps company with a disparate group that includes Eleanor Duchess of Gloucester and Queen Margaret in the *Henry VI* plays, Tamora Queen of the Goths in *Titus Andronicus*, Juliet in *Romeo and Juliet*, Gertrude in *Hamlet*, Helen and Cressida in *Troilus and Cressida*, Goneril and Regan in *King Lear*, Lady Macbeth in *Macbeth*, Cleopatra in *Antony and Cleopatra*, and Volumnia in *Coriolanus*.

The most destructive of these women are those who aspire to male power. Eleanor Duchess of Gloucester stands forth as an example early in Shakespeare's career. Angry at her husband's lack of ambition as Lord Protector over young Henry VI, she declares in an aside, 'Were I a man, a duke, and next of blood, | I would remove these tedious stumbling blocks | And smooth my way upon their headless necks'. Being a woman, she vows to do what she can and 'play my part in fortune's pageant' (*2 Henry VI*, 1.2.63–5, 67). In the event her machinations land her and her husband at the bottom of Fortune's wheel, rather than securing them at the top. In *2 Henry VI* the Duchess has a common counterpart in Simpcox's Wife, arraigned before King Henry VI for helping her husband pose as a blind man who has been miraculously cured by St Alban's shrine. Questioned by the Lord Protector about the lameness that seems to have gone with his supposed blindness, Simpcox explains that he fell from a tree. A blind man climb a tree? Simpcox replies with words that might apply to the Lord Protector's own case: 'Alas, good master, my wife desired some damsons, | And made me climb with danger of my life' (2.1.104–5). The Duchess has a royal counterpart in Margaret of France, Henry VI's queen. Margaret makes one of her earliest entries in the play '*with her hawk on her fist*' (2.1.0. s.d) and through all of *2 Henry VI*, *3 Henry VI*, and *Richard III* plays out a politically robust and rhetorically forceful role. Taunting the discredited Suffolk, she mocks, 'Fie, coward woman and soft-hearted wretch! | Hast thou not spirit to curse thine enemies?' (*2 Henry VI*, 3.2.311–12). Such a spirit she herself possesses in great measure, as Richard, Duke of Gloucester, comes to learn in *Richard III*, 4.4. In the meantime, Margaret's man-like behaviour inspires one of the famous lines of Shakespeare's day: 'O tiger's heart wrapped in a woman's hide!' (*3 Henry VI*, 1.4.138). When weak-willed Henry VI, is persuaded to deny his own son's succession, Margaret takes up arms. On the battlefield she strikes one observer as 'the bloody-minded Queen, | That led calm Henry, though he were a king, | As doth a sail filled with a fretting gust | Command an argosy to stem the waves' (*3 Henry VI*, 2.6.33–6). The woman-led 'argosy', like Cleopatra's on the sea off Alexandria, ends in shipwreck and the hero's death. In the ruin to which she brings her warrior husband Queen Margaret anticipates not only Cleopatra but Lady Macbeth. Like the female others in Shakespeare's later tragedies, she wields annihilating power: the implicit choice facing the male protagonist in such a situation is to destroy the threatening other or to be himself destroyed. From satire to comedy to romance to tragedy containment of the female other demands increasingly extreme tactics.

Foreigners

Appropriately, it is an actual foreigner who provides us with our best account of fictional foreigners on the London stage during the years Shakespeare was writing scripts. During a trip to England in 1599 the Swiss traveller Thomas Platter saw not only *Julius Caesar* at the Globe but another play at a theatre north of the city, in which 'they presented diverse nations and an Englishman struggling together for a maiden; he overcame them all except the German who won the girl in a tussle.' Not giving up hope, the Englishman waited for the German, true to national character, to get drunk, whereupon the Englishman 'stole into the tent and absconded with the German's prize, thus in his turn outwitting the German'.[8] What Platter witnessed on this occasion was the definition of a specifically *English* masculinity. Early modern English facilitated that definition in two dimensions: in space and in time. To space belonged the term *nation*, for people born in the same place and hence constituting a community. To time belonged the term *race*, for people sharing a certain lineage or genealogy.[9] Only later did 'race' come to acquire its biological association with bodily traits and skin colour. The Irish, for example, could be considered both a nation (since they were all born on the same island) and a race (since they were presumed to share a mongrel genealogy that stretched back to Asia

Minor via Spain). Jews, gypsies, and other 'placeless' people presented a special problem: they clearly constituted a race, but any claims they had to nationhood clashed with the prior claims of the people among whom they were living. When Shylock reports that Antonio has 'scorned my nation' (*Merchant of Venice*, 3.1.52), he alludes to just such a clash. In cosmopolitan London, of course, *every* race—French, Italian, German, Hollander, African, Spanish, even Welsh, Irish, and Scottish—presented the same problem of nationality.

In one of the contributions he probably made to the collaborative play *Sir Thomas More* Shakespeare catches the explosive dynamics that races-within-a-nation could touch off. Among young Englishmen one of the rituals of May Day, even in Shakespeare's day, was violence against threatening others, in particular violence against prostitutes (women reduced to their sexual essence) and foreigners (exemplars of alternative models of masculinity). The age of the perpetrators of this violence, young men poised between boyhood and adulthood, helps to explain their sense of vulnerability. Addition II.D to *Sir Thomas More* depicts the famous episode in More's life when he faced down a crowd of apprentices and persuaded them not to attack foreigners. If your forefathers had been peace-breakers like you, More begins, 'the bloody times | Could not have brought you to the state of men'. What do you want, he asks the crowd. 'Marry, the removing of the strangers', comes the reply. More's rejoinder asks for reason—and for human fellow-feeling. Say you did succeed in murdering the strangers and setting fire to their houses. What if the king punished you by banishing you?

> Go you to France or Flanders,
> To any German province, Spain or Portugal,
> Nay, anywhere that not adheres to England—
> Why, you must needs be strangers. Would you be pleased
> To find a nation of such barbarous temper
> That breaking out in hideous violence
> Would not afford you an abode on earth...?
>
> (II.D.74–5, 78, 142–8)

In his full-length scripts Shakespeare both does and does not follow More's advice. Stereotypical foreigners like Don Adriano de Armado in *Love's Labour's Lost* serve as foils to the masculine exemplars they play opposite. Armado's exaggerated chivalry and melancholy drivel in his courtship of Jaquenetta contrast with the humanist suavity and sanguine sonnets with which Navarre and his comrades court the Princess of France and her ladies. The climax comes when '*Armado the braggart*', as he is styled in the stage directions, tries to play Hector in the Pageant of the Worthies that Navarre and his friends sponsor to entertain the ladies. The incongruity of *all* the participants in this charade—Costard the clown as Pompey, Nathaniel the curate as Alexander the Great, Holofernes the schoolmaster as Judas, Mote the boy as Hercules—serves to heighten the true manliness of Navarre, Biron, Longueville, and Dumaine.

The suitors to Portia's hand in *The Merchant of Venice* are cut from the same satiric cloth. Morocco's grandiloquence and Aragon's self-conceit help to confirm Bassanio the local candidate's claims to victory. Morocco's poetic excesses and Aragon's vanity qualify them as examples in Breton's character of 'An Effeminate Fool'. The eliding of gender difference with national difference is writ large in the history plays, in which the French again and again are presented as effeminate foils to English manhood. Harfleur in *Henry V* is a vagina waiting to be entered. If I begin the battery again, Henry warns the elders of the city,

> The gates of mercy shall be all shut up,
> And the fleshed soldier, rough and hard of heart,
> In liberty of bloody hand shall range
> With conscience wide as hell, mowing like grass
> Your fresh fair virgins and your flow'ring infants.

> (3.3.93–7)

The French nobility in the play may, for the convenience of Shakespeare's audience, all speak English, but they do so with a liberal sprinkling of French phrases. '*Dieu de batailles!*' the French Constable exclaims in a burst of Anglophobia. 'Where have they this mettle?' (3.5.15). The '*Dieu de batailles*' is not the same as the 'God of battles' invoked by Henry on the eve of Agincourt (4.1.286). The characters who do speak French in the play are women, Princess Catherine and her maid Alice. The French men in their affected speech, as in their exaggerated *politesse* and lack of valour, are allied with women. Egypt, presided over by a woman in fact, stands in even sharper effeminate opposition to Caesar's Rome.

By granting racial others a measure of independence Shakespeare in other plays seems to heed More's advice. When Shylock asks the audience, as well as his on-stage interlocutors, 'Hath not a Jew eyes?' (*The Merchant of Venice*, 3.1.54), he lays claim to a positive selfhood that exists quite apart from his primary function of embodying everything that Venetian manhood is *not*. He claims a commonality in which 'I' and 'other' are collapsed into one. Whether or not Shylock is able to sustain that tactic through his bloody-minded insistence on Antonio's flesh and his humiliation in the courtroom has been a hotly debated topic for at least 150 years. The verdict on Othello is more certain. With Morocco of *The Merchant of Venice* Othello shares confidence of bearing and pomposity of speech, but his situation as racial other is far more complicated. Othello lays claim to national solidarity with his Venetian employers. Warned that Desdemona's father is going to demand a hearing before the Duke and Senators, Othello acknowledges his race or lineage but rests secure in his adopted nationality:

> My services which I have done the signory
> Shall out-tongue his complaints. 'Tis yet to know—
> Which, when I know that boasting is an honour,
> I shall promulgate—I fetch my life and being
> From men of royal siege, and my demerits
> May speak unbonneted to as proud a fortune
> As this that I have reached.
>
> (1.2.18–24)

Sure enough, he is heralded as 'the valiant Moor' at his entry into the presence of the Duke and Senators. 'Valiant Othello, we must straight employ you | Against the general enemy Ottoman' are the first words said to him in the court scene (1.3.48–9).

The 'general' enemy: that is, *our* enemy and *your* enemy. Iago, like an unregenerate member of More's mob—'I do hate him as I do hell pains', Iago states flatly (1.1.156)—sees to it that the 'us' of Act 1 comes to exclude 'him' by Act 5. 'He' becomes 'not us' but 'one of *them*'. How successful is Iago? Iago may play on every stereotype of Moorishness lurking in the audience's minds—lust, jealousy, perfidy, infidelity—but Othello in his sheer power of speech claims a subjectivity that makes it impossible for the audience simply to distance him as a racial other.[10]

Othello may kill Desdemona as a rash, jealous Moor, but he kills himself as an exemplar of western masculinity, as the hero of a Senecan tragedy who affirms his virtue in the act of suicide. The nationality of Othello as racial other is never more ambiguous than in the final words of his final big speech. Report me to the state as 'one that loved not wisely but too well' (5.2.353).

> Set you down this,
> And say besides that in Aleppo once,
> Where a malignant and a turbaned Turk
> Beat a Venetian and traduced the state,
> I took by th' throat the circumcisèd dog
> And smote him thus.
> *He stabs himself*
>
> (5.2.360–5)

Who is the actor here and who the victim? Does Othello play the part of the valiant Venetian killing a Turk? Or the part of 'our general enemy' the Turk being killed by a valiant Venetian? In his death as in his life he is portrayed as both. Hence his tragedy in a world where masculinity is achieved in opposition to racial others.

Superiors and Inferiors

The hierarchical nature of early modern society meant that men were always defining themselves in yet another way: *vis-à-vis* men above them and below them. As William Gouge observes in his book *Of Domestical Duties*,

even they who are superiors to some are inferiors to others. . . . The master that hath servants under him may be under the authority of a magistrate. Yea, God hath so disposed everyone's several place as there is not anyone but in some respect is under another. The wife, though mother of children, is under her husband. The husband, though head of the family, is under public magistrates. Public magistrates are under another, and all under the king. The king himself under God . . . .[11]

In these circumstances Iago stakes out a radical position when he boasts to Roderigo, 'Were I the Moor I would not be Iago. | In following him I follow but myself.' In claiming 'I am not what I am',

Iago makes a distinction between his own sense of himself ('I *am*') and the position of ensign assigned to him in the military hierarchy of Venice ('*not* what I am') (1.1.57–8, 65). If he cannot be Othello's lieutenant—literally, Othello's 'place-holder'—he will bring down the general and the whole system of distinctions with him. The hierarchy of early modern England was no less full of distinctions than the military hierarchy of Venice. In England there were, according to William Harrison (1577), four 'sorts' or 'degrees' of people: gentlemen who did not have to work for a living, burgesses or citizens in towns and cities, yeomen farmers, and labourers.[12] The implication is starkly clear: a man must occupy one of these 'degrees', and in being one 'sort' of man he cannot be another. Shakespeare and his business partners demonstrate the difference between theory and practice. By law they were servants to gentlemen like the Earl of Southampton, the Lord Chamberlain, or King James; by income and living standards, they were burgesses; by aspiration, gentlemen. Shakespeare achieved the highest of these three distinctions by securing a gentleman's coat of arms for his burgess father. To the rigid social structure set in place by Harrison the theatre posed two serious challenges. To investors it offered a way of moving up the ranks; to audiences, a chance to imagine themselves occupying social positions other than their own.

Is it possible to place Shakespeare's male protagonists with respect to Harrison's typology? Aristotle in the *Poetics* offers us a gauge of sorts in his proposition that the heroes of different kinds of fictions can be placed *vis-à-vis* the audience in three ways: higher, lower, or on the same level. The terms of comparison that Aristotle uses, *spoudaios* and *phaulos*, can be translated 'better' and 'worse', but, as Northrop Frye has pointed out, Aristotle's distinction seems to involve scope of action more than moral considerations. A hero's 'power of action' may be greater than ours, less than ours, or about the same. Recognizing that fiction is a form of representation (*mimesis*), Frye calls the first situation 'high mimetic' and the second situation 'low mimetic' (33). The third situation, in which audience and hero occupy the same plane of action, might be called 'mid-mimetic'. It is all a matter of perspective: 'high mimetic' characters seem larger than life, 'low-mimetic' characters smaller than life, and 'mid-mimetic' characters true to life. Frye does not call attention to the fact, but the hero's mimetic status, the range of possibilities open to him, tends to correlate with his social status, so that the 'high mimetic' heroes of epic and tragedy are usually kings and princes, while the 'low mimetic' heroes of satiric comedy are citizens and servants.

When we apply these distinctions to Shakespeare's scripts, we discover plenty of candidates for 'high mimetic' status among the protagonists of the tragedies and history plays: Titus Andronicus, Richard III, Richard II, Henry Bolingbroke, Henry V, Brutus, Hamlet, Lear, Macbeth, Othello, Antony, Coriolanus, Prospero. Whatever the differences among these characters in ethical terms or in historical period, they occupy high social rank, they speak with an eloquence beyond everyday speech, and they act on a scale far ampler than that afforded by London's streets and lanes. Among 'low mimetic' characters extreme examples are to be found in Jack Cade's rebels in *2 Henry VI* and the plebeians in *Coriolanus*. Occupying a position somewhat closer to the audience, but still definitely 'lower', are the rude mechanicals in *A Midsummer Night's Dream*, the denizens of Eastcheap in *1* and *2 Henry IV* and *Henry V*, Lucio and his brothel buddies in *Measure for Measure*, the country folk in *Love's Labour's Lost*, *As You Like It*, *Much Ado About Nothing*, *The Winter's Tale*, and *The Two Noble Kinsmen*. Who, then, occupies 'mid-mimetic' status? The primary candidates are the heroes of Shakespeare's comedies: Valentine and Proteus, Petruccio, Lysander and Demetrius, Bassanio, Orlando. All of these protagonists, with the exception of Orlando, the slighted younger son of a gentleman, are burgesses who improve their social lot in the course of the play, if not by marrying up then by having their marriages sanctioned by a king, duke, or prince. One could argue that 'mid-mimetic' status in Shakespeare's scripts—the implicit subject position offered to the audience in *all* his scripts—is that of citizen on the make.

The masculinity of men in this middling group is defined with respect to their social others, both below and above. The very fact that the countrymen in *Love's Labour's Lost*, *A Midsummer Night's Dream*, and *The Two Noble Kinsmen* perform for other people's amusement points up their status as convenient reference points against which their betters get their social bearings. The real-life watchers of these plays within plays may not themselves *be* the likes of the King of Navarre or Duke Theseus, but they are invited to *imagine* they are. The men in Shakespeare's audience take their cue from these on-stage protagonists. Nathaniel the curate, Holofernes the schoolmaster, and Anthony Dull the constable in *Love's Labour's Lost*, Nick Bottom the weaver, Peter Quince the carpenter, Francis Flute the bellows-mender, Tom Snout the Tinker, Snug the joiner, and Robin Starveling the tailor in *A Midsummer Night's Dream*, the jailer in charge of Duke Theseus's prison, Gerald the country schoolmaster, Timothy the taborer, the six morris men who dance to his taps in *The Two Noble Kinsmen*—whatever else they may be, the men who watch Shakespeare's plays in performance are presumed to be *not that*. The same holds true for Ned Poins, Francis the tapster, Bardolph, Ensign Pistol, Justice Shallow, Ralph Mouldy, Simon Shadow, Thomas Wart, Francis Feeble, Peter Bullcalf, Abraham Slender, and Peter Simple in the *Henry IV* plays, Constable Dogberry and Verges in *Much Ado About Nothing*, Oliver Martext, Corin, and William in *As You Like It*: these are men to be looked down upon, to be laughed *at*, not *with*. Touchstone, that nimble mover up and down the social ladder, establishes the expected tone of amused condescension in his dialogue with Corin about the relative merits of a shepherd's life and a courtier's life. How do you like the shepherd's life? Corin asks Touchstone. 'Truly, shepherd, in respect of itself, it is a good life; but in respect that it is a shepherd's life, it is naught' (*As You Like It*, 3.2.13–15). And so on for a good three or four minutes. The effect worked by all these simple men is to offset the more accomplished masculinity of their social betters. Recall that Greene's Cloth Britches confesses to enjoying the theatre, even though his ilk are usually presented as fools.[13]

With respect to the men above them in the social hierarchy, the citizen on the make is invited to combine admiration with scepticism. On the one hand, the exploits of kings, dukes, and princes inspire awe. Whatever such men do, they do it with a vision and a rhetorical force far beyond the capacities of the audience—inhabitants of the lords' room included. Richard III achieves his evil ends with an intensity no less than that of Hector and Brutus in their pursuit of honour. Romeo and Troilus love with a passion that leaves no time for mundane affairs like dressing, eating, buying and selling, or making one's way to the theatre. Henry V enacts in a few hours deeds of valour that his historical counterpart took months to accomplish, with lots of marching, waiting, sleeping, and idling in between. Lear makes domestic decisions with cosmic consequences. Even Hamlet plays the part of the obsessive melancholic with a thoroughness that no real-life poseur could match. On the other hand, these larger-than-life exemplars of masculinity meet tragic ends that make the ordinary onlooker quite glad that he is not a king, a prince, or a duke. Even Henry V's triumphs are framed with a sense of loss. Henry left his French conquests to his son, Henry VI, the Chorus reminds the audience, 'Whose state so many had the managing | That they lost France and made his England bleed' (Ep. 11–12).

Where does that leave the ambitious citizen? In an ambiguous position, to say the least. Brash social climbers run the risk of ridicule. The most egregious example is Malvolio. As Lady Olivia's steward, he holds the highest rank among her servants: in managing her house, he manages all the other servants but has trouble controlling Olivia's kinsman Sir Toby Belch and his crony Sir Andrew Aguecheek, gentlemen both—at least by title. Even Maria, as a waiting gentlewoman, is his social superior. What he imagines for himself is something far grander than his present status. If he becomes Lady Olivia's husband, he becomes a gentleman. Prompted by Maria's forged letter, Malvolio seizes on every hint of Olivia's favour: 'when she went away now, "let this fellow be looked to". Fellow!—not "Malvolio", nor after my degree, but "fellow"' (*Twelfth Night*, 3.4.74–6). Just what is Malvolio's degree? His fiscal responsibilities, not to mention his hostility to mirth, connect him with the Puritan citizen class who played the anatagonists to professional theatre in London politics. Malvolio's humiliation is presented as just punishment for presumption on the part of a burgess who hates the theatre. The case of a burgess who *loves* the theatre is something else again. The bravura of the heroes of Shakespeare's histories and tragedies, coupled with the social ambitions of the young men who people his comedies, suggests that masculine ideals for members of his audience are firmly defined *vis-à-vis* men beneath but remain open-ended *vis-à-vis* men above. Not for nothing do Shakespeare's prologues and epilogues address the audience as 'gentlemen'.

Sodomites

The Duke of Exeter's description of the battlefield deaths of the Duke of York and the Earl of Suffolk in *Henry V* is apt to strike listeners today as more appropriate to Romeo and Juliet than to two soldiers. Suffolk is characterized as 'yokefellow' to York's 'honour-owing wounds'. Coming upon Suffolk on the battlefield and discovering his comrade-in-arms already dead, the wounded York is said by Exeter to have taken Suffolk by the beard, kissed the gashes on his face, and begged him to tarry until their two souls could fly to heaven abreast.

> So did he turn, and over Suffolk's neck
> He threw his wounded arm, and kissed his lips,
> And so espoused to death, with blood he sealed
> A testament of noble-ending love.

Exeter's response as onlooker gives the men in Shakespeare's audience their cue: Exeter reports that he tried to hold back the tears, 'But I had not so much of man in me, | And all my mother came into mine eyes | And gave me up to tears' (4.6.9, 24–7, 30–2). Two conflicting ideals of masculinity clash in Exeter's account: emotional control and passionate feeling for one's fellows. The emotional control may be gendered male, the passionate feeling may be gendered female, but Exeter in spite of himself endorses the physical signs of York's love for Suffolk: the grasped beard, the kissed wounds, the embraced neck, the kissed lips, the 'espousal' sealed in blood. Here, if anywhere, is an instance of the erotic, of 'the *passion* of love' (*OED* 'erotic' A, emphasis added). The fact that the expression of such love takes place between two men—and that it is narrated by a third man for the pleasure of several thousand others in the theatre—makes it an instance, for us, of *homo*eroticism. For Shakespeare's original audience the story was first and foremost an emblem of the ideal of male friendship that we considered in Chapter 2. A deconstructive reader might insist that the introduction of womanliness in Exeter's account—the 'man in me' yielding implicitly to the 'woman in me', the 'mother' that forces her way into his eyes, the surrender of 'me' to tears—betrays sexual anxieties that lurk beneath the surface. Alan Bray has called attention to such anxieties generally in the Renaissance cult of male friendship. What a Renaissance man most aspires to be is another man's friend; what he most abhors to be is a sodomite. Unfortunately for a Renaissance man, the signs of male friendship—the grasp, the embrace, the kiss, the 'espousal'—are the same as the signs of sodomy.[14] In his essay 'Of Friendship', for example, Montaigne explicitly raises the question of whether sexual relations between men and boys in the ancient world—'Greek licence', he calls it—ought to be considered a species of friendship. Clearly not, since such relations were not a meeting of equals. Montaigne can nonetheless turn immediately to his friendship with Etienne La Boetie and praise it in passionately physical terms. His feelings for La Boetie cannot be compared to anything else: 'It is I wot not what kind of quintessence, of all this commixture, which having seized all my will induced the same to plunge and lose itself in his, which likewise having seized all his will, brought it to lose and plunge itself in mine, with a mutual greediness and with a semblable concurrence.'[15]

The sodomite constitutes, then, one final other against which masculinity in early modern England is defined. Negotiations of that dilemma in Shakespeare's scripts can be ranged along a continuum from highly romanticized portrayals of erotic friendship at one end to sneering satirizations of sodomy at the other. Keeping company with York and Suffolk at the romanticized end are Palamon and Arcite *The Two Noble Kinsmen*. The eroticism that suffuses this play from first ('New plays and maidenheads are near akin' (Prologue 1)) to last ('He that has | Loved a young handsome wench, then, show his face' (Epilogue 5–6)) extends also to the friendship between Palamon and Arcite. 'Dear Palamon', Arcite begins at their first entrance,

> dearer in love than blood,
> And our prime cousin, yet unhardened in
> The crimes of nature, let us leave the city,
> Thebes, and the temptings in't, before we further
> Sully our gloss of youth.

> (1.2.1–5)

Amid such rhetoric it hardly takes a deconstructive maverick to hear 'crimes *against* nature' in 'crimes *of* nature'. In the play's next scene Emilia describes the love of Pirithous and Theseus for each other in equally extravagant terms, as 'more maturely seasoned' than the love of woman for woman, 'More buckled with strong judgement, and their needs | The one of th'other may be said to water | Their intertangled roots of love' (1.3.56–9). At quite the opposite extreme is Thersites' dismissal of Patroclus' relationship with Achilles in *Troilus and Cressida*. 'Thou art thought to be Achilles' male varlet,' Thersites taunts Patroclus.

PATROCLUS 'Male varlet', you rogue? What's that?

THERSITES Why, his masculine whore. Now the rotten
  diseases of the south, guts-griping, ruptures, catarrhs,
  loads o' gravel i'th'back, lethargies, cold palsies, and the
  like, take and take again such preposterous discoveries.

(5.1.15–21).

'Preposterous', as recent critics have pointed out, is a (homo)sexually
loaded word, meaning to put the backside front. Thersites' focus on
the brute physicality of sodomy accords with the narrow definition of
sodomy as a punishable crime in the statutes of the realm. In practice,
sodomy was construed to be forcible penetration of one male by
another, typically of an underaged boy by an older man.[16] Feelings—
of friendship, of love, of male solidarity—had nothing to do with it.

  In between these extremes are ranged, in varying degrees of ambi-
guity, the friendships of Shakespeare's male protagonists. The place of
homoeroticism in the definition of masculinity thus remains enig-
matic. Antonio's sadness at the beginning of *The Merchant of Venice*
goes unexplained. Solanio's joking suggestion 'Why then, you are in
love' (1.1.46) suddenly seems plausible after Antonio pledges to Bassanio 'My purse, my person, my extremest means' (1.1.138). The Antonio
of *Twelfth Night* is even more forthright in his declaration of love for
Sebastian: 'If you will not murder me for my love, let me be your
servant' (2.1.31–2). Considering that sodomy was a capital offence and
that Sebastian is pointedly referred to as a 'boy', Antonio may have
chosen his words with legal precision. No less radical is the welcome
Aufidius gives to Coriolanus when the Roman hero, Aufidius's sometime arch-enemy, deserts to the Volsces. Lest the force of Aufidius's
comparison go unremarked ('that I see thee here, | Thou noble thing,
more dances my rapt heart | Than when I first my wedded mistress saw
| Bestride my threshold'), Aufidius's serving men comment on the
spectacle: 'Our general himself makes a mistress of him' (4.5.116–19,
199–200). In all of these situations men flirt with sodomy without
declaring it. What is more, the mutuality of erotic feeling remains in
each case uncertain. Does Bassanio understand Antonio's implied
desire? Does he exploit it? Does he return it? What about Sebastian
with respect to the Antonio of *Twelfth Night*? And Coriolanus? Is the
erotic feeling all on Aufidius's side? The mystery of these questions has

given modern actors and directors room for experiment; to the men in Shakespeare's audience it gave room for approaching the sodomite, despite his being a dreaded other.

Opposite Selves and Proximate Selves

Women, foreigners, social inferiors, sodomites: these four sorts of others help to define masculinity in Shakespeare's plays. Even heroes who seem to possess the strongest sense of core identity find them necessary. Take, for example, Henry V. We have observed already how his French adversaries are effeminated, even in the language they speak. Harry's ultimate challenge in the play is to come to terms with this female otherness—in terms that *he* dictates, in English. The key word is 'like'. 'O fair Catherine,' Harry begins his courtship, 'if you will love me soundly with your French heart, I will be glad to hear you confess it brokenly with your English tongue. Do you like me, Kate?' '*Pardonnez-moi*', Catherine replies, 'I cannot tell vat is "like me".' And neither, perhaps, can the listening audience. 'Like' can be heard here as a verb (to 'favour' me or 'fancy' me) or as a preposition ('similar to'). Harry may have begun with a verb, but he encourages the latter sense by quipping, 'An angel is like you, Kate, and you are like an angel.' His real interest in the speech that follows concerns how he and Catherine are like each other. When Catherine protests that it is not the custom in France for women to kiss before they are married, Harry counters, 'Dear Kate, you and I cannot be confined within the weak list of a country's fashion. We are the makers of manners, Kate . . .'. As 'the best king of good fellows', however, his final act is to insist on his male difference. He will kiss her whether she will or no: 'Therefore, patiently and yielding.' The effect of the kiss, however, is to make him back off from what the language of courtly love knows, in French, as *danger*: 'You have witchcraft in your lips, Kate' (*Henry V*, 5.2.104–10, 268–70, 240, 273–4).

The foreign others against which Henry Plantagenet defines his heroic masculinity are not just French but Welsh, Irish, and Scottish. Harry's challenge to the governor of Harfleur has as its immediate foil a round of comic banter among four of his soldiers, the Englishman Gower, the Welshman Fluellen, the Scotsman Jamy, and the Irishman MacMorris, each of whom is scripted to speak his distinctive dialect.

They almost come to blows when MacMorris takes offence at mention of his 'nation': 'What ish my nation? Ish a villain and a bastard and a knave and a rascal? What ish my nation? Who talks of my nation?' (3.3.66–8). Only the brass call to a parley cuts them short. To their petty ethnic rivalries Harry in his oration provides a heroic (and imperialist) corrective. With his social inferiors, as with Catherine, Henry first tries out 'like'—'I think the King is but a man, as I am', he avers as he goes among his men in disguise (4.1.101–2)—but opts ultimately for 'different'. After tricking Fluellen into sporting the challenger's glove that he himself wagered—and reaping the consequences in a box to the ear—the King rewards his 'good countryman' magnanimously with a glove full of what else but *crowns* (4.7.103, 4.8.58). Even sodomites may figure in Harry's self-differentiation. At least one critic has argued that the execution of Scrope serves to distance Harry from suspicions of sodomy. Among the three lords who are arraigned before the king for treason, Scrope is singled out by one onlooker as 'the man that was his bedfellow, | Whom he hath dulled and cloyed with gracious favours' (2.2.8–9). Certainly Henry reserves his greatest show of emotion for Scrope, addressing 49 lines directly to him, compared with just nine lines to Cambridge and none to Grey. Harry's sense of betrayal seems not just political but *personal*, in every sense of the word: 'O how hast thou with jealousy infected | The sweetness of affiance' (2.2.123–4).[17]

The trouble with binary oppositions, as any reader of Derrida will tell you, is this: they are arbitrary. They don't stay put. *Histerica passio* will out. The hated foreigner may turn out to be *you*. The steward may connive to become the master. The comrade-in-arms may strike a critical bystander as the 'masculine whore'. This tendency of X to become A, no matter how carefully one polices the boundaries between the two, has been dubbed by Jonathan Dollimore 'the perverse dynamic'. He describes it as 'that fearful interconnectedness whereby the antithetical inheres within, and is partly produced by, what it opposes'.[18] If 'man' needs 'woman' in order to be 'man', then womanliness will constantly threaten to erupt from within. Effeminacy will be feared more than women themselves. If 'Englishman' needs 'Moor', what about the Moor who speaks eloquent English and behaves according to English ideals of valour? If 'gentleman' needs 'citizen', what about the gentleman who buys his title by trading in fictions? If 'friend' needs 'sodomite', what about the friend who writes to his friend in the language of Petrarchan love poetry? The definition of masculinity in terms of others is an inherently unstable business.

The speaker of Shakespeare's sonnets provides ample testimony that masculine self-definition depends as much on *proximate* selves as on *opposite* selves. In the theatre that dependence is a physical fact. Even a character like Hamlet, who if anyone approaches a lyric poet's autonomy, is who he is because he is part and parcel of others. Michael Pennington, who played Hamlet in John Barton's production for the Royal Shakespeare Company in 1980, concedes that an actor preparing the role has to do more than look into himself. In the course of rehearsals, Pennington reports,

the play began forming itself in my mind as a brilliant narrative exploding on the one hand into set pieces like the first court scene, the play scene and duel; and sustained on the other by a series of essential interviews, duologues that define Hamlet's relations with his neighbours—the Ghost, Ophelia and Gertrude above all, but also Polonius, Rosencrantz and Guildenstern, Horatio and the Gravediggers: a kind of character dialectic that is further refined at four crucial moments into Hamlet's purest and most distinctive encounters, those with his audience.[19]

Tom Stoppard has made famous the existential dependence of Rosencrantz and Guildenstern on Hamlet; Pennington calls attention to Hamlet's existential dependence on Rosencrantz and Guildenstern.

Rather than possessing an essential character, Hamlet participates in a 'character dialectic' with various others. In certain moments Hamlet seems to acknowledge as much. To the Ghost's command 'Remember me' Hamlet responds, 'Remember thee? | ... | ...thy commandment all alone shall live | Within the book and volume of my brain | Unmixed with baser matter' (1.5.91, 95, 102–4). Later Hamlet exclaims to Horatio, 'Give me that man | That is not passion's slave, and I will wear him | In my heart's core, ay, in my heart of heart, | As I do thee' (3.2.69–72). Indeed, at the moment of his death Hamlet bequeathes his story—in a play, all of him that there is—to Horatio. Pennington in his reflections and Hamlet in his confessions both illustrate Paul Smith's point that subjectivity is a *process*: 'the state of being a "subject" is best conceived of in something akin to a temporal aspect—the "subject" is only a moment in a lived life.'[20] In Smith's view, we should think of a character in a fiction, not as *a* subject, but as *several* subjects, as the sum of several distinct identities. Hamlet is his father's son, his mother's son, Ophelia's suitor, Horatio's friend, Laertes' sharer in bereavement as well as his adversary, the player's collaborator, the audience's alter ego. Some of these relationships, like those with Rosencrantz and Guildenstern, with Ophelia, with Gertrude, with Laertes remain 'partly me'; some, like those with the Ghost, with Horatio, perhaps most of all with the audience, seem so enveloping as to constitute 'my next self', an 'other mine'. These circumstances suggest that we need a model of identity-formation that looks beyond deconstructive otherness. Such a model figures as this book's last chapter.

6. Toby Stephens as Coriolanus, Royal Shakespeare Company (1994).

Coalescences

However we choose to consider it—in terms of persons, of ethical ideals, of life passages, of relationships with other people—masculinity in Shakespeare's plays and poems seems precarious. Shakespeare's male protagonists, when they speak of the bodies they inhabit, describe a highly volatile mixture of fluids. With changes in the combination of humours, qualities that are felt to be masculine, like reason and courage, can be overwhelmed by qualities that are felt to be effeminate, like passion and indolence. How a man presents his person to the world is likewise subject to alteration. On the streets of London no less than on the stage of the Globe, a change in dress can mean a change in perceived identity. Ethical ideals, by their very nature, are marks to be aimed at, not possessions to be seized and enjoyed. What counts as appropriate behaviour at one stage in a man's life may not be appropriate behaviour at another. With changes in age come changes in body, in mind, in social role, in self-perception. *Vis-à-vis* other people a man is constantly obliged to negotiate his identity in different, often contradictory ways. He is who he is because he differs from some people but resembles others. All these considerations in the specific case of Shakespeare's works corroborate David Gilmore's conclusion that masculinity, in cultures all over the world, throughout history, is not a natural given, something that comes with possession of male sexual organs, but an achievement, something that must be worked toward and maintained. Masculinity, in this view, is not an *essence* but a *construction*.

Constructionism is one of the basic propositions by which new historicism as a way of reading has distinguished itself from humanism. Where humanism assumes a core essence that unites people otherwise separated in time and social circumstances new historicism insists on cultural differences. *De*construction likewise needs con-structionism. If a man's sense of his own identity is a function of language, and if the meanings marked by language are ultimately arbitrary, then identity is founded on a chimera. Lear seems to antici-pate that condition: 'Nothing will come of nothing. Speak again' (*The Tragedy of King Lear*, 1.1.90)—and, post-structuralist critics would add, again and again and again. In more ways than one, essentialism versus constructionism shapes up as an all-or-nothing proposition. Most recent criticism has stressed the nothing. As a social construc-tion, as an identity made out of words, masculinity has been written off as something that is ultimately impossible to achieve. Lynne Enterline stresses the sense of loss that accompanies male narcissism in Renais-sance texts. For Mark Breitenberg the struggle of writers like Shake-speare to maintain masculine self-identity *vis-à-vis* women involves a permanent state of anxiety.

And yet the case of Lear himself points up the limits of the essentialist/constructionist dichotomy. Reduced to fragments of speech on the heath, his identity literally deconstructed, the once self-possessed autocrat awakes from madness with a more circumspect sense of who he is: 'Pray do not mock. | I am a very foolish, fond old man.' His sense of self-identity, as he realizes, is contingent on those around him. No longer a king, he acknowledges first the simple fact of his manhood, then his fatherhood: 'For *as I am a man*, I think this lady | To be my child, Cordelia' (*The Tragedy of King Lear*, 4.6.52–3, 62–3, emphasis added). Lear's new-found identity is neither the essence he thought it was at the beginning of the play nor the empty nothing it seemed to be after deconstruction on the heath but an *evolving* phenomenon. Michel Serres catches this dynamic state of affairs when he recalls that the word *subject* was originally not a noun but an adjective ('In a state of subjection or dependence; under the control, rule, or influence of something; subordinate', *OED* I.2). The sense of 'subject' as 'the thinking or cognizing agent, the self or ego', dates only from the end of the seventeenth century (*OED* II.9). 'Who am I as a subject?' Serres insists on a qualified answer: 'No, I am not a problem: literally, I am a solution. And I would tolerate writing titles on my visiting card on condition that the title comprise the diverse relations of the substances dissolved in it, their density in the alloy. Who am I?

A fusion of alloys, more coalescent than coalesced."[1] *Coalescence* offers a viable alternative to both *essence* and *construction*. Where *essence* is a state of being (from Latin *esse*, 'to be'), *coalescence* is a process (from Latin *co*, 'with, together', + *alescere*, 'to begin growing'). *Coalescence* recognizes the multiple identities that a protagonist like Lear embraces: autocrat, madman, old man, penitent, father. It recognizes that those identities can be successive or simultaneous or both. It recognizes, not the 'one-and-the-sameness' that the word *identity* denotes, but self-understanding across time, under changing circumstances. As such, *coalescence* offers a way to avoid the impasse between essentialism and constructionism and thus to study the ways in which masculinity *is* achieved, against the odds, in Shakespeare's plays and poems. We can distinguish different sorts of coalescences: with respect to persons, ideals, life passages, even individuals *vis-à-vis* one another.

Persons

Concerning persons as physical bodies, Shakespeare's plays seem designed to restore both the characters and the audience to even temperament. That can come about through a balance of humours (we have discussed at length the case of Prince Hal) or through the purgation of particular humours in characters like Hotspur (choler), Falstaff (phlegm), Hamlet (melancholy), and Macbeth (blood). The case of Falstaff in *The Merry Wives of Windsor* demonstrates how purgation can happen through laughter as well as through tears. Understanding persons as personages and impersonators, one could argue that the circumstances of performance in early modern England made every enactment of every script an affirmation of masculinity. Skill in dramatic impersonation, as we observed in Chapter 1, was thought to be a distinctively masculine trait, depending as it did on a hot, moist temperament for vocal production and for rational control in assuming the passions of other people. By this logic, the force of masculinity was never stronger than in the performance of women's roles, which invited a passionate abandon that the male actor, through his art, had to control. When George Sandys, returning from the Middle East in 1611, stopped off in Messina and saw women performing women's roles, he was not impressed. His complaint? The roles were 'too naturally passionated'.[2] They were not tempered by masculine art. According to Sandys' criteria, Hecuba might stand as the ultimate test of an actor's masculinity.

Or perhaps Cleopatra. However sudden her changes of mood, however keen her sexual appetite, however extreme her outbursts of passion, Cleopatra in her death enacts a masculine ideal of Seneca-inspired suicide. 'Ah, women, women! Look, | Our lamp is spent, it's out': upon Antony's death Cleopatra first addresses Charmian, Iras, and the maids who stand with her 'aloft'. Then she turns to the Romans assembled below: 'Good sirs, take heart; | We'll bury him, and then what's brave, what's noble, | Let's do it after the high Roman fashion, | And make death proud to take us' (4.16.86–90). In that turn the actor playing Cleopatra charts his/her course for the rest of the play—a course that affirms masculine ideals of self-control and bravery. Even Caesar appreciates the gesture. Cleopatra may have studied 'easy ways to die', but 'High events as these | Strike those that make them, and their story is | No less in pity than his glory which | Brought them to be lamented' (5.2.350, 354–7). The last-scene silences of women that have so disturbed feminist critics of Shakespeare fit a pattern in which masculinity—*performing* masculinity no less than *performed* masculinity—is the dominant note.

Shakespeare's two narrative poems, *Venus and Adonis* and *The Rape of Lucrece*, were, in their original printings, likewise exercises in the performance of masculinity. As published by Richard Field, *Venus and Adonis* in 1593 and *The Rape* in 1594, both poems carry dedicatory epistles to the Earl of Southampton that play on Plato's praise in the *Symposium* of soul-authored 'offspring' begotten without the help of women.[3] In the earlier preface Shakespeare apologizes to Southampton for choosing 'so strong a prop to support so weak a burden'. If Southampton is pleased, Shakespeare will honour him 'with some graver labour'. If, on the other hand, 'the first heir of my invention' prove 'deformed', 'I shall be sorry it had so noble a godfather, and never after ear so barren a land' (224). With respect to the poem, the sexual images of 'burden', 'labour', 'heir', and ploughing cast Shakespeare as the mother to Southampton's father as well as a bestower of seed himself. The male readership implied in the epistle is given further definition in the Latin epigraph from Ovid's *Amores*: '*Vilia miretur vulgus; mihi flavas Apollo | Pocula Castalia plena ministret aqua*' ('Let cheap things dazzle the crowd. | For me, may golden Apollo administer full cups from the Castalian spring') (224). Able to read Latin, highly self-conscious of their distance from 'the crowd', appreciative of salacious poems inspired by Ovid, the readership of *Venus and Adonis* is to be identified most closely with the young gentlemen (and gentlemen-to-be) of the inns of court.[4] Reading the poem and its successor, *The Rape of Lucrece*, was, for the books' first buyers, an act of male bonding.

Shakespeare's 'sugared sonnets among his private friends', as Francis Meres described them in 1598, enacted masculinity in even more intimate terms. Anyone with a penny might go and hear a play, a printed book might find readers beyond the coterie implied in a dedication, but poems in manuscript circulated within a circle of friends who knew each other and each other's tastes. By excluding outsiders, manuscripts became a way of affirming the group's social identity.[5] Meres does not specify the gender of Shakespeare's 'private friends', but surviving manuscripts suggest that the readership was by and large made up of men in what Henry Cuffe calls 'our budding and blossoming age' (from pubescence) and 'youth' (up to age 25). Most of these manuscripts contain just one sonnet, the one numbered 2 in Thomas Thorpe's 1609 printing, and most are associated with Oxford colleges. Certainly Thorpe's edition goes out of its way to stress the former privacy of the sonnets, 'never before imprinted', and to heighten the sense of secrets revealed through the volume's mysterious dedication 'to the only begetter of these ensuing sonnets Mr. W.H'. (750). To read a sonnet in manuscript was to affirm one's membership in a highly self-conscious community of male readers. Under such circumstances is it any surprise that the first 126 sonnets in Thorpe's edition should express feelings of male friendship that are alternately tender and angry, candid and guarded, erotic and aloof, while the latter 28 betray varying degrees of misogyny? For the first consumers of *Venus and Adonis*, *The Rape of Lucrece*, and the sonnets, the act of reading was itself an act of masculine self-affirmation.

Ideals

Sir Philip Sidney argues that the exemplifying of heroic masculinity is the very reason for writing, reading, watching, and hearing fiction. In *A Defence of Poesy* Sidney positions 'poesy' (his term for fiction made out of words) halfway between philosophy on the one hand and history on the other. The philosopher, for his part, is 'so hard of utterance and so misty to be conceived' that a man would grow old before he could learn the philosopher's lessons. The historian, for his part, 'is so tied, not to what should be but to what is, to the particular truth of things and not to the general reason of things, that his example draweth no necessary consequence, and therefore a less fruitful doctrine'. Only 'the peerless poet' manages to couple 'the general notion with the particular example'.[6] In all sorts of plays and poems, then, we are invited to look for coalescences of philosophy and history. But in *Shakespeare's* plays and poems those coalescences are not so neat as Sidney assumes.

Under the heading of 'history' we should include not just Holinshed but all of Shakespeare's sources, historical, fictional, dramatic, journalistic. Whether the 'history' in question is Holinshed's *Chronicles* or Lodge's *Rosalynde* or *The True Chronicle History of King Leir* or *A True Repertory of the Wreck and Redemption . . . from the Islands of the Bermudas*, what we discover in Shakespeare's scripts is not a perfect match of ethical ideals with human exemplars but a dialogue between 'history' and 'philosophy', in which the untidy facts of 'history' provide a running critique of the pronouncements of 'philosophy'. The unexpected turns and unresolved issues in Shakespeare's scripts—Kate's 43-line capitulation to Petruccio's will in *The Taming of the Shrew*, news of the Princess's father's death in *Love's Labour's Lost*, Antonio's posture amid the couplings of *The Merchant of Venice*, Don John's refusal to apologize for his treachery at the end of *Much Ado about Nothing*, Isabella's lack of response to the Duke's proposal of marriage in *Measure for Measure*, Bertram's two-line promise to love Helena after all in *All's Well That Ends Well*, Caesar's unexpected celebration of 'a pair so famous' in the last few lines of *Antony and Cleopatra*, Sebastian's unscripted, unrepentant presence in the denouement of *The Tempest*—all suggest that Shakespeare wrote from 'history' upward and not from 'philosophy' downward. The result is certainly coalescence, but of *competing* stories that stand in an awkward relationship to ethical ideals. It is as if Shakespeare combined the imperative mood of philosophy ('Do this') with the subjunctive mood of fiction ('What if . . .?').

Each of the masculine ideals we surveyed in Chapter 2 is subject to this kind of qualification. The chivalric idealist exemplified in

Henry V (as Prince of Wales he offers 'courtesy' to the vanquished Hotspur by covering his foe's mangled face with tokens from his own knightly regalia (*1 Henry IV*, 5.4.93–5)) sorts oddly with the Machiavellian pragmatist who realizes that the only thing separating him from his common soldiers is 'idol ceremony' (*Henry V*, 4.1.237). The Herculean hero whose eyes 'have glowed like plated Mars' (*Antony and Cleopatra*, 1.1.4), whose legs 'bestrid the ocean', whose raised arm 'crested the world', whose voice 'was propertied | As all the tunèd spheres' (5.2.81–3), bungles his own suicide. Hamlet, the student trained in humanist ideals at Wittenberg University, is not able to restrain himself from rashly thrusting his dagger through the arras in his mother's bedroom, an action that ultimately costs him his life. Master George Page, the burgess of Windsor, avoids the ultimate infamy of his social type, being cuckolded by his wife, but fails to realize the mercantile ideal of investing his daughter's dowry to what he supposes is maximum advantage. The saucy jacks of Shakespeare's plays—Tranio, Bottom, Lancelot Gobbo—get what they want in the way of sexual satisfaction but never manage to emulate Deloney's Jack of Newbury in turning themselves into heroes of capitalist success stories.

In every case, coalescences of ideals and realities remain approximate, problematical, incomplete. In part that is a result of the way each of these protagonists functions as more than the exemplar of an ideal. He enters the fiction with all the baggage of his involvement in someone else's story—Holinshed's, Plautus', Cinthio's—and he finds his identity in Shakespeare's story not only with respect to abstract precepts but in cooperation with all of the other characters who crowd the same story, some of them coming from quite different sources, with quite different histories of their own. Coalescence of ideals and realities is complicated further by the fact that multiple ideals often compete for one particular character's allegiance. Bassanio, for example, presents himself as both *chivalric* adventurer and *merchant* adventurer. 'In Belmont is a lady richly left', Bassanio tells Antonio. 'Nor is the wide world ignorant of her worth.' Worth by what measure? According to her 'wondrous virtues'? Or according to her dowry? Bassanio likens the Portia of Belmont to Brutus's Portia, even as the name itself suggests a marriage 'portion'. Imagining Portia's bright hair as 'a golden fleece', Bassanio longs to join the 'Jasons' who 'come in quest of her' (*Merchant of Venice*, 1.1.161–72). Equally remarkable among the coalescences of ideals and realities is the fact that many of Shakespeare's most famous heroes—Romeo, Richard III, Lear, Macbeth—conspicuously fail to exemplify an ethical ideal. Indeed, they are who they are because they are *not*, after all, the paragons of virtue that Sidney seems to expect in serious works of literature. And yet each of these heroes commands the audience's imaginative sympathy. They do so because they are *tragic* heroes. What we witness in such cases is an existential realization about ideals that is beyond Sidney's ken.

Just as we cannot expect to find a paradigm of male identity that transcends all times and all cultures, so should we be wary of assuming a single paradigm of tragedy. J. M. R. Margeson in *The Origins of English Tragedy* has demonstrated a number of different paradigms all operating at the same time in the late sixteenth century and early seventeenth century. Each of those paradigms positions the hero differently *vis-à-vis* the world around him.[7] At least three of the paradigms seem relevant here. In a romance tragedy like *Romeo and Juliet* the protagonists/lovers are overthrown by the forces of Fortune. In a Senecan tragedy like *Julius Caesar*, a morally upright protagonist, beset by the forces of an inimical evil world, affirms his self-identity in a heroic act of suicide. In tragedies inspired by morality plays, a hero like Macbeth or Lear or Antony is confronted with moral choices. In choosing wrong, he seals his destiny. The ethical situation in each of these three types of tragedy may be different, but common to them all is the destruction of the hero for the very reason that he is who he is. Common to all three is a gap between masculinity as a cultural ideal and its achievement on the part of the protagonist. Perhaps it is the fact that this cultural ideal is ultimately unachievable that gives the situation its claims to universality. With respect to masculine identity, Shakespeare's tragedies mourn the gap between cultural ideals and the human possibility of achieving those ideals.

Passages

Coalescences in life passages can be considered in two dimensions: in the horizontal dimension of time, as a protagonist moves from one life stage to another, and in the vertical dimension of space, as he aligns the microcosm of his changing person with the macrocosm of the universe. What is desired in time is a coalescence of one's changed physical body with the social milieu in which one lives. As we observed in Chapter 3, many of Shakespeare's plays seem designed to achieve just such a coalescence. The young men of the early comedies—Valentine and Proteus, Petruccio, Demetrius and Lysander, Bassanio and Graziano, Master Fenton—find in marriage a rooted base for the juices of 'our budding and blossoming age', as Henry Cuffe calls early youth. The complications of the later comedies stem in part from a lack of coalescence between body and social identity: Benedick is a confirmed bachelor with a past history of failed courtship, Orsino is governed by melancholy rather than blood, the Duke of Vienna takes on the role of father-confessor to his wife-to-be, Bertram seems underscripted as he moves from soldier-adventurer to married man. The history plays shape up even more obviously as rites of passage whereby a young man—Henry Bolingbroke, Prince Hal, Henry VI, the Earl of Richmond—takes possession of his role as king, in effect negotiating a fit between his youthful person and his social role. Coalescence in the tragedies is perhaps harder to discern. In their deaths figures like Titus Andronicus, Romeo, Brutus, Hamlet, Hector, Othello, Timon, Lear, Macbeth, and Antony experience, not integration of body with society, but isolation. Extirpation of the hero seems to be the end toward which these tragedies drive. If there is coalescence in such a situation, it is to be found beyond society, beyond indeed the tragic hero himself. 'The tragic hero is very great as compared with us,' Northrop Frye observes, 'but there is something else, something on the side of him opposite the audience, compared to which he is small. This something else may be called God, gods, fate, accident, fortune, necessity, circumstance, or any combination of these, but whatever it is the tragic hero is our mediator with it.'[8]

The coalescence of body with cosmos takes place in horizontal time—it occurs at the end of the tragedy, at the moment of death—but its primary axis is vertical. 'Look up,' Edgar exclaims, perhaps to the swooning Lear, perhaps to the witnesses to the old king's grief. Kent rejoins, 'Vex not his ghost. O, let him pass' (*The Tragedy of King Lear*, 5.3.288–9). The coalescence of microcosm with macrocosm is not peculiar, however, to tragedy. Performances of masculinity in comedy, history, and romance also involve gestures toward metaphysical correspondences. In *As You Like It* Rosalind's disguise as Ganymede may expose masculinity as a performance—and insist on that circumstance right to the end of the epilogue—but the identities of the male protagonists are secured by nature and validated by divinity. The Forest of Arden is a proving ground for masculine virtues of endurance, bravery, and self-reliance. 'Now, my co-mates and brothers in exile,' Duke Senior begins his encomium of the greenwood.

> Here feel we not the penalty of Adam,
> The seasons' difference, as the icy fang
> And churlish chiding of the winter's wind,
> Which when it bites and blows upon my body
> Even till I shrink with cold, I smile, and say
> 'This is no flattery. These are counsellors
> That feelingly persuade me what I am'.
>
> (2.1.1, 5–11)

The appearance of Hymen, titular deity of marriage, in the final scene gives sanction to the rite of passage the play is bringing to conclusion: 'Then is there mirth in heaven | When earthly things made even | Atone together' (5.4.106–8). Macrocosmic reverberations in the history plays are even louder. Aspirants to royal power—Richard III is a notable exception—stake their claims on divine authority. The language of triumph that Richmond speaks on Bosworth Field is replete with images of coalescence:

> We will unite the white rose and the red.
> Smile, heaven, upon this fair conjunction,
> That long have frowned upon their enmity.
> What traitor hears me and says not 'Amen'?
>
> (*Richard III*, 5.8.19–22)

Coalescences of the individual with the universal are strongest of all in Shakespeare's late romances. Diana asserts her protection over Pericles toward the end of his peregrinations, Time witnesses Leontes' expiation of his jealousy in *The Winter's Tale*, Jupiter assures the ghosts of Posthumus's parents and siblings 'Your low-laid son our godhead will uplift' (*Cymbeline*, 5.5.197), Cranmer speaks for heaven in celebrating Henry VIII's paternity and in prophesying that Elizabeth will prove 'A pattern to all princes living with her, | And all that shall succeed' (*All Is True*, 5.4.22–3), Palamon and Arcite fight to the death under the aegis of Mars and Venus.

In comparison with these blatant endorsements, the achievement of heroic masculinity in *The Tempest* is much more complicated. Post-structuralist critics read Prospero's mastery largely as a function of the power he asserts over various others: his dead wife, Miranda, Sycorax, Ariel, Caliban. Prospero himself offers a more self-searching account. The story of his life that he narrates to Miranda in Scene 2 of *The Tempest* is a dramatised counterpart to the autobiographies we noted in Chapter 3. How does Prospero read his own life? Far from presenting himself as an all-powerful magus or confident imperialist, Prospero describes himself as a deeply divided man. As 'prime duke', he tells Miranda,

> —being so reputed
> In dignity, and for the liberal arts
> Without a parallel—those being all my study,
> The government I cast upon my brother,
> And to my state grew stranger, being transported
> And rapt in secret studies.

Let us attend to the oppositions here: 'liberal arts' versus 'government', 'I' versus 'my brother', 'my state' versus 'secret studies', 'stranger' versus 'rapt'. The oppositions are expanded as Prospero continues:

> I, thus neglecting worldly ends, all dedicated
> To closeness and the bettering of my mind
> With that which but by being so retired
> O'er priced all popular rate, in my false brother
> Awaked an evil nature . . . .

> (*The Tempest*, 1.2.72–7, 89–93)

To the earlier oppositions are added 'neglecting' versus 'dedicated', 'worldly ends' versus 'closeness' and 'bettering of my mind', 'retired' pursuits versus things valued at 'popular rate'. The most fundamental opposition of all occurs near the beginning of the story: 'reputed' versus its implied opposites 'was' or 'am'.

Guided by Prospero's account of his divided self, the audience-spectators are invited to hear and see *The Tempest* as an attempt to bring these oppositions into coalescence. Prospero promises to finish the play as he began it, with the story of his life. Come to my poor cell, Prospero invites Alonso and his train, where he will pass away part of the night

> With such discourse as I not doubt shall make it
> Go quick away: the story of my life,
> And the particular accidents gone by
> Since I came to this isle.

(5.1.307–10)

What shape will that story take? The 'rise and fall' pattern of a tragedy modelled on Boccaccio's *De Casibus Virorum Illustrium* might have suited Prospero's story at the beginning of the play, but the outcome here is a second rise. The humility of Prospero's final speech does not promise such a turn. With respect to Prospero's art, it is also possible to imagine the 'before' and 'after' pattern of religious visionaries like Rhys Evans. Prospero's key word 'accidents' may imply, however, the kind of episodic life-story narrated by Captain John Smith, another man who ventured overseas into parts unknown. Whichever form Prospero adopts, the story he tells this time will be one of oppositions reconciled, of the private scholar regaining public rule, of liberal arts put into the service of government, of 'I' and 'my brother' atoned, of reputation and reality being made one and the same. It will be a story of coalescences.

Others

In Shakespeare's plays the forging of masculine identity *vis-à-vis* others can be charted along a continuum from extreme isolation at one end to full integration at the other. At first glance, the poles might seem to be defined by tragedy and comedy. Tragedy, after all, involves the isolation of the protagonist; comedy, a celebration of his connectedness. The circumstances of individual characters, however, call such a neat equation into question. Among Shakespeare's tragic heroes there are certainly those whose selfhood seems to be demarcated by their extreme isolation: Titus Andronicus, Timon of Athens, and Coriolanus come to mind immediately. As Bert States would remind us, however, no dramatic protagonist exists in total isolation. Character onstage is always a function of other characters. Titus may finish the play bereft of all his family, but in his final self-assertive speech he *needs* interlocutors in the persons of his tormentors Saturninus and Tamora. Coriolanus, the man who has declared 'Wife, mother, child, I know not' (5.2.82), is finally estranged from his solitary ally, Aufidius, and positively begs his own destruction from those with whom he shares the stage in the play's last scene. Timon's is surely the greatest isolation of all. His last words in the play are not even addressed to another on-stage character but are written out in an epitaph posted on his cave-tomb and read out to the audience by Alcibiades.

At quite the opposite extreme are comic protagonists like Valentine and Proteus, Demetrius and Lysander, Orlando, and Orsino, whose masculine identities are achieved as part of a community that includes not only their male companions but their wives-to-be. Assured of the lady over whom they have fallen out, Valentine declares to Proteus, 'Our day of marriage shall be yours, | One feast, one house, one mutual happiness' (*The Two Gentlemen of Verona*, 5.4.170–1). Two commonly held sentiments coalesce in Valentine's speech: that a man's friend is another self and that husband and wife are one flesh. Concerning the former relationship, Francis Bacon observes that a man with a friend 'hath as it were two Lives in his desires. A man hath a Body, and that Body is confined to a Place, but where *Friendship* is, all Offices of Life are as it were granted to Him and his Deputy. For he may exercise them by his *Friend*.' Concerning husbands and wives Thomas Gainsford pronounces a woman 'the wonder of nature, for she maketh two bodies one flesh and two hearts one soul, so that the husband and wife truly loving so conspire in all their actions that they have in a manner but one motion'.[9] Both sentiments entertain the possibility of merging 'other' into 'me' and 'I' into 'other'—a consummation that gender ambiguities certainly help to facilitate. When Orsino, the effeminate melancholic lover, insists on calling Viola 'Cesario'—'For so you shall be while you are a man' (*Twelfth Night*, 5.1.382)—he is choosing, for the moment at least, to subsume difference into sameness.

It is the range of possibilities between these extremes that gives Shakespeare's plays their life-likeness. Tragic protagonists like Brutus, Hamlet, Hector, Othello, Macbeth, and Antony find their masculine identities, not in isolation, but in complicated relationships with both men and women. We observed in Chapter 4 how even so independent a spokesman as Hamlet is who he is because he is partly his father, partly Ophelia, partly Gertrude, partly Laertes, partly Horatio, partly Fortinbras. Hamlet in fact charges Horatio to take up his story at the end, even as he endows Fortinbras with his dying voice. The play closes with coalescence between the man who has spoken in his own right and the men with whom he chooses to merge himself in death. Hector's case in *Troilus and Cressida* is different. Starting out as a man whose identity is very much that of son, brother, warrior, he dares to speak his own mind in the council scene—'If Helen then be wife to Sparta's king, | As it is known she is, these moral laws | Of nature and of nations speak aloud | To have her back returned'—but then retreats to his group identity:

> Hector's opinion
> Is this in way of truth—yet ne'ertheless,
> My sprightly brethren, I propend to you
> In resolution to keep Helen still;
> For 'tis a cause that hath no mean dependence
> Upon our joint and several dignities.

> (2.2.182–5, 187–92)

Hector's capitulation at this crucial moment ends ultimately in his isolated death at the hands of Achilles and his Myrmidons. By his own account, Hector's masculine identity is a coalescence of two kinds of dignity, 'joint' and 'several'. In death, the dignity in question is not 'joint' but one of the 'several'. It is Hector's alone. Perhaps the most affecting instance of coalescence is Lear's. Surrounded by a stageful of others in the play's first scene, Lear is stripped of his retainers until he finds himself alone on the heath with his fool as his main interlocutor. Emerging from the total isolation of his sleep, he is reconciled with Cordelia. When they are captured and sent to prison, he imagines a world inhabited only by the two of them, a world in which they will coalesce into one all-sufficient whole: 'We two alone will sing like birds i'th'cage. | When thou dost ask me blessing, I'll kneel down | And ask of thee forgiveness...' (*The Tragedy of King Lear*, 5.3.9–11). The poignancy of that speech is all the greater when Cordelia's death leaves Lear as profoundly other-less as any of Shakespeare's tragic protagonists.

Toward the integrative pole of the continuum some of the protagonists in Shakespeare's comedies find themselves in equally complicated positions *vis-à-vis* others. To some degree, masculine identity in the comedies involves an exclusion of others: Don Armado the loquacious incompetent lover, Shylock the Jew, Malvolio the spoilsport social climber, Antonio the sea-captain sodomite. The position of women among these signifying others is not so easy to plot. The main drift of the play-within-the-play in *The Taming of the Shrew*, for example, would seem to be an affirmation of masculine power against a sharply defined female other. Kate's speech of submission, despite its seeming acceptance of mysogynist dogma, upsets the power dynamics whereby women remain true to form and allow men to be men. In refusing their husbands' bidding, Bianca and Hortensio's wife behave just as men, whatever they say they *want*, in fact *expect* their wives to behave. In the very act of coming when Petruccio calls and saying what he wishes to hear, Kate affirms a connectedness to her husband that the others lack—a connectedness that is to be sealed in bed. Petruccio's response to Kate's speech is a careful positioning of 'us' against 'them': 'Come, Kate, *we'll* to bed. | *We three* are married, but *you two* are sped' (5.2.189–90, emphases added). Whether 'sped' here means 'done for' or 'having done it' is a nice question. Hortensio and Lucentio have consummated their marriages; Petruccio's interruption of his own wedding banquet (3.3.57) implies that he and Kate have not. The coalescence of man and wife in the play's last scene, as compared to the separation of the other couples, makes Petruccio's masculine identity a less isolated affair than it might seem.

In this respect, Kate as a strong woman anticipates the strong women of Shakespeare's later comedies: Portia, Nerissa, Rosalind, Beatrice, Helena. To the degree that these female others assert their own power they demand a place in their spouses' self-identity. For Bassanio, Benedick, and Bertram, if not for Orlando, those demands produce anxiety that promises to spill over into Act 6, after the play is over. Portia vows to 'answer all things faithfully', but Graziano worries about 'keeping safe Nerissa's ring', both as vagina and as band of gold (*The Merchant of Venice*, 5.1.299, 307). Benedick perhaps hints at his own anxieties about cuckolding when he teases Don Pedro, 'There is no staff more reverend than one tipped with horn' (*Much Ado About Nothing*, 5.4.122–3). And Bertram manages only a single lame couplet—a conditional one, addressed not to his wife but to the king—when he acknowledges Helena's trickery in trapping him in marriage: 'If she, my liege, can make me know this clearly | I'll love her dearly, ever ever dearly' (*All's Well That Ends Well*, 5.3.317–18).

The late romances seem more unified than the earlier comedies in charting a clear course from isolation to coalescence. At the beginning of *The Winter's Tale*, for example, Leontes finds his identity in his childhood friend, in his wife, in his son. A flash of jealousy destroys those bonds and leaves Leontes in a position quite as isolated as Lear's. The comic resolution to this tragic situation restores the harmonious interconnectedness of self, friend, wife, and offspring that Leontes enjoyed at the beginning. He acknowledges those signifying others one by one, beginning with Hermione:

> What, look upon my brother. Both your pardons,
> That e'er I put between your holy looks
> My ill suspicion. This' your son-in-law
> And son unto the King, whom heavens directing
> Is troth-plight to your daughter.

Last to be addressed is the lone interlocutor with whom he has passed sixteen long years: 'Good Paulina, | Lead us from hence' (5.3.148–53). Leontes' insistence that Paulina take Camillo as a husband may be inspired not so much by the demands of symmetry as by his need to distance himself from her as he reconnects with his former self. Pericles, Posthumus, and Prospero make similar moves from isolation to coalescence.

Along the continuum from isolation to integration the history plays offer sharp contrasts. Defeated protagonists like Henry VI, Richard III, Richard II, and King John parallel Lear's career from integrated self to isolated self. The most poetic of these king-figures provides the sharpest image of the situation they all come to share. 'I have been studying how I may compare | This prison where I live unto the world', Richard II begins;

> And for because the world is populous,
> And here is not a creature but myself,
> I cannot do it. Yet I'll hammer it out.
> My brain I'll prove the female to my soul,
> My soul the father, and these two beget
> A generation of still-breeding thoughts;
> And these same thoughts people this little world
> In humours like the people of this world.

First he imagines himself a contemplative divine who accepts his imprisonment with faith, then an ambitious man who strives to escape, then a contented man who takes comfort that others have been in the same position. 'Thus play I in one person many people, | And none contented.' Lacking others with whom he may coalesce, Richard attempts to beget them within himself. In his extreme isolation he inevitably ends in nullity:

> But whate'er I be,
> Nor I, nor any man that but man is,
> With nothing shall be pleased till he be eased
> With being nothing.

> (5.5.1–10, 31–2, 38–41)

In sharp contrast stands Henry Bolingbroke, who ends the play of *Richard II*, not in solitary soliloquy, but in dialogue with others. Those others fall into two groups: allies (in the persons of York, Northumberland, Fitzwalter, and Percy) and enemies (in the person of Carlisle and the corpse of Richard). In that situation of coalescence and exclusion Bolingbroke figures as a prototype of Richmond in *Richard III*, Prince Arthur in *King John*, and Prince Hal in the trilogy of *1* and *2 Henry IV*, and *Henry V*.

The middle of the continuum between isolation and integration is defined precisely by the circumstances of Arcite and Palamon in *The Two Noble Kinsmen*. Finding their identities in each other at the beginning of the play ('We are one another's wife,' Arcite declares, 'ever begetting | New births of love' (2.2.80–1)), the two friends fall out over Emilia. With respect to masculine identity Emilia poses a threat not only as a female other but as a force that disrupts the friends' coalescence with one another. However varied Shakespeare's handling of this particular dilemma in his earlier plays, the resolution here seems radically arbitrary. Deciding their differences in a tournament, Arcite dies, while Palamon lives on to claim Emilia. The play ends with Arcite in tragic isolation and Palamon in comic integration. Palamon is left in a position, however, to appreciate the irony of his situation: 'That we should things desire which do cost us | The loss of our desire! That naught could buy | Dear love, but loss of dear love' (5.6.110–12). The need for others is a given; that need is satisfied through 'losing' and 'buying', through excluding and incorporating.

Among the prime candidates for this position of self-irony, halfway between isolation and coalescence, is Henry V: boon companion, prodigal son, valiant warrior, husband, politic king.

Performances

It is possible, then, to read each of Shakespeare's scripts as a particular instance of coalescence, as an achievement of masculinity in a particular set of circumstances. In theatre, as in life, masculinity may be a performance, but the event in question is not always the same. The protagonists are different, and the story is different, but so are the actors and the audience. Performance of masculinity is contingent on all four variables. Over the past 400 years Shakespeare's scripts have been performed tens of thousands of times in places all over the world, in languages other than English, by actors trained in acting traditions different from Shakespeare's own, before audiences knowing little or nothing about Renaissance England, amid social and political concerns radically different from those of 1600, within different cultural assumptions about what constitutes masculinity. In these performances masculinity must inevitably represent the coalescence of ideas shared by actors and audiences, whoever they are, wherever they may be, with ideas coded in Shakespeare's scripts. The result is a cultural hybrid, a coalescence of early modern ways of performing masculinity with ways belonging to another place and time. The production history of any of Shakespeare's plays will illustrate the point. As examples let us consider the four protagonists with whom we began: Lear, Macbeth, Coriolanus, and Hamlet.

By his own admission, Lear's masculinity is a function of reason, power, and difference from women. '*Histerica passio* down, thou climbing sorrow; | Thy element's below' (*The Tragedy of King Lear*, 2.2.232–3): when Lear locates himself *vis-à-vis* these three coordinates, he does so in distinctly early modern terms. In stark contrast stands Paul Scofield's Lear in one of the landmark productions of the twentieth century (stage 1962, film 1971). The director, Peter Brook, had been excited by Jan Kott's argument, eventually published in *Shakespeare Our Contemporary* (1965), that Lear plays out with his Fool an existential *folie à deux* not unlike that between Vladimir and Estragon in Samuel Beckett's *Waiting for Godot* or Hamm and Clov in *Endgame*. In this situation masculinity remains the function of binaries that it is in Shakespeare's script, but the binary opposites themselves have lost their historical specificity. Closer to the sense of *histerica passio*, perhaps, was the hypermasculinity in Max Stafford-Clark's production of *Lear* with the English Stage Company in 1992–3. Inhabiting a militaristic, all-male social world, Tom Wilkinson's mustachioed Lear strode onstage in Edwardian riding-coat and breeches. The barrackroom jokes of his entourage, including his camp, cross-dressed Fool, more than merited the fury of Goneril and Regan. More usual in contemporary productions is to present Lear as a failed father, as in Deborah Warner's production for the Royal National Theatre in 1990, with Brian Cox as Lear.[10] King troubled in his person, struggler with existential anxiety, failed father: the coalescences in each case are different.

With such disparities in contemporary productions of *King Lear* in England, it should come as no surprise to discover quite different constructions of masculinity in productions elsewhere. Even a production that aims faithfully to reproduce Shakespeare's text in another language cannot avoid the distinctive constructions of masculine identity that come with a different dramatic tradition—and with a different language. Discussing the challenges of translating *King Lear* into Japanese, Tetsuo Anzai has insisted that the text of a play is not just a verbal artefact. 'Instead, it stands for the dramatic or theatrical experience embodied in it. The experience is the thing. What we have to aim at in translating a dramatic text is therefore not to translate its literal meaning but to re-create this latent theatrical experience.'[11] In the case of *Lear* in Japanese that means tempering Lear's assertiveness. In Anzai's translation, the imperative, exclamation, and declaration in 'Howl, howl, howl, howl! O, you are men of stones. | Had I your tongues and eyes, I'd use them so | That heaven's vault should crack' (*The Tragedy of King Lear*, 5.3.232–4) become a series of interrogatives demanded by what Anzai describes as the Japanese language's 'inadequacy in direct, forceful assertion': 'Are you stones? Have you no voice, no eyes? | If you have any voice, why don't you howl so | That heaven's vault should crack and fall?' (Anzai 125–7). With the change from imperative to interrogative comes a change in how a man like Lear is expected to *speak* and, with that change, in who he *is* for Japanese actors and audiences. Ania Loomba offers another example in her discussion of *King Lear* as performed in the Kathakali dance-drama tradition of Kerala in India. In that tradition it is impossible for a king to appear without his headgear. How, then, to show a man who is both king and madman? Widespread criticism of a Kathakali adaptation of *Lear* that ignored this prohibition illustrates Loomba's argument that postcolonial Shakespeare, far from being an acknowledgement of colonial authority, can function as an affirmation of native traditions.[12]

'Are you a man?' (*Macbeth*, 3.4.57): Lady Macbeth's taunt to her swooning husband has been answered in quite disparate ways since the play was first produced, probably in 1606 or 1607. For Simon Forman, who witnessed a performance of the play in 1611, Macbeth's guilt was immediate, collaborative, and visceral: 'When Macbeth had murdered the king, the blood on his hands could not be washed off by any means, nor from his wife's hands, which handled the bloody daggers in hiding them, by which means they became much amazed and affronted.'[13] Eighteenth-century actors and audiences were disposed to construct masculinity in much less judgemental terms. David Garrick's Macbeth (played 1744 to 1768) was a man of sensibility, in the specifically eighteenth-century sense of the word as 'quickness and acuteness of apprehension or feeling' (*OED* '*sensibility*' 5.a). Playing opposite Mrs Hannah Pritchard as Lady Macbeth, Garrick portrayed a paragon of high moral consciousness who was instantly struck with guilt once he had succumbed to his wife's temptations. Construing Macbeth along similar lines, Jean-François Ducis produced a version for the Comédie Française in 1784 in which the hero was made to appear as noble, innocent, and remorseful as possible. In both of these eighteenth-century versions Macbeth's suicide was designed to engage pity, not the moral opprobrium implied by Forman.[14] Sensibility as Macbeth's dominant trait becomes courage in John Philip Kemble's interpretation of the role, both on the stage from 1778 to 1817 and in an essay on Macbeth and Richard III published in 1786. Kemble sets out in his essay to rescue Macbeth from Thomas Whately's claim that Richard shows true 'intrepidity', whereas Macbeth shows mere 'resolution'. Commenting on the Captain's description of Macbeth in battle in 1.2.7–23, Kemble asks, 'Could Shakespeare call a man brave, and insist upon his well deserving that appellation; could he grace a man with the title of valour's minion, and deem him, as he does in a subsequent passage, worthy to be matched even with the goddess of war;—could he do this, and not design to impress a full idea of the dignity of his courage?'[15] All of Macbeth's subsequent actions, including his murder of Banquo and his defiance of Macduff in the end, follow from this trait.

Twentieth-century answers to Lady Macbeth's question have been just as varied. Where Forman saw wickedness, Garrick sensibility, and Kemble courage, interpreters since Max Reinhardt (1916) have tended to see a conflicted Freudian psyche. Derek Jacobi, who played Macbeth in Adrian Noble's production for the Royal Shakespeare Company in 1993, typifies this approach when he finds Macbeth's dominant note to be fear. To explain that emotion Jacobi draws a contrast between 'Macbeth the warrior, whose duty is killing and maiming, and Macbeth the husband, the lover, the domestic, cultured man who dances and listens to music'. In the course of preparing their roles, he and the actress playing Lady Macbeth decided that 'somewhere in the past of their relationship they had lost a child'.[16] The killer of kings is to be understood not only as husband and lover but as the possessor of post-nineteenth-century subconsciousness. Symptomatic in a different way of twentieth-century ways of constructing masculinity is Roman Polanski's film version of the play (1971), which parallels Michel Foucault's work in presenting Macbeth, not as a moral agent in his own right, but as the victim of a corrupt society.[17]

The 'Voodoo' *Macbeth* produced by Orson Welles (original stage performances 1936, film versions 1947 and 1950, stage revival under Afro-American auspices 1977) illustrates yet another modern formation of masculine identity, this time *vis-à-vis* 'primitive' culture. Although designed to offer positive role models to African-Americans—in 1936 they had few opportunities to perform in professional theatre and lived in even worse poverty than other Depression-era Americans—Welles's production was conceived, produced, and funded mostly by European-Americans.[18] With the paintings that Picasso and other mid-century artists produced in response to African art Welles's 'Voodoo' *Macbeth* shares a fetishization of things black. Finding his identity among the bloody revolutions of the Caribbean in the nineteenth century, Welles's Macbeth is violent, passionate, and superstitious. In the original production drums and chanting established a primitive pulse that had its visual counterpart in colours that grew ever more vivid and intense, reaching a peak in the banquet scene

(Shakespeare's 3.4). The grandeur of this scene, complete with Viennese waltzes and waiters serving champagne, was apparently designed to make clear the hedonistic pleasures after which Macbeth and Lady Macbeth were lusting. The 'Voodoo' *Macbeth*, at least in its 1936 and 1947–1950 incarnations, was all about a black 'other', a white construction of black masculinity that served to affirm the ways in which white masculinity is *not that*.

Just before he dashes into the city of Corioles, Caius Martius cries to his comrades in arms, 'Mark me, and do the like' (*Coriolanus*, 1.5.16). In the event, no one follows him. Instead, they stand back and comment on his manliness. 'Thou art lost, Martius', one of them laments to his fellow soldiers.

> A carbuncle entire, as big as thou art,
> Were not so rich a jewel. Thou wast a soldier
> Even to Cato's wish, not fierce and terrible
> Only in strokes, but with thy grim looks and
> The thunder-like percussion of thy sounds
> Thou mad'st thine enemies shake as if the world
> Were feverous and did tremble.
>
>   (1.5.25–32)

At that moment Martius reappears, bleeding, and quickly achieves the victory that earns him his new name, Coriolanus. 'Mark me, and do the like': in his fierce isolation Coriolanus presents himself as a heroic exemplar of masculinity. As such, he has been subject to the different ideas of masculinity assumed by actors and audiences across the past four hundred years.

Nahum Tate's adaptation, *The Ingratitude of a Commonwealth: Or, the Fall of Caius Martius Coriolanus* (first acted 1681), not only uses Shakespeare's script as Tory propaganda against the Whigs but turns Coriolanus himself into a stalwart family man. His leave-taking of Volumnia and Virgilia in the equivalent of Shakespeare's 4.1 is centred on his attachment to his son. 'Where is my little Life?' the doting father says.

> Pray let me see him,
> Leave him a hasty blessing, and away.
>   *Young* Martius *brought in*; Coriolanus *take[s] him in his arms.*
> Oh! How I grudge ingrateful Rome this Treasure!

Make much of him, Virgilia. I shall live
To train him up in war, and he shall choose
Some country to defend, and make his own:
My absence in some part he shall supply;
And with his innocent prattling, chide thy sights,
When thou shalt wake, and miss me from thy bed.[19]

The homely domesticity invoked in this speech is emphasized again in the scene in which Volumnia and Virgilia beg Coriolanus to spare Rome (the equivalent of Shakespeare's 5.3) as well as in the extensively rewritten ending. The final scene of *The Ingratitude of a Commonwealth* shows Coriolanus, not only in juxtaposition with his military rival Aufidius but reunited with his wounded wife, his dying mother, and his mutilated son. Coriolanus himself dies as the centrepiece in a family tableau: 'So, grasping in each arm my treasure, I | Pleas'd with the prize, to Death's calm region fly' (64). The fierce soldier and the tender husband coalesce in an observation made earlier in the play by Valeria: 'He's the dearest obstinate man! Which I confess in a vulgar person, were most inordinately, unsufferable; but in him it looks so grand, heroic, and august, that no era, catalogue, chronicle, register, or annals of time can ever...'. But she is cut short by the appearance of the 'little soldier', Coriolanus's son (52).

Rivalry at the beginning of the nineteenth century between John Philip Kemble's Coriolanus (acted 1789–97 and 1811–17) and Edmund Kean's (first acted 1820) defines the difference between a neo-classical ideal of manhood and a romantic ideal. It was Kemble's interpretation that put Shakespeare's original text of *Coriolanus* back on the boards. John Ripley in his stage history of the play describes a hero *à l'antique* who might have strode onto the stage of Drury Lane out of a painting by Jacques-Louis David: 'Complexities, ambiguities, and contradictions are not to be tolerated.... His aristocratic integrity and fatal arrogance blaze in ever-growing splendor from his first appearance with the citizens to his final defiance of Aufidius.' Coriolanus dies in a blaze of 'patriotic arrogance'—as well he might, considering the havoc being wrought by The People across the English Channel in France.[20] Kean revolutionized the role by presenting Coriolanus as a passionate, rough-edged idealist whose integrity is destroyed by the corrupt, temporizing world in which he is forced to act. That is to say, Kean's Coriolanus sounded a lot like Byron. Some critics found Kean's portrayal altogether too emotional. 'Alone I did it' (5.6.117): comparing Kemble's performance with Kean's, one observer claimed, 'the one was a mighty mind betrayed unwillingly into the expression of an exulting consciousness of his great deeds, the other the egotism of a bully' (quoted in Ripley 157). Despite their return to Shakespeare's text, both versions of Coriolanus, Kemble's and Kean's, offered exemplars of masculinity that men of the time might imagine themselves emulating. As such, both versions of Coriolanus avoided any hint of homoeroticism in Coriolanus's relations with Aufidius. The suspect sentences in Aufidius's welcoming speech—'Let me twine | Mine arms about that body...' (4.5.107–27)—were simply dropped. The fact that Nahum Tate could retain those sentences in 1681 while Kemble and Kean excised them corroborates Randolph Trumbach's argument that it was only in the eighteenth century that the sodomite emerged as a recognized social type and that true manhood was ideologically separated from homoeroticism. Kemble's later performances in the role of Coriolanus and all of Kean's coincided with the greatest number of prosecutions for sodomy in English history.[21]

The homoeroticism so conspicuously absent from nineteenth-century productions of *Coriolanus* began to reappear in the mid-twentieth century but in a thoroughly Freudian guise. Coriolanus in Michael Langham's production for the Stratford, Ontario, festival in 1961 and in Tyrone Guthrie's production for the Nottingham Playhouse in 1963 both presented cases of arrested development. In Langham's production 39-year-old Paul Scofield, playing opposite Eleanor Stuart's dominating mother-figure, displayed what Ripley describes as 'male narcissism and aggression caused by infantile deprivation' (303). In Guthrie's production John Neville as Coriolanus and Ian McKellen as Aufidius directed toward each other behaviour that the printed programme describes as 'the hysterical and homosexual element which seems so useful and powerful an ingredient in the composition of intensely vigorous men of action' (quoted in Ripley 304). The symmetry here between 'hysterical' and 'homosexual' locates Guthrie's primary reference point not in the Band of Sparta but in the theories of Sigmund Freud. Implicitly at least, Volumnia was held responsible for Coriolanus's self-defeating behaviour. The conflicting elements in Coriolanus's role—warrior, aristocrat, son, father, lover of manliness in himself and other men—coalesce in these two Freudian interpretations but in ways radically different from Shakespeare's original.

Many of the best contemporary productions of Shakespeare's plays make a point of their historical difference. David Thacker's production of *Coriolanus* for the Royal Shakespeare Company in 1993–4 is a particularly apt example, since it invoked no fewer than four historical reference points: Plutarch's Rome, Shakespeare's England, Napoleon's France, and the audiences' own present.[22] Against a backdrop of an unfinished version of Eugène Delacroix's 'Liberty Leading the People' and to the accompaniment of brass music that recalled Beethoven's *Coriolan* overture, Toby Stephens played a Coriolanus whose speech, costume, and bearing suggested Napoleon (see Figure 6). Precedent for putting *Coriolanus* into Napoleonic dress goes back to Langham's production for Stratford, Ontario, and Guthrie's for the Nottingham playhouse in the 1960s. (In addition to having produced a warrior-autocrat in Napoleon, the French seemed to the British, even in Napoleon's day, to combine a habit of pushing political theory too far with a penchant for homoeroticism.[23]) This time, however, the effect was postmodern. Instead of trying to realize a modernist coalescence of character, ideology, and historical period, Thacker's production seemed calculated to play up the separateness of those elements—a dis-coalescence, if that is possible. Spilling of the action out into the theatre meant, in Ripley's formation, that 'the twentieth-century audience, willingly or unwillingly, became a participant in a Napoleonic reading of a Jacobean artistic treatment of a Roman event' (332). Within these disparate cultural coordinates Stephens plotted a Coriolanus whose manhood was very much in the making. At age 24 Stephens combined psychological vulnerability with physical self-containment. Even his blaring voice seemed to ward off the possibility of coalescence with those around him, with the citizens of Rome, his companions-at-arms, his political allies, his wife, his son, his mother, even Aufidius. In this production homoerotic attraction was all on Aufidius's side: Coriolanus bore Aufidius's embraces with stiff unease. Thacker's *Coriolanus*, for some viewers at least, pulled back the illusionistic scenery and exposed the dramatic mechanisms by which masculinity is produced in the theatre.

'To be or not to be': Hamlet stakes his identity on taking action rather than talking. In all three early printed versions of the script, the first quarto (1603), the second quarto (1604), and the folio (1623), *Hamlet* the play queries the coalescence of word and action. When the Hamlet of the folio advises the players to 'suit the action to the word, the word to the action', he articulates an ideal to which he, too, aspires. The already existing script of *Hamlet* that Shakespeare took in hand—there are references to it from 1589 onwards—apparently portrayed the crafty man of action who figures in François de Belleforest's *Histoires Tragiques*, the revenger who traps his victims in a great hall and sets it afire, thereby claiming his father's kingdom for himself. As Anthony Dawson points out in his performance history of Shakespeare's *Hamlet*, the protagonist of the second quarto differs from the protagonist of the folio in being more loquacious—he is given an additional soliloquy in 'How all occasions do inform against me' (fragment J, p. 689)—and in the graveyard scene he, like the protagonist of the folio, lacks the stage direction of the first quarto, '*Hamlet leaps in after Laertes*'. Dawson reads these disparities as an indication that speech and action coalesced in different ways at different points in the play's original production run.[24] Certainly the Hamlet who lived on in performances in Germany after English troupes had toured there speaks much more to the point than Shakespeare's Hamlet and in the play's last scene is choreographed to carry out a triumphant series of stabbings. 'Stab away until the blade is broken!' pleads the contrite last victim in the German *Tragedy of Fratricide Punished or Prince Hamlet of Denmark*.[25]

The Hamlet of the Restoration and eighteenth-century stage was, by contrast, a talker as well as a doer, and a more polished and stately talker than Shakespeare's original Hamlet. Cuts made to the texts of Hamlet's soliloquies by Sir William Davenant allowed Thomas Betterton to display his elegant, restrained acting style to the full. Where original audiences had heard a series of false starts and leaps of thought in Hamlet's first soliloquy Betterton's listeners heard verse that aspired to heroic couplets. In the original script Hamlet fractures standard English syntax as his racing mind pursues the image of his mother forgetting his father and marrying Claudius:

> Must I remember? Why, she would hang on him
> As if increase of appetite had grown
> By what it fed on, and yet within a month—

Let me not think on't; frailty, thy name is woman—
A little month, or ere those shoes were old
With which she followed my poor father's body,
Like Niobe, all tears, why she, even she—
O God! a beast that wants discourse of reason
Would have mourned longer!—married with mine uncle,
My father's brother, but no more like my father
Than I to Hercules; within a month,
Ere yet the salt of most unrighteous tears
Had left the flushing of her gallèd eyes,
She married.

(1.2.143–56)

In Davenant's revision Hamlet's mind, and his syntax, are altogether
more controlled:

She used to hang on him,
As if increase of appetite had grown
By what it fed on, and yet within a month,
Let me not think on't, frailty thy name is woman,
[CUT] married with my uncle,
My father's brother; but no more like my father
Than I to Hercules: [CUT].[26]

What is being constructed in the cuts of 1676 is nothing less than a
different sort of man from the Hamlets of 1603, 1604, and 1623.
Betterton's Hamlet, however keen on revenge, is better mannered,
having been schooled in France, rather than Wittenberg, during the
Interregnum. Restraint becomes an index to manliness. Describing
Betterton's response to the elder Hamlet's ghost, Colley Cibber notes
that 'the boldness of his Expostulation was still govern'd by Decency,
manly, but not braving' (quoted in Dawson 31). Altogether different
was the man of feeling that David Garrick found in the role in the later
eighteenth century. When Garrick pronounced the phrase 'so excellent a king', he would allow tears of grief to fall. A young German
traveller, Georg Lichtenberg, who often saw Garrick act in the 1770s,
describes such a display of tender emotion as the very essence of
masculinity: 'This manner of shedding tears . . . betrays both the heavy
burden of grief in his heart and the manly spirit which suffers under it.'
So moved was Lichtenberg by the first soliloquy that he and his

(presumably male) neighbour turned to each other for the first time and spoke. 'It was quite irresistible' (quoted in Dawson 35). Garrick's Hamlet, no less than his Macbeth, was a man of exquisite sensibility, altogether reasonable but susceptible at the same time to delicate feelings.

It was the qualities Hamlet was perceived to share with Goethe's young Werther, the man of sorrows, that made for such a ready transition from Garrick's Hamlet to the romantic Hamlet of the nineteenth and early twentieth centuries. This is the Hamlet who lives on in popular imagination even today. Where earlier interpreters had found unity, a natural coalescence of traits, Edmund Kean, who acted Hamlet from 1810 to 1833, and Sir Henry Irving, who acted the part from 1874 to 1885, found multiplicity, disjointedness, sudden flashes of thought and feeling. In Irving's case such disunity was the very proof of Hamlet's individuality (Dawson 46, 62). When Samuel Johnson in the preface to his edition of Shakespeare (1765) praised the *universality* of Shakespeare's characters—'In the writings of other poets a character is too often an individual; in those of Shakespeare it is commonly a species'—he was articulating the principle that informed Betterton's portrayal of Hamlet and Garrick's.[27] Betterton and Garrick sought to project traits perceived to be typical; Irving and his successors, traits perceived to be unique. Nineteenth- and early-twentieth-century actors took their cue from Hamlet himself: 'I have that within that passeth show' (1.2.85). That something within has provided, for post-Romantic interpreters of the role, the point of coalescence once provided by revenge, filial duty, or sensibility. For Laurence Olivier (stage 1937, film 1948) the point of coalescence, the something within that passes show, is Freud's Oedipus complex.

What the history of performance of *Hamlet* shows us is a succession, not of unique individuals, but of exemplars of changing cultural constructions of masculinity. John Gielgud's Hamlet of 1929 and later was praised at the time as a 'very human' modern young man, displaying qualities that Dawson enumerates as 'restless intelligence', 'lightning sensitivity of reaction', and 'princely elegance and courtly assurance' (99–100). Laurence Olivier's Hamlet may have been, famously, 'a man who could not make up his mind', but he showed himself, given the right motive, quite capable of action. That characteristic he shared with his 1930s contemporaries, Gustav Gründgen's Hamlet at the

German National Theatre in Berlin and the Hamlet of Koreya Senda's production for the New Tsukiji Theatre Company in Japan.[28] David Warner's Hamlet in 1965 was an angry young man of the sort who had created an impression in John Osborne's *Look Back in Anger* (1956). Kenneth Branagh's Hamlet (stage 1988, film 1996) has struck some observers as no less confined than its predecessors to the masculine ideals of the actor's own time and place: in this case, sexiness, domesticity, patriotism, and career sense (Dawson 18–22, 132–46).

In *Black Hamlet* (1937) Wulf Sachs, psychoanalysing a South African Negro named John Chavafambira, argues for the universality of 'Hamletism' as a condition of 'indecision and hesitancy when action is required'.[29] Productions of *Hamlet* outside Britain and North America, however, demonstrate decidedly more local coalescences of Shakespeare's script with cultural constructions of masculinity. Goro Suzuki, for example, locates the appeal of Hamlet to Japanese audiences in Zen philosophy: 'What is designated in Zen as the "experience of original inseparability", going back to the prelapsarian state of "this goodly frame, the earth", is exactly what the Prince of Denmark, upon his return to the Danish royal castle of Elsinore, is desperately after throughout the play'. According to this perspective, the moment of truth for Hamlet comes, not in his acts of revenge, but in his death speech: Hamlet moves 'from an outrageous sea of words to a world of silence, a world impregnated with fullness. Paradoxical as this may sound, it is indeed a world of rich language, a world of constant change and dynamism.'[30] Hamlet is most a man when he neither acts nor speaks.

By contrast, the Hamlet of the first professional production of the play in Iraq in 1973 was lifted out of Shakespeare's text and set down in cultural circumstances where decisive action was to be assumed. A careful translation into Arabic by Jabra Ibrahim Jabra put into Hamlet's mouth words that were close to Shakespeare's original script; the directorial concept by Sami Abdul-Hamid Nuri required Hamlet to act, however, according to the traditional values of feudal Arab culture in the desert or on the Arabian island—values that would have demanded forthright revenge for deprivation of one's land. Hamlet was imagined as having returned to his native culture after education elsewhere, perhaps in the West. 'This was my chance', Nuri explained, 'to put a person like Hamlet in an Arab society, give him circumstances to face like those described in the original text—and see what he would do.' Hamlet's predicament, according to Nuri, was not so much psychological as political.[31] In effect, *Hamlet Arabian*, as the production was called, explored the crisis of masculinity in contemporary Arab society, a crisis in which traditional values and Western values compete for a man's allegiance.

Every time a script by Shakespeare is brought to the stage, in Baghdad or in Stratford-upon-Avon, masculinity is being performed. It is achieved through a series of coalescences: of individual protagonists with other characters in the play, of philosophical ideals with narrative contingencies, of present concerns and the history of past performances, of actors' and audience's ideas of appropriate male behaviour with ideas belonging to other times and places. István Géher catches these complexities in his description of 'Hamlet the Hungarian: A Living Monument'. To take Jan Kott's cue and call Hamlet 'our contemporary' would require, Géher argues, some qualification. Géher begins with language. In the translation by János Arany (1867), Hamlet the Hungarian speaks a nineteenth-century language associated with romance and nationalism—but with a difference: 'His diction, though refined and civilized in its high moral seriousness, is invigorated by a broader and more daring use of the comic potentialities inherent in down-to-earth popular language, not refraining from "country matters" and ever "relishing" of the "old stock".' If Shakespeare qualifies Hungarian romanticism, so does Hungarian romanticism qualify Shakespeare: 'Shakespeare's protagonist has a wit more elegantly sparkling, a more acrobatic speech spoken more "trippingly on the tongue", whereas the "accent" of Hamlet the Hungarian is more full-bodied, his "gait" heavier under the "pressure" of the "fardel" of being. His blood is thicker, his passions are more haemorrhaging . . .'. These coalescences happen, not in the nineteenth century or the seventeenth century, but *now*: 'The speech of Hamlet the Hungarian is both solid and fluid, his voice carries through the distance of centuries, has the living ring of here and now, with ghostly undertones of bygone ages.'[32]

'This is I, | Hamlet the Dane' (5.1.253–4): Hamlet is never only that. He is Hamlet the Briton, Hamlet the German, Hamlet the American, Hamlet the Arabian, Hamlet the Australian, Hamlet the Japanese, Hamlet the South African, Hamlet the Hungarian. As such, he is perfectly situated to hold the mirror up to nature, to show the age and body of the time its form (shape) and pressure (impressed character). In early modern terms that is an act, not simply of self-observation, much less of self-celebration, but of self-critique: it serves 'to show virtue her own feature, scorn her own image' (3.2.22–3). In fine, Shakespeare's plays and poems offer ways of finding a perspective on masculinity in the here and now. In teaching us that masculinity is contingent in all sorts of ways, productions of Shakespeare's plays and readings of Shakespeare's poems give us the opportunity to imagine versions of masculinity that may be more equitable and more fulfilling than those we know already.

INTRODUCTION

1. This and all other quotations from Shakespeare's plays and poems are taken from *The Complete Works*, ed. Stanley Wells and Gary Taylor (Oxford: Clarendon Press, 1989). The passage quoted here comes from *The Tragedy of King Lear*, as printed in the 1623 folio, one of two quite different texts of *Lear* included in the Oxford edition. Act, scene, and line numbers will vary from other editions of the play.

2. James I, *Witty Observations Gathered from Our Late Sovereign King James in His Ordinary Discourse* (London, 1643), 8. In keeping with the style of the Oxford Shakespeare Topics series, this and all other quotations from early modern sources have been edited to accord with modern spelling and punctuation.

3. Judith Butler, *Gender Trouble: Feminism and the Subversion of Identity* (New York: Routledge, 1990), 25.

4. David Gilmore, *Manhood in the Making: Cultural Conceptions of Masculinity* (New Haven: Yale University Press, 1990), 17.

5. Lynn Enterline, *The Tears of Narcissus: Melancholia and Masculinity in Early Modern Writing* (Stanford: Stanford University Press, 1995).

6. Mark Breitenberg, *Anxious Masculinity in Early Modern England* (Cambridge: Cambridge University Press, 1996).

CHAPTER I

1. Philippe de Mornay, *The True Knowledge of a Man's Own Self*, trans. Anthony Munday (London: William Leake, 1602), Aᵢᵢ.

2. Helkiah Crooke, *Microcosmographia: A Description of the Body of Man* (London: Jaggard, 1618), 12, 646. Further references to this, and to all other sources cited more than once, are provided in parentheses in the main text.

3. Rolf Soellner, *Shakespeare's Patterns of Self-Knowledge* (Columbus, Oh: Ohio State University Press, 1972), 3–40, lays out received ideas about self-knowledge before exploring Shakespeare's responses to those ideas in three phases: (1) acceptance of received opinion in plays up through *Henry V*, (2) sceptical exploration of problems and ambiguities in the mid-career plays *Julius Caesar*, *Hamlet*, *Troilus and Cressida*, and *Measure for Measure*,

and (3) affirmation that self-knowledge is possible in *Othello, King Lear, Macbeth*, and *The Tempest*.

4. Anne Ferry, *The 'Inward' Language: Sonnets of Wyatt, Sidney, Shakespeare, Donne* (Chicago: University of Chicago Press, 1983), 31–70.

5. George Trosse, *The Life of the Late Reverend Mr. George Trosse*, ed. A. W. Brink (Montreal and London: McGill-Queen's University Press, 1974), 86–7.

6. On this point, see Donald K. Hedrick, 'Male Surplus Value', in Jean Howard and Scott Shershow, eds., *Marxist Shakespeares* (London: Routledge, 2000).

7. Simonds D'Ewes, *Autobiography and Correspondence*, ed. J. O. Halliwell (2 vols., London: Richard Bentley, 1845), i. 263.

8. J. B. Bamborough, *The Little World of Man* (London: Longman, 1932), 52–81; Nancy G. Siraisi, *Medieval and Early Renaissance Medicine: An Introduction to Knowledge and Practice* (Chicago: University of Chicago Press, 1990), 97–114; Thomas Laqueur, *Making Sex: Body and Gender from the Greeks to Freud* (Cambridge, Mass.: Harvard University Press, 1990); Gail Kern Paster, *The Body Embarrassed: Drama and the Disciplines of Shame in Early Modern England* (Ithaca: Cornell University Press, 1993); David Hillman and Carla Mazzio, eds., *The Body in Parts: Fantasies of Corporeality in Early Modern Europe* (London: Routledge, 1997).

9. Cynthia Marshall, 'Wound Man: *Coriolanus*, Gender, and the Theatrical Construction of Interiority', in Valerie Traub, M. Lindsay Kaplan, and Dympna Callaghan, eds., *Feminist Readings of Early Modern Culture: Emerging Subjects* (Cambridge: Cambridge University Press, 1996), 93–118.

10. Levinus Lemnius, *De habitu et constitutione corporis*, trans. Thomas Newton as *The Touchstone of Complexions* (London: Thomas Marsh, 1576), 135.

11. Levinus Lemnius, *De miraculis occultis naturae*, anon. trans. as *The Secret Miracles of Nature* (London: Humphrey Mosley, 1658), 131.

12. U. C. Knoepflmacher, 'The Humours as Symbolic Nucleus in *Henry IV, Part 1*', *College English* 24 (1963), 497–501; Yumiko Yamada, 'Shakespeare's Humour Plays', *Shakespeare Studies* (Japan) 21 (1981–2), 35–64; Robert L. Reid, 'Humoral Psychology in Shakespeare's Henriad', *Comparative Drama* 30 (1996–7), 471–502.

13. Laurent Joubert, *Traité du Ris*, trans. Gregory David de Rocher as *Treatise on Laughter* (University, Alabama: University of Alabama Press, 1980), 60.

14. For a succinct statement of early modern understanding of the soul, see Bamborough, *The Little World of Man*, 29–51.

15. Walter Ralegh, *The History of the World*, ed. C. A. Patrides (Philadelphia: Temple University Press, 1971), 126.

16. Sir Philip Sidney, *A Defence of Poetry*, ed. J. A. Van Dorsten (Oxford: Oxford University Press, 1966), 29.

17. Leeds Barroll, *Artificial Persons: The Formation of Character in the Tragedies of Shakespeare* (Columbia: University of South Carolina Press, 1974), 74. Barroll defines 'transcendentalism' as 'that mode of thought which assumes the existence of an agency governing man from a supernatural plane of existence which is unavailable to the human senses' (p. 41).

18. Fulke Greville, *Selected Poems*, ed. Thom Gunn (Chicago: University of Chicago Press, 1968), 149.

19. For a full treatment of this doctrine, its origins and its afterlife in early modern Europe, see Ernst Hartwig Kantorowicz, *The King's Two Bodies: A Study in Medieval Political Theology* (Princeton: Princeton University Press, 1957).

20. A chronologically extended account of English coronation rituals is provided by Percy Ernst Schramm, *A History of the English Coronation*, trans. L. P. Wickham (Oxford: Clarendon Press, 1937). On Elizabeth in particular, see C. G. Bayne, 'The Coronation of Queen Elizabeth', *English Historical Review* 22 (1907), 650–73; A. L. Rowse, 'The Coronation of Queen Elizabeth I', *History Today* 3 (1953), 301–10; and Neville W. Williams, 'The Coronation of Queen Elizabeth', *Quarterly Review* 597 (1953), 397–411.

21. Wilfrid Hooper, 'The Tudor Sumptuary Laws', *English Historical Review* 30 (1915), 433–49; F. A. Young, Jr., *The Proclamations of the Tudor Queens* (Cambridge: Cambridge University Press, 1976), 161–70; Anne Jones and Peter Stallybrass, *Renaissance Habits: Clothing and the Materials of Memory* (Cambridge: Cambridge University Press, 2000).

22. 24 Henry VIII cap. 13 in *A Collection in English of All the Statutes Now in Force* (London: Thomas Wight & Bonham Norton, 1598), 13^v–16.

23. Untitled proclamation (London: Christopher Barker, 1597), collected in Humphrey Dyson, ed., *A Book Containing All Such Proclamations as Were Published during the Reign of the Late Queen Elizabeth* (2 vols., London; Bonham Norton & John Bill, 1618), ii. 379.

24. Robert Greene, *A Quip for an Upstart Courtier* (1602) in *The Life and Complete Works in Prose and Verse*, ed. Alexander B. Grosart (repr. London: Russell & Russell, 1964), ix. 223.

25. Philip Stubbes, *The Anatomy of Abuses* (London: Richard Jones, 1583), sig. C2^v.

26. 'Articles for the due execution of the Statutes of Apparell' (2 vols., London: Richard Jugge & John Cawood, 1562), in Dyson, *Proclamations*, i. 65.

27. Strong, no. 100, p. 154.

28. William Shakespeare, *The First Folio*, facsimile edn., ed. Charlton Hinman (New York: Norton, 1968), 37.

29. Transcribed in R. A. Foakes and R. T. Rickert, eds., *Henslowe's Diary* (Cambridge: Cambridge University Press, 1961), 318–23.

30. Quoted in Andrew Gurr, *The Shakespearean Stage 1574–1642*, 3rd edn. (Cambridge: Cambridge University Press, 1992), 194.

31. Stephen Gosson, *The School of Abuse* (London: Thomas Woodcock, 1579), C6.

32. Roslyn Lander Knutson, *The Repertory of Shakespeare's Company 1594–1613* (Fayetteville: University of Arkansas Press, 1991), 86–7.

33. Joseph R. Roach, *The Player's Passion: Studies in the Science of Acting* (Newark: University of Delaware Press, 1985), 23–57.

CHAPTER 2

1. M629, M75, M353, M254, M602 in Morris Palmer Tilley, *A Dictionary of the Proverbs in England in the Sixteenth and Seventeenth Centuries* (Ann Arbor: University of Michigan Press, 1950).

2. Thomas Nashe, *Piers Penniless* (1592), quoted in William Shakespeare, *The Complete Works*, ed. Stanley Wells and Gary Taylor (Oxford: Clarendon Press, 1986), 153.

3. Thomas Heywood, *An Apology for Actors* (London: Nicholas Oakes, 1612), B4.

4. Included in Gāmini Salgādo, ed., *Eyewitnesses of Shakespeare: First-Hand Accounts of Performances 1590–1890* (London: Chatto & Windus, 1975), 33.

5. William Gouge, *The Dignity of Chivalry, set forth in a sermon preached before the Artillery Company of London, June 23, 1626* (London: Ralph Mab, 1626), 5–6.

6. William Harrison, *The Description of England*, ed. Georges Edelen (Ithaca: Cornell University Press, 1968), 94.

7. C. L. Barber, *The Idea of Honour in the English Drama 1591–1700* (Gothenburg: University of Gothenburg Press, 1957), 330–1.

8. William Segar, *Honour Military and Civil* (London: Robert Barker, 1602), p. iii.

9. Keith Wrightson, *English Society 1580–1680* (London: Hutchinson, 1982), 130–42.

10. Roger B. Manning, *Hunters and Poachers: A Cultural and Social History of Unlawful Hunting in England 1485–1640* (Oxford: Oxford University Press, 1993).

11. On cult of chivalry in Elizabethan painting, see Roy Strong, 'Fair England's Knights: The Accession Day tournaments', in *The Cult of Elizabeth:*

Elizabethan Portraiture and Pageantry (London: Thames & Hudson, 1977), 129–64. Frances Yates has studied 'Elizabethan Chivalry: The Romance of the Accession Day Tilts', in *Astrea: The Imperial Theme in the Sixteenth Century* (London: Routledge, 1975), 88–111. On *The Comedy of Errors* as a feature of the 1594 *Gesta Grayorum*, see Bruce R. Smith, 'A Night of Errors and the Dawn of Empire: Male Enterprise in *The Comedy of Errors*', in Michael Collins, ed., *Shakespeare's 'Sweet Thunder'* (Newark: University of Delaware Press, 1997), 102–25.

12. Richard C. McCoy, *The Rites of Knighthood: The Literature and Politics of Elizabethan Chivalry* (Berkeley: University of California Press, 1989), 3–4.

13. Baldasar Castiglione, *The Book of the Courtier*, trans. Sir Thomas Hoby (London: Dent, 1928), 35–7.

14. Eugene M. Waith, *The Herculean Hero in Marlowe, Chapman, Shakespeare, and Dryden* (New York: Columbia University Press, 1962), 11.

15. Roger Ascham, *The Schoolmaster*, ed. Lawrence V. Ryan (Ithaca: Cornell University Press, 1967), 41.

16. Robert Cleaver and John Dod, *A Godly Form of Household Government: For the Ordering of Private Families According to the Direction of God's Word* (London: Thomas Man, 1614), A7.

17. Thomas Platter, *Travels in England 1599*, trans. Clare Williams (London: Cape, 1937), 166.

18. Printed in Charles Read Baskervill, *The Elizabethan Jig and Related Song Drama* (Chicago: University of Chicago Press, 1929), 444–9. The version printed by Baskervill, revised for a later performance, cuts Simpkin and the wife off by having the husband return and catch them in their intrigue. In the original version, Baskervill reports, Simpkin and the wife seem to have outsmarted him.

19. Raymond Williams, 'Base and Superstructure in Marxist Cultural Theory', *New Left Review* 82 (1973), 3–16.

20. Henry Peacham, *The Complete Gentleman*, ed. Virgil B. Heltzel (Ithaca: Cornell University Press, 1962), 13.

21. Richard Brathwait, *The English Gentleman, Containing sundry excellent rules or exquisite observations tending to direction of every gentleman of selecter rank and quality how to demean or accommodate himself in the manage of public or private affairs* (London: Robert Bostock, 1630), Q2.

22. Francis Bacon, *The Essays or Counsels, Civil and Moral*, ed. Michael Kiernan (Oxford: Clarendon Press, 1985), 86.

23. Aristotle, *The Ethics*, trans. J. A. K. Thomson, rev. Hugh Tredennick (Harmondsworth: Penguin, 1976), 258.

24. Michel de Montaigne, *Essays*, trans. John Florio, introd. Thomas Seccombe (3 vols., London: G. Richards, 1908), i.232.

25. Plutarch, *Lives of the Noble Grecians and Romans Compared Together*, trans. Thomas North, introd. George Wyndham (6 vols., London: David Nutt, 1895), i. 4–5.

26. Paul Smith, *Discerning the Subject* (Minneapolis: University of Minnesota Press, 1988), 37–8.

27. Eric Auerbach, 'The Weary Prince', in *Mimesis: The Representation of Reality in Western Literature*, trans. Willard R. Trask (Princeton: Princeton University Press, 1953), 312–33.

CHAPTER 3

1. See e.g. *Timaeus* 27E ff.: 'we must make a distinction and ask, What is that which always is and has no becoming; and what is that which is always becoming and never is? That which is apprehended by intelligence and reason is always in the same state; but that which is conceived by opinion with the help of sensation and without reason, is always in a process of becoming and perishing and never really is': Plato, *Dialogues*, trans. B. Jowett (New York: Random House, 1937), 2.12.

2. An accessible and thorough primer of Freudian theory can be found in J. A. C. Brown, *Freud and the Post-Freudians* (Harmondsworth: Penguin, 1961), 17–35.

3. Coppélia Kahn, *Man's Estate: Masculine Identity in Shakespeare* (Berkeley: University of California Press, 1981), 10–12, 47–81. See also Peter Erickson, *Patriarchal Structures in Shakespeare's Drama* (Berkeley: University of California Press, 1985), and Janet Adelman, *Suffocating Mothers: Fantasies of Maternal Origin in Shakespeare's Plays* (London: Routledge, 1992).

4. Erik H. Erikson, *Identity and the Life Cycle* (New York: Norton, 1980), 51–107, 129.

5. Madan Sarup, *Jacques Lacan* (Toronto: University of Toronto Press, 1992), 101–7.

6. Cynthia Marshall, 'Wound-Man: *Coriolanus*, Gender, and the Theatrical Construction of Interiority' in Valerie Traub, M. Lindsay Kaplan, and Dympna Callaghan, eds., *Feminist Readings of Early Modern Culture: Emerging Subjects* (Cambridge: Cambridge University Press, 1996), 93–118. See also Marshall's essays 'Man of Steel Done Got the Blues: Melancholic Subversion of Presence in *Antony and Cleopatra*', *Shakespeare Quarterly* 44 (1993), 385–408; 'Portia's Wound, Calpurnia's Dream: Reading Character in *Julius Caesar*', *English Literary Renaissance* 24 (1994), 471–88; and 'The Doubled Jacques and Constructions of Negation in *As You Like It*', *Shakespeare Quarterly* 49 (1998), 375–92. Cf. Joel Fineman, *Shakespeare's Perjured Eye* (Berkeley: University of California Press, 1986)

and *The Subjectivity Effect in Western Literary Tradition* (Cambridge, Mass.: MIT Press, 1991).

7. J. A. Burrow, *The Ages of Man: A Study in Medieval Writing and Thought* (Oxford: Oxford University Press, 1986), 5–54.

8. Walter Raleigh, *The History of the World*, ed. C. A. Patrides (Philadelphia: Temple University Press, 1971), 127–8.

9. Henry Cuffe, *The Differences of the Ages of Man's Life* (London: Arnold Hatfield for Martin Clearke, 1607), 90.

10. Evidence, demographic and anecdotal, about infancy and childhood in early modern England is digested in Keith Wrightson, *English Society 1580–1680* (London: Hutchinson, 1982), 104–18; Ralph A. Houlbrooke, *The English Family 1450–1700* (London: Longman, 1984), 127–65; and Ilana Ben-Amos, *Adolescence and Youth in Early Modern England* (New Haven: Yale University Press, 1994), 39–68.

11. Sydnam Poyntz, *A True Relation of These German Wars from Mansfield's Going Out of England (1624) until This Last Year 1636*, ed. A. T. S. Goodrick, Camden Society 3rd ser., 14 (1908), 45.

12. On later childhood and youth, see Houlbrooke, *The English Family*, 150–5, 166–88, and Ben-Amos, *Adolescence and Youth*, 39–68.

13. Y48 in Morris Palmer Tilley, *A Dictionary of the Proverbs in England in the Sixteenth and Seventeenth Centuries* (Ann Arbor: University of Michigan Press, 1950).

14. The English translator of *The Problemes of Aristotle, with other Philosophers and Phisitions* (London: Arnold Hatfield, 1597) specifies ages where the original text does not when he questions, 'Why doth the voice change in men and women, in men at 14, in women at 12, in men when they begin to yield seed, in women when their breasts begin to grow?' (C1^{v}). On the mean age of marriage, see Houlbrooke, *The English Family*, 65–8; Wrightson, *English Society*, 66–88; and Ben-Amos, *Adolescence and Youth*, 32.

15. Roger Ascham, *The Schoolmaster*, ed. Lawrence V. Ryan (Ithaca: Cornell University Press, 1967), 40.

16. Steve Rappaport, *Worlds Within Worlds: Structures of Life in Sixteenth-Century London* (Cambridge: Cambridge University Press, 1989), 69; Houlbrooke, *The English Family*, 202, 217–18.

17. Very little external information links Burbage to certain roles, but Martin Holmes speculates about the internal evidence of the scripts in *Shakespeare and Burbage: The Sound of Shakespeare as Devised to Suit the Voice and Talents of His Principal Player* (London: Phillimore, 1978).

18. M616 in Morris Palmer Tilley, *A Dictionary of the Proverbs in England in the Sixteenth and Seventeenth Centuries* (Ann Arbor: University of Michigan Press, 1950).

19. Ronald Hutton, *The Stations of the Sun: A History of the Ritual Year in Britain* (Oxford: Oxford University Press, 1996), 1–24, 151–68, 295–303, 332–47; C. L. Barber, *Shakespeare's Festive Comedies* (Princeton: Princeton University Press, 1959); Maynard Mack Jr., *The Killing of the King: Three Studies in Shakespeare's Tragic Structure* (New Haven: Yale University Press, 1973); Naomi Liebler, *Shakespeare's Festive Tragedy: The Ritual Foundations of Genre* (London: Routledge, 1995); François Laroque, *Shakespeare's Festive World: Elizabethan Seasonal Entertainment and the Professional Stage*, trans. Janet Lloyd (Cambridge: Cambridge University Press, 1991).

20. Victor Turner, *From Ritual to Theatre: The Human Seriousness of play* (New York: Performing Arts Journal, 1982), 24–7, citing Arnold van Gennep, *The Rites of Passage* (1908; repr. Chicago: University of Chicago Press, 1960).

21. David Cressy, *Birth, Marriage, and Death: Ritual, Religion, and the Life-Cycle in Tudor and Stuart England* (Oxford: Oxford University Press, 1997), p. vii.

22. If rites of passage in unified traditional cultures are 'liminal', then theatrical performances in decentred capitalist cultures like Shakespeare's and ours are 'liminoid': they are *like* traditional rites of passage but are not the genuine article. They lack the ritual occasion and unified audience of traditional rites. Cf. Turner, *From Ritual to Theatre*, 20–60.

23. Phillip Stubbes, *The Anatomy of Abuses*, ed. F. J. Furnivall (London: New Shakespeare Society, 1877–9), 145. On ritual customs of marriage, see Cressy, *Birth, Marriage, and Death*, 336–76.

24. Marilyn L. Williamson, *The Patriarchy of Shakespeare's Comedies* (Detroit: Wayne State University Press, 1987).

25. Quoted in Wrightson, *English Society*, 91. On the two models of marriage that obtained in early modern England, see Houlbrooke, *The English Family*, 96–126, and Wrightson, *English Society*, 90–104.

26. According to Cressy, more than 90 per cent of those reaching adulthood in the sixteenth century married, compared with more than 80 per cent in the seventeenth century (p. 285). On the rites of death, see Cressy, *Birth, Marriage, and Death*, 379–482.

27. Michael Neill, *Issues of Death: Mortality and Identity in English Renaissance Tragedy* (Oxford: Clarendon Press, 1997), 1–22.

28. 1 Corinthians 13: 12 in *The Geneva Bible*, introd. Lloyd E. Berry (Madison: University of Wisconsin Press, 1969).

29. Thomas Whythorne, *Autobiography*, ed. James M. Osborne (London: Oxford University Press, 1962), pp. xv, 12–13.

30. Sir Simonds D'Ewes, *Autobiography and Correspondence*, ed. J. O. Halliwell (2 vols., London: Richard Bentley, 1845).

31. Richard Norwood, *Journal*, ed. Wesley Frank Craven and Walter B. Hayward (New York: Scholars' Facsimiles and Reprints, 1945), 71.

32. Rhys Evans, *An Eccho to the Voice from Heaven: Or a narration of the life, and manner of the special calling and visions of Arise Evans* (London: printed for the author, 1652), 8.

33. George Trosse, *The Life of the Late Reverend Mr. George Trosse*, ed. A. W. Brink (Montreal and London: McGill-Queen's University Press, 1974), 86.

34. Robert Parsons, *Memoirs*, ed. A. H. Pollen (2 vols., Catholic Record Society Miscellanea, n.d.) ii: 12–36.

35. Richard Baxter, *Reliquiae Baxterianae: Or Mr. Richard Baxter's Narrative of the Most Memorable Passages of His Life and Times*, abr. J. M. Lloyd Thomas, ed. N. H. Keeble, Everyman Library (London: Dent, 1974), 103–32.

36. Phineas Pett, *Autobiography*, ed. W. G. Perrin ([place not specified] Navy Records Society, 1918), 100.

37. Adam Martindale, *Life*, ed. Richard Parkinson (London: Chetham Society, 1895).

38. Thomas Raymond, *Autobiography*, ed. G. Davies, Camden Society 3rd ser., 28 (1917), 19.

39. John Smith, *The Complete Works*, ed. Philip L. Barbour (3 vols., Chapel Hill: University of North Carolina Press, 1986), iii.153.

CHAPTER 4

1. Bert O. States, *Hamlet and the Concept of Character* (Baltimore: Johns Hopkins University Press, 1992), 6–7.

2. Both Derrida's ideas and Lacan's are lucidly explained in Catherine Belsey, *Critical Practice* (London: Methuen, 1980) and are given practical application in her *The Subject of Tragedy: Identity and Difference in Renaissance Drama* (London: Methuen, 1985).

3. The map is reproduced as plate 161 and catalogued in Rodney W. Shirley, *The Mapping of the World: Early Printed World Maps 1472–1700* (London: Holland Press, 1983), no. 198, p. 219. The unique surviving copy resides in the British Library (BL maps 188.k.1 (5)).

4. Thomas Gainsford, *The Rich Cabinet Furnished with variety of excellent descriptions, exquisite characters, witty discourses, and delightful histories divine and moral* (London: Roger Jackson, 1616), 38.

5. Nicholas Breton, *The Good and the Bad*, repr. in *English Character Writings of the Seventeenth Century*, ed. Henry Morley (London: Routledge, 1891), 274–5.

6. Coppélia Kahn, *Roman Shakespeare: Warriors, Wounds, and Women* (London: Routledge, 1997), 79.

7. My categorizations are inspired by Northrop Frye's typology of myths in *Anatomy of Criticism* (Princeton: Princeton University Press, 1957), 163–239. Frye's four-part cycle better fits the complexities of Shakespeare's 39 scripts than Marilyn French's bipartite scheme in *Shakespeare's Division of Experience* (New York: Summit Books, 1981).

8. Thomas Platter, *Travels in England 1599*, trans. Clare Williams (London: Cape, 1937), 166.

9. For the historical specificity of these terms I am indebted to Margo Hendricks, 'Introduction', in Margo Hendricks and Patricia Parker, eds., *Women, 'Race', and Writing in the Early Modern Period* (London: Routledge, 1994), 1–2. The distinction between space and time is my own.

10. On traits of blackness, see Kim F. Hall, *Things of Darkness: Economies of Race and Gender in Early Modern England* (Ithaca: Cornell University Press, 1995).

11. William Gouge, *Of Domestical Duties* (London: John Haviland, 1622), 5.

12. William Harrison, *The Description of England*, ed. Georges Edelen (Ithaca: Cornell University Press, 1968), 94.

13. Robert Greene, *A Quip for an Upstart Courtier* (1602), in *The Life and Complete Works in Prose and Verse*, ed. Alexander B. Grosart (repr. 15 vols., London: Russell & Russell, 1964), xi. 291–2.

14. Alan Bray, 'Homosexuality and the Signs of Male Friendship in Elizabethan England' (1990), repr. in Jonathan Goldberg, ed., *Queering the Renaissance* (Durham, NC: Duke University Press, 1994), 40–61.

15. Michel de Montaigne, *Essays*, trans. John Florio, introd. Thomas Seccombe (3 vols., London: G. Richards, 1908), i. 235.

16. On 'preposterous', see especially Patricia Parker, *Shakespeare from the Margins: Language, Culture, Context* (Chicago: University of Chicago Press, 1996), 20–55. On early modern sodomy laws and the record of court prosecutions, see Bruce R. Smith, *Homosexual Desire in Shakespeare's England: A Cultural Poetics* (Chicago: University of Chicago Press, 1991), 46–53.

17. Richard Corum, 'Henry's Desires', in Louise Fradenburg and Carla Freccero, eds., *Premodern Sexualities* (London: Routledge, 1996), 71–97.

18. Jonathan Dollimore, *Sexual Dissidence: Augustine to Wilde, Freud to Foucault* (Oxford: Clarendon Press, 1991), 33.

19. Michael Pennington, 'Hamlet', in Philip Brockbank, ed., *Players of Shakespeare: Essays in Shakespearean Performance by Twelve Players with the Royal Shakespeare Company* (Cambridge: Cambridge University Press, 1985), 119.

20. Paul Smith, *Discerning the Subject* (Minneapolis: University of Minnesota Press, 1988), 37.

CHAPTER 5

1. Michel Serres, *The Troubadour of Knowledge*, trans. Sheila Faria Glaser and William Paulson (Ann Arbor: University of Michigan Press, 1997), 147.

2. George Sandys, *A Relation of a Journey Begun A.D. 1610*, 2nd edn. (London: W. Barrett, 1615), 245–6.

3. Plato, *Symposium*, ss. 208–9. On the importance of this trope for understanding collaborative authorship in early modern England, see Jeffrey Masten, *Textual Intercourse: Collaboration, Authorship, and Sexualities in Renaissance Drama* (Cambridge: Cambridge University Press, 1997).

4. Arthur Marotti, *John Donne, Coterie Poet* (Madison: University of Wisconsin Press, 1986), 25–34.

5. Harold Love, *Scribal Publication in Seventeenth-Century England* (Oxford: Clarendon Press, 1993), 177–230, and Arthur Marotti, *Manuscript, Print, and the English Renaissance Lyric* (Ithaca: Cornell University Press, 1995), 135–208.

6. Sir Philip Sidney, *A Defence of Poetry*, ed. J. A. Van Dorsten (Oxford: Oxford University Press, 1966), 31–2.

7. J. M. R. Margeson, *The Origins of English Tragedy* (Oxford: Clarendon Press, 1967).

8. Northrop Frye, *Anatomy of Criticism* (Princeton: Princeton University Press, 1957), 207.

9. Francis Bacon, *The Essays or Counsels, Civil and Moral*, ed. Michael Kiernan (Oxford: Clarendon Press, 1985), 86; Thomas Gainsford, *The Rich Cabinet Furnished with variety of excellent descriptions, exquisite characters, witty discourses, and delightful histories divine and moral* (London: Roger Jackson, 1616), 163.

10. On the performance history of *King Lear*, see Marvin Rosenberg, *The Masks of King Lear* (Berkeley: University of California Press, 1978) and Alexander Leggatt, *King Lear* (Manchester: University of Manchester Press, 1991). Brook's production is described ibid. 32–52; Stafford-Clark's and Deborah Warner's in Peter Holland, *English Shakespeares: Shakespeare on the English Stage in the 1990s* (Cambridge: Cambridge University Press, 1997), 154–6 and 44–9.

11. Tetsuo Anzai, 'Directing *King Lear* in Japanese Translation', in Takashi Sasayama, J. R. Mulryne, and Margaret Shewring, eds., *Shake-*

speare and the Japanese Stage (Cambridge: Cambridge University Press, 1998), 125.

12. Ania Loomba, ' "Local-Manufacture Made-in-India Othello Fellows": Issues of Race, Hybridity and Location in Post-colonial Shakespeare', in Ania Loomba and Martin Orkin, eds., *Post-Colonial Shakespeares* (London: Routledge, 1998), 143–63.

13. Gāmini Salgādo, ed., *Eyewitnesses of Shakespeare: First-hand Accounts of Performances 1590–1890* (London: Chatto & Windus, 1975), 31.

14. The production history of *Macbeth* is surveyed in Marvin Rosenberg, *The Masks of Macbeth* (Berkeley: University of Calfornia Press, 1978) and Bernice W. Kliman, *Macbeth* (Manchester: University of Manchester Press, 1992). Garrick's portrayal is described ibid. 24–9; Ducis's version in Marion Monaco, *Shakespeare on the French Stage in the Eighteenth Century* (Paris: Didier, 1974), 139–45.

15. John Philip Kemble, *Macbeth Reconsidered* (London: T. & J. Egerton, 1786), 7.

16. Derek Jacobi, 'Macbeth', in *Players of Shakespeare 4* (Cambridge: Cambridge University Press, 1998), 199, 201.

17. Bernice W. Kliman, 'Gleanings: The Residue of Difference in Scripts: The Case of Polanski's *Macbeth*', in Jay L. Halio and Hugh Richmond, eds., *Shakespearean Illuminations: Essays in Honor of Marvin Rosenberg* (Newark: University of Delaware Press, 1998), 131–46.

18. Kliman, *Macbeth*, 86–99.

19. Nahum Tate, *The Ingratitude of a Commonwealth: Or, the Fall of Caius Martius Coriolanus* (London: Joseph Hindmarsh, 1682), 36–7. Further references are cited in the text.

20. John Ripley, *Coriolanus on Stage in England and America, 1609–1994* (Madison, NJ: Fairleigh Dickinson University Press, 1998), 122. See also Barbara Puschmann-Nalenz, 'Using Shakespeare? The Appropriation of *Coriolanus* and *King Henry V* in John Philip Kemble's 1789 Productions', in Holger Klein and Jean-Marie Maguin, *Shakespeare and France* (Lewiston, NY: Mellen, 1995), 219–32. Further references to Ripley's production history are cited in the text.

21. Randolph Trumbach, *Sex and the Gender Revolution* (Chicago: University of Chicago Press, 1998), 3–8. On the heightened rate of prosecutions for sodomy, see Louis Crompton, *Byron and Greek Love: Homophobia in Nineteenth-century England* (Berkeley: University of California Press, 1985), 12–62.

22. In addition to Ripley, *Coriolanus*, 332–3, see Holland, *English Shakespeares*, 202–6. I have also drawn on my own experience as a member of the audience in August 1994.

23. Crompton, *Byron and Greek Love*, 159–60.

24. Anthony Dawson, *Hamlet* (Manchester: Manchester University Press, 1995), 27.

25. *Tragedie of Fratricide Punished or Prince Hamlet Punished*, 5.6.78, as translated in Ernst Brennecke, *Shakespeare in Germany 1590–1700* (Chicago: University of Chicago Press, 1964), 290.

26. *The Tragedy of Hamlet Prince of Denmark, As it is now acted at His Highness the Duke of York's Theatre* (London: J. Martyn & H. Herringham, 1676), 9. On the changing punctuation of Hamlet's first soliloquy as a key to different constructions of the character, see Bruce R. Smith, 'Prickly Characters', in David M. Bergeron, ed., *Reading and Writing in Shakespeare* (Newark: University of Delaware Press, 1996), 25–44.

27. Samuel Johnson, 'Preface [to Shakespeare]', in *Works*, vii, ed. Arthur Sherbo (New Haven: Yale University Press, 1959), 62.

28. On Olivier's interpretation, see Dawson, *Hamlet*, 110–18; on Gründgen's interpretation, Wilhelm Hortmann, *Shakespeare on the German Stage: The Twentieth Century* (Cambridge: Cambridge University Press, 1998), 156–7; on Senda's production, Sasayama et al., *Shakespeare and the Japanese Stage*, 59–60.

29. Andreas Bertoldi, 'Shakespeare, Psychoanalysis and the Colonial Encounter: The Case of Wulf Sachs's *Black Hamlet*', in Loomba and Orkin, *Post-Colonial Shakespeares*, 235–58.

30. Goro Suzuki, 'The Japanese Character as Reflected in Shakespeare's Great Tragedies', in Tetsuo Anzai, Soji Iawasaki, Holger Klein, and Peter Milward, eds., *Shakespeare in Japan* (Lewiston, NY: Mellen, 1998), 41–2.

31. Abedalmutalab A. Alsenad, 'Professional Production of Shakespeare in Iraq: An Exploration of Cultural Adaptation' (Ph.D. dissertation, University of Colorado, 1988), 103–5, 120–38.

32. István Géher, 'Hamlet the Hungarian: A Living Monument', in Holger Klein and Péter Dávidházi, eds., *Shakespeare and Hungary* (Lewiston, NY: Mellen, 1996), 75–6.

Suggestions for Further Reading

The theoretical issues that have informed most discussions of gender since the 1980s are set forth in Judith Butler, *Gender Trouble: Feminism and the Subversion of Identity* (New York: Routledge, 1990). David Gilmore, *Manhood in the Making: Cultural Conceptions of Masculinity* (New Haven: Yale University Press, 1990) summarizes the work of historians and anthropologists and provides a comprehensive comparison of how masculinity has been constructed in several different historical eras, in numerous cultures all over the world.

With respect to the physical bodies that early modern men imagined they inhabited, see J. B. Bamborough, *The Little World of Man* (London: Longman, 1932); Nancy G. Siraisi, *Medieval and Early Renaissance Medicine: An Introduction to Knowledge and Practice* (Chicago: University of Chicago Press, 1990), 97–114; Thomas Laqueur, *Making Sex: Body and Gender from the Greeks to Freud* (Cambridge, Mass.: Harvard University Press, 1990); Gail Kern Paster, *The Body Embarrassed: Drama and the Disciplines of Shame in Early Modern England* (Ithaca: Cornell University Press, 1993); and David Hillman and Carla Mazzio, eds., *The Body in Parts: Fantasies of Corporeality in Early Modern Europe* (London: Routledge, 1997). Anne Jones and Peter Stallybrass, *Renaissance Habits: Clothing and the Materials of Memory* (Cambridge: Cambridge University Press, 2000) offer the best account of clothing as an index to personal identity. Early modern ideas about persons as performers in plays are Joseph R. Roach's subject in the first chapter of *The Player's Passion: Studies in the Science of Acting* (Newark: University of Delaware Press, 1985).

Ideals governing manly behaviour in Shakespeare's England varied according to social standing. The social hierarchy is set in place by Keith Wrightson in chapter 1 of *English Society 1580–1680* (London: Hutchinson, 1982). On the chivalric code that governed the lives of men at the top, see Richard C. McCoy, *The Rites of Knighthood: The Literature and Politics of Elizabethan Chivalry* (Berkeley: University of California Press, 1989). Ideals for other sorts of men are discussed by Eugene M. Waith, *The Herculean Hero in Marlowe, Chapman, Shakespeare, and Dryden* (New York: Columbia University Press, 1962); Margo Todd, *Christian Humanism and the Puritan Social Order* (Cambridge: Cambridge University Press, 1987); and Louis B. Wright, *Middle-Class Culture in Elizabethan England* (1935; repr. London: Methuen, 1964).

Concerning life passages, J. A. Burrow's *The Ages of Man: A Study in Medieval Writing and Thought* (Oxford: Oxford University Press, 1986) offers the best account of traditional schemes like the ones that inspire Jaques's disquisition 'All the world's a stage' (*As You Like It*, 2.7.139–66) and Feste's song 'When that I was and a little tiny boy' (*Twelfth Night*, 5.1.385–404). For historical evidence of how different stages of life were socially organized, see Keith Wrightson, *English Society 1580–1680* (London: Hutchinson, 1982); Ralph A. Houlbrooke, *The English Family 1450–1700* (London: Longman, 1984); Ilana Ben-Amos, *Adolescence and Youth in Early Modern England* (New Haven: Yale University Press, 1994); and David Cressy, *Birth, Marriage, and Death: Ritual, Religion, and the Life-cycle in Tudor and Stuart England* (Oxford: Oxford University Press, 1997). Michael Neill's book *Issues of Death: Mortality and Identity in English Renaissance Tragedy* (Oxford: Clarendon Press, 1997) discusses dramatic representations of the rite of passage that concludes all the schemes.

On 'otherness' in the formation of self-identity, see the theoretical explanation of Jacques Derrida's deconstructionist model and Jacques Lacan's psychoanalytical model in Catherine Belsey's *Critical Practice* (London: Methuen, 1980). These models are put to practical use in Belsey's *The Subject of Tragedy: Identity and Difference in Renaissance Drama* (London: Methuen, 1985). Numerous books and articles address the role of women as 'other' in Shakespeare's England. The best overview is provided by Anthony Fletcher in *Gender, Sex, and Subordination in England, 1500–1800* (New Haven: Yale University Press, 1995). Applications specific to Shakespeare are collected in Deborah E. Barker and Ivo Kamps, eds., *Shakespeare and Gender: A History* (London: Verso, 1995). On otherness and race, see Kim F. Hall, *Things of Darkness: Economies of Race and Gender in Early Modern England* (Ithaca: Cornell University Press, 1995). Otherness with respect to social class is brought to the fore in Alan Sinfield and Jonathan Dollimore's *Political Shakespeare*, 2nd edn. (Ithaca: Cornell University Press, Manchester: Manchester University Press, 1994). Alan Bray, 'Homosexuality and the Signs of Male Friendship in Elizabethan England' (1990), repr. in Jonathan Goldberg, ed., *Queering the Renaissance* (Durham, NC: Duke University Press, 1994), 40–61, discusses the sodomite as other.

Self-identity as a matter of coalescences is explored by Paul Smith in *Discerning the Subject* (Minneapolis: University of Minnesota Press, 1988) and Michel Serres, *The Troubadour of Knowledge*, trans. Sheila Faria Glaser and William Paulson (Ann Arbor: University of Michigan Press, 1997). Historical differences in how masculinity has been constructed on stage can be followed in the volumes on individual plays in the series Shakespeare in Performance, published by Manchester University Press. See especially Alexander Leggatt on *King Lear* (1991), Bernice W. Kliman on *Macbeth* (1992), and Anthony Dawson on *Hamlet* (1995). In addition to volumes on various countries in *The Shakespeare Yearbook* series (Lewiston, NY: Edwin Mellen), three readily available books will suggest the range of interpretations in theatres beyond England and North America: Wilhelm Hortmann, *Shakespeare on the German Stage: The Twentieth Century* (Cambridge: Cambridge University Press, 1998); Takashi Sasayama, J. R. Mulryne, and Margaret Shewring, eds., *Shakespeare and the Japanese Stage* (Cambridge: Cambridge University Press, 1998); and Ania Loomba and Martin Orkin, eds., *Post-Colonial Shakespeares* (London: Routledge, 1998).

Index